Stone not only makes the case that religious naturalism can incorporate a sense of sacredness that underwrites environmentalism; he also demonstrates that he is not alone in thinking this possible. This book describes a plethora of religiously naturalistic environmentalist positions, and makes clear that there has been for some time a community of the similarly-minded in this area.

Andrew Dole,
Amherst College, USA

SACRED NATURE

Sacred Nature examines the crisis of environmental degradation through the prism of religious naturalism, which seeks rich spiritual engagement in a world without a god. Jerome Stone introduces students to the growing field of religious naturalism, exploring a series of questions about how it addresses the environmental crises, evaluating the merits of public prophetic discourse that uses the language of spirituality. He presents and defends the concept of religious naturalism while drawing out the implications of religious naturalism for addressing some of the major environmental issues facing humans today. This book is designed for undergraduate and graduate students, as well as scholars specializing in contemporary religious thought or environmental studies.

Jerome A. Stone is a Professor Emeritus, Department of Philosophy, William Rainey Harper College, and formerly taught at Meadville Lombard Theological School. He is also a Community Minister affiliated with the Unitarian Church of Evanston, Illinois, USA.

SACRED NATURE

The environmental potential of religious naturalism

Jerome A. Stone

LONDON AND NEW YORK

First published 2017
by Routledge
2 Park Square, Milton Park, Abingdon, Oxon OX14 4RN

and by Routledge
711 Third Avenue, New York, NY 10017

Routledge is an imprint of the Taylor & Francis Group, an informa business

© 2017 Jerome Stone

The right of Jerome Stone to be identified as author of this work has been asserted by him in accordance with sections 77 and 78 of the Copyright, Designs and Patents Act 1988.

All rights reserved. No part of this book may be reprinted or reproduced or utilized in any form or by any electronic, mechanical, or other means, now known or hereafter invented, including photocopying and recording, or in any information storage or retrieval system, without permission in writing from the publishers.

Trademark notice: Product or corporate names may be trademarks or registered trademarks, and are used only for identification and explanation without intent to infringe.

British Library Cataloguing-in-Publication Data
A catalogue record for this book is available from the British Library

Library of Congress Cataloging-in-Publication Data
Names: Stone, Jerome Arthur, 1935– author.
Title: Sacred nature : the environmental potential of religious naturalism / Jerome A. Stone.
Description: 1 [edition]. | New York : Routledge, 2017. | Includes bibliographical references and index.
Identifiers: LCCN 2016054574| ISBN 9781138897847 (hardback) | ISBN 9781138897854 (pbk.) | ISBN 9781315708942 (ebook)
Subjects: LCSH: Naturalism—Religious aspects. | Nature—Religious aspects. | Ecotheology.
Classification: LCC BL183 .S764 2017 | DDC 146—dc23
LC record available at https://lccn.loc.gov/2016054574

ISBN: 978-1-138-89784-7 (hbk)
ISBN: 978-1-138-89785-4 (pbk)
ISBN: 978-1-315-70894-2 (ebk)

Typeset in Bembo and Stone Sans
by Florence Production Ltd, Stoodleigh, Devon, UK

 Printed in the United Kingdom by Henry Ling Limited

*To Sue, Debbie, Eric, Faith, Aaron,
my UU friends, and the Religious Naturalist Association.*

Prudence never kindled a fire in the human mind; I have no hope for a conservation born of fear.

—Aldo Leopold

CONTENTS

Foreword   *xiii*
Acknowledgements   *xv*
Introduction   *xvii*

1   Introducing religious naturalism   1

2   Alternative starting points: experiences of the sacred and the big picture   13

3   Appreciative perception   31

4   Spirituality for naturalists   67

5   The "G_d" word   83

6   Needed paradigm shifts   97

7   Learning from indigenous peoples   107

8   Religious naturalism in the public square: toward a public ecotheology   121

     Conclusion   137

Index   *141*

FOREWORD

Jerome Stone has established himself as a major thinker in the theory and practice of religious naturalism, and this book tackles one of the issues that must be tackled if this "forgotten alternative" (as Stone calls it in an earlier book) is to become the powerful worldview it promises to be (as Michael Hogue has argued), namely how to ground a viable morality in religious naturalism. To be sure, other authors have made some progress on that task, but in this book, Stone examines a very specific area, concentrating especially on the interface between theory and practice.

What I find exciting about the book is the way it lifts up and emphasizes the interplay between the general and the particular, urges us to alternate our consideration of the general and the particular, and uses that emphasis to ground a spirituality. I will never be able to think of my religious naturalism quite the same after reading how so many former heroes of environmentalism (such as Thoreau, Muir, and Leopold) presaged exactly the needed interplay between the overall understanding of environmental science and the localized attention to detail that will motivate each of us to be good citizens of the earth. Indeed, I will never be able to see a vacant lot the same way, much less my own back yard or even a highway ditch. National parks and German forests also now must loom both larger and smaller as I learn to practice "appreciative perception," a concept that in Stone's hands not only reflects on such concepts as mindfulness, but both builds on them and grounds them in a satisfying theory.

This is profound. Each of us is healthier and happier, I judge, when we have a philosophy of life that is intellectually sound, and yet emotionally fulfilling on a day-by-day basis. There is still work to do to work out a personal morality for religious naturalism, but this contribution to a social morality has many personal implications, implications that will make the future work of Stone and other thinkers so much easier. In fact, I would suggest that his emphasis on health (of the planet) can become a touchstone for cultural and personal morality as well. But, that is for another time. You are in for a treat as you read this book.

Michael Cavanaugh, 2016

ACKNOWLEDGEMENTS

Thanks go to my wife, Sue, for encouragement, wise counsel and stimulating my interest in the environment. Creighton Peden, and Revs. Constance Grant and Bret Lortie were more helpful than they realize. Rev. Dr. Thandeka gave me a blessing, which I shall never forget. Susan Stone, Donald Crosby, and John Tobin read all or parts of the manuscript and gave helpful criticism. Michael Cavanaugh, William Dean, Kathleen Dyrda, Ursula Goodenough, Chad Meister, and Hilde Whalley all played vital roles. Lisa Sideris was very helpful. Two anonymous reviewers for the publishers made helpful comments. Tim Philbin of William Rainey Harper College, the United Library of Garrett Evangelical Theological Seminary, and the Interlibrary Loan Department of the Evanston Public Library were most helpful. Eve Mayer, Sarah Gore, and Rebecca Shillabeer of Taylor and Francis deserve a special thanks for their faith in this project, and especially, Eve's persistence in locating me.

INTRODUCTION

This book is an attempt to draw out some of the environmental implications of religious naturalism. Specifically, it explores the possibilities of holding nature as sacred. In this book, by *nature*, I mean everything that is, this entire universe, without reference to a transcendent deity, soul, realm of spirits, or heaven. The term *nature* will include the human world of culture and history. It does not, in this volume, refer exclusively to pristine wilderness or pastoral settings. By *sacred*, I mean anything that is of very great importance or value. A case for this wide definition will be made in Chapter 2.

This book will introduce religious naturalism in the first chapter. The remaining chapters will draw out the implications of religious naturalism for addressing some of the major environmental issues facing humans today. These chapters will outline the position of major contemporary writers, many of them naturalists of a religious bent, and then draw on these writers to develop an original position. Thus, this book, in the final seven chapters, aims both to illustrate how major contemporary naturalists address environmental problems and to develop seven fresh approaches.

This book will be of interest to the general reader as well as specialists in environmental studies. The writing is clear enough that it should be accessible to undergraduates. The survey of parts of the landscape of religious naturalism in each chapter is designed to make it useful for the beginning student, and the development of the new approaches by the author should make it of interest to both graduate students and people already advanced in environmental studies. The notes at the end of each chapter are kept to a minimum, while there are plenty of bibliographical references, again for each chapter.

"Is there anything you would not do for money?" This is a question that I often used when I taught ethics. I could not, of course, just teach my own values, though my values shaped the way I taught the class. But, I could get students to think about values, possibly even to develop their character. After some thought, the students always realized that there was something that they would not do, even for several million dollars. Now, whatever we would not hurt, destroy, or damage, even for much money, power, or prestige, we can say we hold that to be sacred.

Perhaps, Stuart Kauffman's recollection of the words of N. Scott Momaday can help elicit the attitude for which I use the word "sacred."

> Momaday told us that the central issue we confront is to reinvent the sacred. He told of a sacred shield of the Kiowa, sanctified by the sacrifices and suffering of the warriors who had been honored to hold it in battle. . . . He told of the recent discovery and return of the shield from the family home of the post-Civil War general who had taken it. Momaday's deep voice fell gently over us as he described the welcome set forth for that shield and the place it holds, quiet, somber, still, revered for the passion and suffering distilled within its arc.
>
> (Kauffman, 1995, 4)

I suggest that we need to "rediscover," rather than "reinvent" the sacred. And, I have high regard for Kauffman's search for the laws of self-organization and complexity as our way today of rediscovering the sacred, although the validity of his approach is beyond my ability to evaluate. But, I join him in his appreciation of Momaday's attempt to point to the sacred. What if all of the universe were as sacred as the Kiowa shield?

By itself, religious naturalism will not solve our environmental problems. By itself, it will not solve the technical problems of sustainability, cost-benefit analysis, preservation versus conservation, or habitat protection in the midst of an exploding human species. But, religious naturalism, with its sense of the sacredness of both human life and of other lives and habitats, indeed of far-flung galaxies and incredibly small bosons and quarks, can provide motivation for the long haul, perspective, insight, and perhaps encouragement in the face of disaster and our moral failures.

Since my years teaching a course on Racism in America and participating on the margins of the struggle for desegregated housing in a northern city, I am acutely aware that my perspective is considerably limited to that of a middle-class, well-educated "white person" in the suburban Midwestern United States. Social location does matter, though it offers no excuse for a narrow outlook. I have also learned that you cannot fight all battles at once, though this should not be misused as an excuse for inaction.

Concern for non-human life and its habitats is not just for middle or upper-class elites. There is a strong tradition of African American appreciation for the non-human world (See Alice Walker's *The Color Purple*, 164–168, Walker, 1982; Johnson and Bowker, 2004; Kimberly Smith, 2004; Kimberly Smith, 2005). In addition, people in poverty often have a keen awareness of the cost of environmental destruction. (See Rob Nixon, *Slow Violence and the Environmentalism of the Poor*, Nixon, 2011).

I have had second thoughts about the word "religious" in religious naturalism. For some people, the word "religious" has unfortunate connotations of organized or institutional religion. This often underlies the phrase, "I am not religious, but I am spiritual." However, the word "spiritual" also has unfortunate baggage, suggesting something non-material. Besides, the phrase "religious naturalism" is beginning to enter the vocabulary of the culture.

The word "nature" is used frequently in this book. It is often taken to mean the non-human or perhaps non-urban aspects of this world. In this book, when I use the word "nature," I definitely include humans, their products, and their built environment. Nature is all that there is, but with the understanding that there is no transcendent deity, soul, or heaven.

The first chapter is devoted to explaining religious naturalism. It starts with a general description of religious naturalism, followed by a brief history. Then, there is a discussion of ideas that are close to religious naturalism, but which should be distinguished from it, including pantheism, atheism, agnosticism, and the Gaia movement.

The second chapter proposes that in seeking for the sacred, we should alternate between a focus on specific experiences and attention to the broad picture of the universe that science is sketching. Reflection on specific experiences leads to a naturalistic theory of "sacred" events. Four writers are then examined on how they find meaning in the overall scientific account of the universe. These viewpoints are then used to develop a theory on the relationship between science and meanings. These two theories, one of sacred events and the other on drawing meanings from science, are key to the rest of the book.

Then, the notion of "appreciative perception" is developed. This will be a key element in a recovery of a sense of the sacred. Three examples are given: West Point cadets on top of Mount Katahdin, the photographing of a polar bear, and a student journal assignment. There follow analyses of the practice of appreciative perception by Henry David Thoreau, Aldo Leopold, Delores LaChapelle, and Gary Snyder. This third chapter ends by drawing together these analyses into a general theory of appreciative perception.

The first part of Chapter 4 analyzes the thoughts of various writers who practice what could be called a naturalized spirituality. In the second part of the chapter, drawing on these thinkers, I develop my own theory of naturalized spirituality. The practice of naturalized spirituality is another key component in a recovery of a sense of the sacred.

Chapter 5 presents a naturalistic conception of god as an alternative to the traditional supernaturalistic idea. Two main varieties are depicted. After analyzing a number of thinkers who develop a naturalistic conception of god, this approach is evaluated as helpful, but ultimately dangerous.

The next chapter offers reconstructions of the ways we engage with our earth. First, there needs to be a resacralization of the earth. Our revised theory of the sacred provides a basis for this. Second, a reconception of spirit and matter is proposed, which incorporates spirit with body. Third, we need to broaden our care beyond the human world. Fourth, we must learn to re-envision the feminine side of the divine. These paradigm shifts have immediate and immense practical significance for our dealings with the environment.

Indigenous peoples have much to teach us. The seventh chapter seeks to find inspiration and general clues we may adopt from them without stealing their spirituality. One way of addressing the obstacles to learning from indigenous peoples is to point out that the distinction between modern Western culture and that of indigenous peoples is often exaggerated. A second way is to rethink the superiority of humans. Third, we must recognize that the ideas of indigenous peoples are not simply pre-scientific. We need to deepen our understanding of gender, of ritual, of what it means to be embodied. We need multiple images of time. Finally, we should drop the question of which religious tradition is better.

In the last chapter, the possibility of creating a public ecotheology on a naturalistic basis is explored. The notion of a public theologian using recognizable symbols of transcendence is developed. The chapter is carried on in dialog with contemporary thinkers.

In many ways, this book is a response to Michael Hogue's challenge in *The Promise of Religious Naturalism* to work out the practical implications of religious naturalism (Hogue, 2010). Unfortunately, I was unable to take account of his forthcoming *American Immanence* (Hogue, 2018).

Bibliography

Hogue, Michael. 2010. *The Promise of Religious Naturalism*. Lanham, MD: Rowman & Littlefield.
Hogue, Michael. 2018. *American Immanence: Democracy for an Uncertain World*. New York, NY: Columbia University Press.
Johnson, Cassandra and J.M. Bowker. 2004. "African-American Wildland Memories," *Environmental Ethics*, 26, 57–75.
Kauffman, Stuart. 1995. *At Home in the Universe: The Search for the Laws of Self-Organization and Complexity*. New York: Oxford University Press.
Nixon, Rob. 2011. *Slow Violence and the Environmentalism of the Poor*. Cambridge, MA: Harvard University Press.
Smith, Kimberly K. 2004. "Black Agrarianism and the Foundations of Black Environmental Thought," *Environmental Ethics*, 26, 267–286.
Smith, Kimberly K. 2005. "What is Africa to Me? Wildness in Black Thought from 1860 to 1930," *Environmental Ethics*, 27, 279–298.
Walker, Alice. 1982. *The Color Purple*. New York, NY: Harcourt Brace Jovanovich.

1
INTRODUCING RELIGIOUS NATURALISM

Religious naturalism is a philosophy of life that points out how to lead a robust religious (or spiritual) life while believing that the natural world, including humans, is all there is. Religious naturalism claims that you can be religious (or spiritual) without: 1) belief in a God who is different from the rest of the world, 2) without looking for a heaven (and maybe hell) after this life, and 3) without believing that there is a special eternal part of people (their souls), which survives this life. In other words, religious naturalism is the attempt to lead a religious or spiritual life without the traditional beliefs in God, afterlife, and a soul.

Naturalists believe that this world, this universe, is all there is. The meaning of life is to be found in relating to this world, not to a God and heaven apart from this world. Nature, including humans and their civilizations, is all there is. That is what naturalism means.[1] Religious naturalism is an attempt to lead a religious life as a naturalist.

Explaining what constitutes a religious or spiritual life is a large and hotly contested topic. Here is my working definition of religion. It is a tentative definition, subject to revision. Religion is our attempt to make sense of our lives and to act appropriately within the total scheme of things. In other words, religion is an effort to orient ourselves to the big picture.

Is nature enough? Perhaps not. It would be nice to have a God to comfort and console us. It would be nice to have a heaven in which the suffering and pain of this world is relieved and our deepest longings are satisfied and the injustices of this world are made right. It would be nice, but I do not think there is any evidence for it. There is no big rock candy mountain. Is nature enough? No, but it will have to do. And, it will often suffice, especially when understood and appreciated for what it can and cannot do.

Now this idea seems dangerous, even downright subversive. But, do not worry. The religious naturalists I know are not out to subvert the moral order. We advocate learning to be moral without worrying about heaven or hell. We try to be moral because it is the right thing to do. In fact, many of us religious naturalists think that there are good scientific reasons for trying to be moral.

I am not writing these pages to change your religious beliefs. I could not do that anyway. Rather, I am trying to paint a picture of religious naturalism, especially its value in the struggle to save our planet—to keep it as a suitable home for us humans and our non-human relatives. Religious naturalism is a guess, what I call a surmise. I shall next try to make a case for it, but in the end, it will be an insight; an insight that makes sense to me and many other people. It is a surmise, not a scientific theory, although I try to have it informed by the best scientific thinking.

A case for religious naturalism

A rigorous proof for the adequacy of religious naturalism or any other philosophy of life cannot be provided. However, a case for religious naturalism can be made, even though it will not be a conclusive argument. It will be a wager, a reasoned, weighted wager, and one side will appear more likely to be true.

Naturalism should not be thought of as an empirical generalization from scientific facts. Naturalism, religious or otherwise, is a philosophical position. It is deeply informed by the results of scientific inquiry, but it is not simply based on them. It is a philosophical position and, at the same time, a way of living. As such, it cannot be dismissed simply because it goes beyond strict empirical evidence or the canons of scientific inquiry.

A negative argument for the ontological restraint involved in any kind of naturalism is that the arguments for the reality of God conceived of as an ontological ultimate are unsound. A complete critique of all the arguments for a maximally conceived deity (as opposed to the naturalistic theism treated in Chapter 5) is not possible here. (For a fuller treatment, see Stone, 1992, 28–30.) However, an indication of the weakness of some of the more popular of these arguments can be sketched here.

The ontological arguments for the existence of God, which claim to prove that because God is by definition a necessary being, God must necessarily exist, have been usually thought to be invalid. Charles Hartshorne and Schubert Ogden have recently set forth vigorous defenses of the ontological arguments based on what is technically known as modal logic. Using a criticism similar to that of John Hick, I have critiqued Hartshorne and Ogden in terms of a distinction between the necessity of a proposition and the necessity of an entity (Stone, 1992, 170–181).

The cosmological arguments for the existence of God were given classic expression by Thomas Aquinas in five arguments. He argued from the existence of the universe to the existence of a cause for the universe. In these arguments, he makes three assumptions, the second and third of which are untenable. The first is that all finite beings are dependent on other beings for motion, efficient causation, or existence. The second is that an infinite regress in the chain of dependence is impossible. The third is that the anchor of this chain, the first cause or necessary being, is the proper object of religious devotion.

The human imagination is very fertile, and there is a human propensity for wish fulfillment. These tendencies make constant caution advisable. We need an agnosticism, an intellectual humility, about religious and philosophical ultimates.

A more positive case for religious naturalism can be made. Living as a *naturalist* means that you can avoid many of the disadvantages of some traditional religious outlooks. You do not have to wonder why God is allowing bad things to happen to you. You do not have to worry about the conflicts between science and religion. You do not have to go through the mental gymnastics of the standard attempts of theodicy or reconciliation of science and religion. And, you can avoid the unnecessary sense of guilt and the old-fashioned ideas that sometimes accompany traditional religion. You do not fan the flames of religious bigotry and wars. Many religious people also share these freedoms, but naturalists do not have to fight rearguard actions against the sorrier aspects of organized religion as many religious liberals do. And, living as a *religious* naturalist means that you do not have to live in a totally alien world. Granted that nature as a whole is indifferent to you, that the tsunami does not ask about your religion nor God helps you hit a home run, nevertheless, the universe has set the stage for the physical, biological, and historical evolution that produced you. And, living as a religious naturalist means that you can have many of the positive values of a religious or spiritual life.

What is "religious" about religious naturalism? To lead a religious life, I suggest, is to "*attempt to make sense of our lives and behave appropriately within the total scheme of things*" (Stone, 2008, 226). This definition, incomplete though it may be, points out two important things. First, making sense of something is not an empirical issue in the strict sense. On the other hand, making sense should not side-step empirical inquiry. Insight should be informed by the best sciences available. Second, when we try to make sense of our lives, there is a dimension to this that is "about everything." We ask, how does my joy, my sorrow, my dilemmas fit into the grand scheme of things? This attempt to make sense "of it all" can be thought of as what makes us religious. It is what unites religious naturalism with other religious orientations. As a naturalist, I try to be open to the challenges and graces, which this life affords to me. Occasionally, I imagine myself as a minor partner on one of the growing edges of the cosmos. This is my naturalist analog to being a "created co-creator," as Lutheran theologian Philip Hefner develops the idea (Hefner, 1993).

To lead a religious life does not mean to identify with any particular religion or join any of the normally recognized religious groups. A religious naturalist might find resources and discipline in a compatible religious body or even more than one religious tradition, but need not.

There is a downside to religious naturalism. You do not have the comfort of a God who makes everything turn out alright or of immortality. There is no cosmic companion to alleviate your loneliness. You cannot use God to make sense of all of the suffering and chaos in the world. It is our job, not God's, to strengthen the levees and prepare for emergencies. It is our job to comfort the bereaved, to strive for justice, and to remember those who have perished. For many people, God also offers an explanation for specific events, such as why the flood devastated New Orleans or smallpox decimated Boston in 1721–1722. God also seems to offer an explanation for why there is anything, not nothing. But, God does not suffice as an explanation, either in particular or in general. Why is there a God? These are limit questions. Naturalism should respect the asking of limit questions, but retain an agnosticism toward any alleged answers to them. To live without a God or hope of immortality may take some grieving. However, mourning sometimes is a part of maturity.

Nature is not enough. It is not self-explanatory. It is not completely meaningful. Nature does not give complete satisfaction to our deepest longings. It does not answer our moral dilemmas. It does not provide a foundation for our epistemological, ontological, or valuational searches. But, nature, including human culture, is all that we have and it will have to do. And, often, it suffices magnificently (adapted from Stone, 2003).

Who are the religious naturalists?

There are a number of religious naturalists—some of whom call themselves religious naturalists, some of whom do not—who would agree with what I have written up to this point. This section introduces a few of these figures in order to give the reader a sense of the variety of religious naturalists and also some common themes that appear in their works.

We could start with indigenous traditions. However, we shall discuss these in Chapter 7. We could also start with the Carvaka writers (the materialistic Hindu thinkers), with the Mahayana Buddhist tradition that nirvana is samsara, the Daoist notion of the Dao, and the neo-Confucian idea of forming one body with Heaven and Earth (Stone, 2008, 19). However, for sake of brevity, we shall restrict ourselves to the Western tradition. The monk Giordano Bruno developed a version of pantheism and was burned at the stake for his heresy in 1600. Pantheism is close to religious naturalism, and often, is a variety of it. In the enlightenment, John Toland was the first to use the term "pantheism" (Toland, 1751). Interpreters of the philosopher Spinoza disagree, but surely his phrase "God or nature" is a clear forerunner of religious naturalism (Stone, 2008, 18, 42–44). The American Ralph Waldo Emerson had a strong sense of the immanence of the divine, but his idealism kept him from being a consistent naturalist (Stone, 2008, 18–19). Perhaps, Henry David Thoreau belongs. (See the detailed study of Thoreau by Bron Taylor in *Dark Green Religion*, Taylor, 2010, 50–58, 227–247.) There are important twentieth-century philosophers in the United States who can be considered religious naturalists. These include George Santayana, John Dewey, John Herman Randall, and Roy Wood Sellars. Mention can also be made of the philosophers Samuel Alexander in England and Jan Christiaan Smuts in South Africa (Stone, 2008, 17–58). It would take several pages to explain the people and movements mentioned in this paragraph. For the sake of brevity, therefore, we shall make a selective presentation of prominent twentieth-century religious naturalists.

The humanists

In the 1920s and 1930s, there were a number of agnostic or atheist humanist writers whose passion for intellectual honesty and social justice combined with a non-theistic outlook could be considered as making them religious naturalists. This is because these passions acted as relatively transcendent factors in their lives and writings, similar to the religious element of other naturalists.

John Dietrich and Curtis Reese

One of these was John Dietrich, minister of the First Unitarian Society in Minneapolis from 1916 to 1938 (Olds, 1996, 53–97; Dietrich, 1989; Stone, 2008, 69–70). Although he wished to drop all talk about God, he did not consider himself an atheist, which for him implied both crude materialism and dogmatism (Olds, 1996, 73). In 1917, at the annual meeting of the Western Unitarian Conference in Des Moines, Iowa, Dietrich talked with Unitarian minister Curtis Reese about their very similar views. Soon, Reese started using the term "humanism." In 1919, Reese became the secretary of the Western Unitarian Conference. This is extremely significant. As the chief Unitarian denominational executive in the Midwestern United States, he was able to facilitate the placement of humanist ministers in pulpits, thus providing an institutional home for religious humanism (Olds, 1996, 99–124).

The Humanist Manifesto

The first *Humanist Manifesto* of 1933 is probably the most well-known statement of the Humanist position, at least in the United States (*Humanist Manifestos I and II*, 1973). The sense of the manifesto can be gathered from the following quotations:

> Religious humanism considers the complete realization of human personality to be the end of man's life and seeks its development and fulfillment in the here and now. . . . In place of the old attitudes involved in worship and prayer the humanist finds his religious emotions expressed in a heightened sense of personal life and in a cooperative effort to promote social well-being. . . . Man is at last becoming aware that he alone is responsible for the realization of the world of his dreams, that he has within himself the power for its achievement. He must set intelligence and will to the task.
> (*Humanist Manifestos I and II*, 1973, 9. 10)

Julian Huxley

Biologist Julian Huxley, first Director General of UNESCO, was an important humanist writer during the 1920s and 1930s. He called for a radical transformation of Western religion in *Religion without Revelation*. The reconstruction is to be based on agnosticism (thus without referring to a supernatural divine power), evolutionary natural science, and psychology (Huxley, 1941, v, 17). The agnosticism extends to God, heaven, and hell.

> Until ... the idea of God [is] relegated to the past with the idea of ritual magic and other products of primitive and unscientific thought, we shall never get the new religion we need. In that new religion, man must make up his mind to take upon himself his full burden, by acknowledging that he is the highest entity of which he has any knowledge, that his values are the only basis for any categorical imperative, and that he must work out both his own salvation and destiny, and the standards on which they are based.
> (Huxley, 1941, vi-vii)

Huxley saw the core of religion as reverence or a sense of the sacred. As grounds for this assertion, he drew upon the anthropological and phenomenological studies of religion by Robert Lowie, R.R. Marett, and Rudolf Otto (Huxley, 1941, 8, 41–47). Mature religion should move beyond convention and superstition and be linked with intelligence and morality (Huxley, 1941, 16–17, 41–47, 48, 54).

Kenneth Patton

Kenneth Patton was a minister of the Universalist experimental Charles Street Meeting House in Boston from 1949 to about 1964. In *Man's Hidden Search: An Inquiry into Naturalistic Mysticism*, Patton develops the theme of "being at home in the universe" (Patton, 1954). In poetic language, he writes,

> The wind comforts him as fondly as his mother's arms / The sunlight is like his best friend's recognizing laughter. A caterpillar crawling on the back of his hand is as rich and welcoming as his brother's arms across his shoulders. The children on the street of another country are as near to him as his own children.... The earth is his home and its creatures are his family.
> (Patton, 1954, 54)

Coupled with this sense of "at home-ness" is the sense of mystery, "The sheer wonder of the 'thereness,' the 'thatness' of any object, the simple, profound mystery of existence itself, of the texture, the presence of anything" (Patton, 1954, 71).

Patton makes the religious dimension of this naturalism clear, using the term naturalistic mysticism. "Mysticism is the means whereby men outreach themselves, extend themselves beyond previous confines, stretch the tent of their comprehension and observation to cover a larger plot of the universe" (Patton, 1954, 98).

Patton finds a major cause for our inadequacy as mystics in the fact that our emotions and thoughts have, for centuries, been accommodated to the two-storied world. "Religion was primarily the staircase by which men could get upstairs" (Patton, 1954, 96).

To one who believes in the two realms, an explanation of life and man in terms of one realm may seem meager and stultifying. The only answer is that expanse and splendor have little to do with the number of realms. One room can be larger than two smaller rooms together. In qualitative terms, the material realm may come to appear so abounding in variety, subtlety, beauty, depth, and mystery that it will include within it the qualities of existence and experience that once were thought to belong to a spiritual realm (Patton, 1954, 100).

The religion of the future will celebrate the universe, centering especially on life. It will be an impassioned affirmation, a celebration of life (Patton, 1964, 119, 125, 151).

More recent religious naturalists

Albert Einstein

The physicist Albert Einstein inspired much discussion in the media. His views of religion, scattered in various places in his writings, probably fit within our conception of religious naturalism. He definitely rejected any notion of a personal God. For him, genuine religiosity involved a pursuit of rational knowledge of the natural world together with a humility about achieving it (Jammer, 1999, 95, 117, 121–122). He described his own spiritual life as a "cosmic religious feeling," admired Spinoza's "intellectual love" of God (*amor Dei intellectualis*), and spoke of the wonder of nature and the harmony of the universe (Jammer, 1999, 78–80, 97, 121–122). He once declared that: "My views are near to those of Spinoza: admiration for the beauty of and belief in the logical simplicity of the order and harmony which we can grasp humbly and only imperfectly" (quoted in Jammer, 1999, 138–139). Einstein was a determinist, thus separating him from many recent naturalists (Jammer, 1999, 80 and elsewhere). He separated morality and religion (Jammer, 1999, 135). The possible difficulty of including him among the religious naturalists comes out in his reference to "the existence of a spirit vastly superior to that of men" and the phrase, "The divine reveals itself in the physical world" (Jammer, 1999, 93, 151). These two quotations aside, the general thrust of Einstein's thought is in a religious naturalist mode. Perhaps, the vagueness of "a spirit" and "the divine" allowed him to use expressions that he would not have used if he were trying to achieve philosophical clarity. Recently, Ronald Dworkin, in *Religion Without God*, developed an approach similar to that of Einstein (Dworkin, 2013, 1–43).

Sharon Welch

Sharon Welch, the Provost of Meadville Lombard Theological School, has been reflecting on how to work for social justice with limited knowledge about the consequences of our actions and no assurance about their success. Her thinking about the theological dimension of social action falls into two periods.

8 Introducing religious naturalism

In both periods, the divine is not a separate entity. In her earlier period, the divine is a characteristic of relationships or of the capacity to enter into right relationships with other people, with nature, and with ourselves (Welch, 2000, 173, 175). Rather than the word "God", she uses "divine" as an adjective to refer to grace or the power of relations.

I detect at least three functions of the divine for Welch in this period. One is that "divine" refers to the unexpected healing of relationships. Grace is "a power that lifts us to a larger self and a deeper joy as it leads us to accept blame and begin the long process of reparation and re-creation" (Welch, 2000, 174). A second function of the divine is as the compassion and anger needed to nurture and protect (Welch, 2000, 173). A third function is as a focus of respect, orientation, and worship. "Divinity then connotes a quality of relationships, lives, events, and natural processes that are worthy of worship, that provide orientation, focus, and guidance to our lives" (Welch, 2000, 176).

In her later writing, Welch is even more reticent to use traditional religious language. This is in part because she is keenly aware of how religious people can be cruel and destructive.

Slave owners and abolitionists, participants in the Civil Rights Movement, and members of the Ku Klux Klan, alike drew comfort and challenge from their religious beliefs and their participation in religious communities (Welch, 1999a, 127).

Chet Raymo

In his delightful *Skeptics and True Believers*, Chet Raymo has given us a very readable account of the attitudes of these two groups, skeptics and true believers. A former teacher of physics and astronomy, for years he had a weekly column in the *Boston Globe*. "Science cannot nor should be a religion, but it can be the basis for the religious experience: astonishment, experiential union, adoration, praise" (Raymo, 1998, 255).

Basic to Raymo is his sense that all the "scientific knowledge that we have of this world, or will ever have, is as an island in the sea [of mystery].... We live in our partial knowledge as the Dutch live on polders claimed from the sea" (Raymo, 1998, 47, quoted from his previous *Honey from Stone*). As a corollary, "the growth of the island increases the length of the shore along which we encounter mystery" (Raymo, 1998, 48). Also important is that Raymo rejects the idea of Wordsworth that the "meddling intellect" really "murders to dissect." Instead, he agrees with Richard Feynman's reply that scientific knowledge adds to the excitement of a flower. It adds. It does not subtract (Raymo, 1998, 52–53). Readers will also find his *When God is Gone, Everything is Holy* very delightful reading (Raymo, 2008).

Donald Crosby

In his book, *A Religion of Nature*, philosopher Donald Crosby develops the viewpoint that nature is the religious ultimate. He does this by articulating a theory of the functions of a "religious object," that is, the fundamental focus of thought and practice in a religion. The six functions are uniqueness, primacy, pervasiveness of everything else, rightness in the sense of being the goal and standard for human life, permanence in the face of declining health and approaching death, and hiddenness in the sense of being a source of mystery and awe and something that can only be spoken of indirectly. Crosby then goes on to show how nature fulfills each of these functions, and is thus, the appropriate religious object.

It is important for Crosby to refer to the mixture of good and evil in nature. Life brings pain, suffering, and death. Nature is partly good and partly evil. However, we need to remember that nature can often rejuvenate, inspire, and redeem us.

To the objection that this viewpoint does not provide an explanation for nature, Crosby replies that no explanation is needed. If God is posited as the explanation for nature, the question as to the explanation for God raises its head. If it is replied that God is self-caused, the same can also be said of nature.

Nature is not personal and has no conscious awareness. Thus, we are relieved of the problems of wondering how a good God can be the author of so much evil and apparently not display impartiality. The universe has no overall purpose or plan. But, there are creatures in the universe who have purposes and make plans. Yet, even though nature is not personal, humans can express gratitude, trust, and resolve in meditations on nature.

Nature, while not itself good, is the principal source of good for all its creatures. It has produced the beauty and sublimity of the universe. Through the process of evolution, it is the source, sustainer, and restorer of life. It is the ultimate source of human life and the goods of history and culture, and has evolved humans to create and preserve various goods. Thus,

> we have no need of God, gods, animating spirits . . . nor do we need to pine for another life. . . . Nature itself, when we rightly conceive of it and comprehend our role within it, can provide ample context and support for finding purpose, value, and meaning in our lives.
>
> (Crosby, 2002, 169)

After publishing *A Religion of Nature*, Crosby has written a number of books that further develop his approach. *Living with Ambiguity* focuses on the issue of the destructive aspect of nature. *The Thou of Nature* elaborates his proposal for an environmental ethic. *More than Discourse* is an analysis of religious symbols or their analogs, which can be used in a naturalistic spirituality. *Nature as Sacred Ground: A Metaphysics for Religious Naturalism* develops one possible approach to major philosophical issues (Crosby, 2002, 2008, 2013, 2014, 2015).

Since 1978, there have been many writings by people who fit under the umbrella term of religious naturalism. They are too numerous to mention here. A summary of their work up to 2007 can be found in Jerome A. Stone, *Religious Naturalism Today* (Stone, 2008). I wish to mention the following, written since 2007: Victor

Anderson's *Creative Exchange: A Constructive Theology of African American Religious Experience*, Ronald Dworkin's *Religion Without God*, and Carol Wayne White's *Black Lives and Sacred Humanity* (Anderson, 2008; Dworkin, 2013; White, 2016). Michael Hogue has written a helpful analysis and evaluation in *The Promise of Religious Naturalism* (Hogue, 2010). He focused on four figures: Donald Crosby, Ursula Goodenough, Loyal Rue, and Jerome Stone.

There are many more writers who could be mentioned. However, this will give the reader a sense of the variety of writers who could be categorized as religious naturalists. For a discussion of several of them, see my *Religious Naturalism Today* (Stone, 2008).

Boundary issues

This characterization of religious naturalism as the attempt to explore and encourage religious ways of responding to the world on a completely naturalistic basis has some boundary issues.

One idea that overlaps religious naturalism is materialism or physicalism. By materialism, I do not mean old-fashioned mechanism. Rather, it is an affirmation of the physical basis of all reality. Now, this is logically difficult to maintain because of the word "all." However, in order to keep dialog open with indigenous and neo-pagan religious people who have experienced what they term immaterial spirits and also in order not to block inquiry in this area by dogmatically denying the possibility of such experiences, I do not affirm physicalism unequivocally. In the final analysis, however, I suggest that whatever spirits there are will be found to have a material basis. The universe is full of patterns that can be replicated across time and space. That is the basis of both life and information technology. However, I believe that these patterns always have a basis in physical reality. Naturalism does not logically entail physicalism, but most religious naturalists tend toward a generous materialism that allows for much of what we designate by the terms "purpose," "mind," and "value."

Religious humanism can be viewed as a type of religious naturalism. The commitment of many humanists to the search for truth and the struggle for justice is the naturalistic analog to commitment to the transcendent in traditional religions. (At one time, I drew a line between religious naturalism and humanism. See Stone, 1999.) William Murry, in his *Reason and Reverence: Religious Humanism for the 21st Century*, declares that religious naturalism gives humanism "both a solid philosophical foundation and an inspiring sacred story. It gives humanism a cosmology, a deeper spiritual dimension, an environmental ethic, and a larger vision." Calling this stance "humanistic religious naturalism," he goes on to write that humanism "is greatly enriched by grounding it in religious naturalism" (Murry, 2007, 72, 61–74).

Whether pantheism is a form of religious naturalism need not detain us long. Probably, many pantheists could be considered religious naturalists.

There is a similarity between some religious naturalists and people who speak of the earth as a Goddess named Gaia. However, many religious naturalists have a religious or spiritual orientation to the entire universe, not just the planet earth.

Is process theology a form of naturalism? Process theology is a technical form of theology rooted in the philosophies of Alfred North Whitehead and Charles Hartshorne and developed especially at the University of Chicago's Divinity School and the Center for Process Studies at Claremont, California. As I understand process theology, although God is deeply immersed within this world, God is so distinct and superior as to fall outside of naturalism as I understand it. Thus, process theology is immanentist, but not naturalist.

Another boundary issue is about a group of theologians that can be called "ground of being" theologians. These include Paul Tillich's notion of God as the ground of being, Robert Neville's notion that "God's individuality emerges in the act of creating; it is not antecedent," and Wesley Wildman's idea of the self-transcendent ground of nature (Tillich's phrase "ground of being" is found throughout his writings, but see especially his *Systematic Theology*, I, 1951; Neville, 1991, 16; Wildman, 2006). While there is an affinity between this "ground of being naturalism" and the naturalism of this book, most naturalists utilized in this book would not use the term in Wildman's sense. I feel affinity to these ideas, particularly because they depict the immanence of the sacred. Indeed, I once considered myself a Tillichean. Nevertheless, I moved away from this position when I decided that the concept of a "ground of being" was finally unintelligible and that much of the value of this viewpoint could be had at less intellectual cost in my minimalist vision of transcendence.

In this chapter, we have described religious naturalism as a philosophy of life that points out how to lead a robust religious (or spiritual) life while believing that the natural world, including humans, is all there is. We now turn to two issues that will provide the starting points for what follows: our experiences of sacredness and how we draw meaning from the picture of the universe that science is describing.

Note

1 Portions of this chapter are adapted from the Introduction to my *Religious Naturalism Today* (Stone, 2008) and "What is Religious Naturalism?" (Stone, 2000).

Bibliography

Anderson, Victor. 2008. *Creative Exchange: A Constructive Theology of African American Religious Experience*. Philadelphia, PA: Fortress Press.
Crosby, Donald A. 2002. *A Religion of Nature*. Albany: State University of New York Press.
Crosby, Donald A. 2008. *Living with Ambiguity: Religious Naturalism and the Menace of Evil*. Albany: State University of New York Press.
Crosby, Donald A. 2013. *The Thou of Nature: Religious Naturalism and Reverence for Sentient Life*. Albany: State University of New York Press.
Crosby, Donald A. 2014. *More than Discourse: Symbolic Expressions of Naturalistic Faith*. Albany: State University of New York Press.
Crosby, Donald A. 2015. *Nature as Sacred Ground: A Metaphysics for Religious Naturalism*. Albany: State University of New York Press.
Dietrich, John H. 1989. *What if the World Went Humanist? Ten Sermons*. Edited by Mason Olds. Yellow Springs, OH: Fellowship of Religious Humanists.

Dworkin, Ronald. 2013. *Religion Without God*. Cambridge, MA: Harvard University Press.
Hefner, Philip. 1993. *The Human Factor: Evolution, Culture, and Religion*. Minneapolis, MN: Fortress Press.
Hogue, Michael. 2010. *The Promise of Religious Naturalism*. Lanham, MD: Rowman & Littlefield.
Humanist Manifestos I and II. 1973. Buffalo: Prometheus Books.
Huxley, Julian. 1941. *Religion Without Revelation*. London: Watts & Co.
Jammer, Max. 1999. *Einstein and Religion: Physics and Theology*. Princeton: Princeton University Press.
Murry, William R. 2007. *Reason and Reverence: Religious Humanism for the 21st Century*. Boston: Skinner House Books.
Neville, Robert Cummings. 1991. *Behind the Masks of God: An Essay Toward Comparative Theology*. Albany: State University of New York Press.
Olds, Mason. 1996. *American Religious Humanism*, revised ed. Minneapolis, Fellowship of Religious Humanists.
Patton, Kenneth L. 1954. *Man's Hidden Search: An Inquiry into Naturalistic Mysticism*. Boston: Meeting House Press.
Patton, Kenneth L. 1964. *A Religion for One World: Art and Symbols for a Universal Religion*. Boston: Beacon Press.
Raymo, Chet. 1998. *Skeptics and True Believers: The Exhilarating Connection Between Science and Religion*. New York: Walker and Company.
Raymo, Chet. 2008. *When God is Gone, Everything is Holy: The Making of a Religious Naturalist*. Notre Dame, IN: Sorin Books.
Stone, Jerome A. 1992. *The Minimalist Vision of Transcendence: A Naturalist Philosophy of Religion*. Albany: State University of New York Press.
Stone, Jerome A. 1999. "The Line Between Religious Naturalism and Humanism: G.B. Foster and E. Haydon," *American Journal of Theology and Philosophy*, 20 (September), 217–240.
Stone, Jerome A. 2000. "What is Religious Naturalism?" *Journal of Liberal Religion* (Fall). www.meadville.edu. [Reprinted with addendum, *Religious Humanism*, Winter/Spring 2001, 60–74].
Stone, Jerome A. 2003 "Is Nature enough? Yes," *Zygon: Journal of Religion and Science*, 38, 783–800
Stone, Jerome A. 2008. *Religious Naturalism Today: The Rebirth of a Forgotten Alternative*. Albany: State University of New York Press.
Taylor, Bron. 2010. *Dark Green Religion: Nature Spirituality and the Planetary Future*. Berkeley: University of California Press.
Tillich, Paul. 1951. *Systematic Theology*, Volume One. Chicago: The University of Chicago Press.
Toland, John. 1751. *Pantheistikon*. Sam Paterson, London; reprinted by Garland Publishing, London.
Welch, Sharon D. 1999. *Sweet Dreams in America: Making Ethics and Spirituality Work*. New York: Routledge.
Welch, Sharon D. 2000. *A Feminist Ethic of Risk*, revised ed. Minneapolis: Fortress Press.
White, Carol Wayne. 2016. *Black Lives and Sacred Humanity: Toward an African American Religious Naturalism*. New York, NY: Fordham University Press.
Wildman, Wesley J. 2006. "Ground-of-Being Theologies," in Edited by Philip Clayton and Zachary Simpson. *The Oxford Handbook of Religion and Science* (pp. 612–632). New York: Oxford University Press.

2
ALTERNATIVE STARTING POINTS

Experiences of the sacred and the big picture

In our exploration of religious naturalism, we shall alternate between two perspectives: experiences of the sacred or events of overriding importance and the scientifically informed big picture or epic of creation. These two could be called specific feelings and abstract generalizations. They could also be called our feelings with minimal thought and our attitudes after careful, rational reflection upon our best-tested scientific theories. Which comes first? Sometimes, it is important to start with one or the other. The key thing is to keep alternating between immediate experience and reflection on the big picture. It is something like walking. For some purposes, it is important to start off with the correct foot. But, whichever way you start, the important point is to alternate between one foot and the other.

It is important for the reader to remember that although many of the illustrations of sacred events will be drawn from the non-human world, such as a brown pelican or Horicon Marsh, many events and processes within the human world, such as creative interchange, can be thought of as sacred. The inspiration of religious naturalism is not limited to sunsets and wilderness areas.

To illustrate a specific feeling of the sacred, I cite Donald Crosby's account of watching a pelican soaring over land near the Gulf of Mexico.

> Its great wings outstretched, the brown pelican spirals in the thermal air. Scarcely a flicker of those magnificent wings is required for it to soar further and further aloft. Finally reaching an apogee of the spiral, it gently banks and slowly descends, only to be uplifted again in its circling flight. The pelican's course through the air, its feet tucked behind its breast and its giant beak thrust boldly before it, seems effortless. For me, at that moment, this pelican's flight is a compelling symbol of the numinous powers, presences, and wonders of the natural order to which we both miraculously belong.
>
> (Crosby, 2014, 3)

On the other hand, to illustrate the big picture, I refer to Ursula Goodenough's best-selling book, *The Sacred Depths of Nature* (Goodenough, 1998). Goodenough is a microbiologist and author of a widely used textbook on genetics. After years of research, she reflected on the religious implications of what she had learned as a scientist and wrote her book. We shall develop her position further on in this chapter.

Actually, it may become clear from these two illustrations that it is impossible to completely separate the immediate feeling of importance and the scientifically informed big picture. There is thoughtful reflection going on in Crosby's account of the brown pelican and plenty of feeling in Goodenough's *Sacred Depths*. Nevertheless, we can think of immediate experiences of the sacred and reflection on the big picture as end points of a spectrum. Thus, we can describe our exploration of sacred nature as based on both specific feelings of overriding importance and reflection on the scientifically informed picture of the entire universe.

For another illustration of a specific experience of the sacred, let me refer to a visit that my wife and I made to Horicon Marsh in Wisconsin. It is a mid-October day in 2014. The sky has a medium high overcast. The breeze is chilly, but I am okay under my topcoat and heavy sweater. I am a little apprehensive about how cold it will be when we get on the pontoon boat and sit still as we move into the wind. But, it will be worth it, I tell myself. I remember our previous trip here in the spring bird migration season several years ago. It was warm and sunny then. I do not even tell myself not to be disappointed if this time it is not as great as last time.

My wife and I were on one of our pilgrimages to Wisconsin. Yes, I know that's a religious term, but even an old agnostic like me has an appreciation for those well-honed words. To talk about "going on a pilgrimage" is more illuminating than obfuscating. The leaves had lost much of their color on our drive up from the northern Chicago suburbs, but it was still nice to get away—even though we are retired. That morning we had left our motel after a good breakfast and had refreshed our knowledge of the history of Horicon Marsh at the visitor's center. After lunch (I am not much for fasting, I chuckle to myself), we find the little, low sign that invites us to go on a marsh boat ride. We park, approach, and get our tickets.

We are asked to watch a video about the cranes at the International Crane Foundation (ICF). Not as relevant to the day's visit, but the story of cranes, their restoration, and the lighter-than-air pilots teaching the young cranes how to migrate is fascinating the nth time you learn about it. Besides, the ICF needs publicity and the folk gathered here are the perfect audience.

We climb on board the little pontoon craft. There were eight of us (if I remember right). The engine catches right away and slowly we are off, up the little river, under the bridge, past the John Deere factory, toward the south end of the marsh. Our pilot and guide talks appreciatively about the care that John Deere takes with this river: the plants and carefully placed rock piles to cut down on erosion, and the barriers that keep the oil slicks contained around their discharge hoses. Of course, they have some self-interest here in reducing erosion, and the Clean Water Act is enforced. Still, care seems taken with the river that drains the marsh.

Our boat takes us up near the west side of the marsh and back down the other. The southern part of the marsh through which we go is a mix of open water, cattails, and small wooded islands. Most of the birds in this part of the marsh have either migrated or are out feeding in the surrounding farmland. We do spot some ducks and other water birds and a couple of double-crested cormorants.

This is a special place. The southern third is a wildlife area cared for by the Wisconsin Department of Natural Resources, the northern two-thirds are a national wildlife area protected by the U.S. Fish and Wildlife Service. People seem to care about protecting this wetland as a habitat for wildlife. Years earlier, we had made a similar boat trip in May during the spring migration season and had seen or heard a number of different warblers. My soul felt nourished by our boat ride.

This was not a deeply ecstatic experience, such as the time I was overwhelmed by the stars on a dark clear night in Giant City State Park in southern Illinois, so moved that I stayed awake most of the night with a visceral excitement. Nevertheless, I felt this visit to the marsh was an experience of overriding significance. The use of the word *sacred* seems appropriate.

Even though I use a visit to a Wisconsin marsh as an illustration of an experience of the sacred, we should not be misled by this example. For a religious naturalist, such experiences are not to be limited to the non-human world, such as a park or nature preserve. The birth of a child or standing at a graveside or a moment of hard-won reconciliation between enemies often show us that the sacred can be found in the human realm. Furthermore, a sacred place of what we call "the natural world" need not be a set-aside place, such as a park or nature preserve, as is Horicon Marsh. Often, a vacant lot or backyard will suffice.

Religious naturalism stresses that humans are an integral part of nature. When naturalists with a spiritual bent write or talk about "nature," the human world is included. Even when Thoreau writes about his experience about the timberline on Mount Ktaadn or Donald Crosby writes about the graceful flight of a brown pelican, focusing on what might be called their intrinsic or inherent value, there are humans involved doing the experiencing and the writing, and in the case of many religious naturalists, there is self-aware reflection on these engagements with the other-than-human.

One more example may illustrate my notion of an experience of the sacred. The young bird landed on her back. The fledgling swallow (or swift?) was just learning to fly and had found a nice landing place on 17-year-old Dottie. Startled and delighted, Dottie stood still on the verandah as the little bird worked its way up to her shoulder and then under her dark tresses. It seemed like a long time as Dottie kept still and onlookers tried not to scare the little creature. Finally, Dottie said, in a hushed, emotional voice, "I feel like God has picked me." Meanwhile, the mother bird was flying back and forth overhead, screeching, clearly in distress. After pictures were taken, someone gently pulled back her hair and coaxed the bird onto his finger. "That was so cool!" exclaimed Dottie.

16 Alternative starting points

We can use this anecdote as an illustration of a particularly intense experience of sacredness. Let us look at the two things the girl said. "I feel like God has picked me." This is clearly traditional religious language, and whether true or not, was used appropriately in the sense that what she said made sense to everyone. This was clearly an experience of major importance to her. She also said that the event was "cool." Given my use of the term "sacred," we can say that this was a sacred event for her. It was the felt major significance of the event, not her use of traditional religious language, that allows us to use the term "sacred."

When I asked the girl's father if we could say that this was a sacred event for his daughter, "No," he replied. (Both of her parents are academics, so the question was appropriate.) My point here is that while the term "sacred" is clearly apt at some times, like many vague words, there is no bright line around its appropriate extension. There is no set of criteria to clearly demarcate the situations in which the term "sacred" is used appropriately. The father was not wrong in rejecting the use of the term (especially if he had a developed theoretical definition of "sacred" based on his academic discipline). On the other hand, given my theory of the "sacred" as "any thing, event or process of major felt importance," it is entirely appropriate to say that, to her, this was a sacred event. For our purpose in this book, which is not that of religious studies, a certain latitude in the use of this word is allowable, if not taken to an extreme post-modern excess.

This is, of course, a very wide and unusual definition of the word "sacred." The word usually has connotations of "coming from" or "pointing to" or "symbolizing" or "participating" in a transcendent or otherworldly dimension; in short, the word "sacred" has connotations of the supernatural. Given that naturalism, which is the viewpoint of this book, does not recognize the existence of the transcendent, otherworldly, or supernatural, the term "sacred" is not used here in its traditional meaning.

The word "sacred," as used in this book, refers to any thing, event, process, or action of very great felt importance. This is a naturalistic analog of the standard meaning of the word. This naturalistic meaning is non-standard, and therefore, controversial. This is similar to other uses of traditional words with new meanings. For example, the denotation of the word "family" by many English speakers in recent times includes a same-sex couple with an adopted child. This is not yet a standard usage, but it is probably on its way to becoming so. It is still controversial. Words change their meanings over time. One cannot legitimately defend the restriction of the word "family" to a same-sex couple or a single parent and child or children merely by saying that "the word family *means* either a man and a wife plus any children or else a single parent plus any children." One cannot say that this *is* what the word means, because the word is changing its meaning. One could adopt a conservative stance and say that "the word family *should be restricted* to either a man and a woman plus any children or else a single parent plus any children." But, then, this restriction needs to be defended. In controversial cases, there is a burden of proof (or at least of justification) on *both* those who wish to expand the meaning of a term *and* on those who wish to restrict its meaning. So, it is with the term "sacred."

Our justification for this wider use of the term "sacred" is first that our naturalistic stance requires widening the use of the term past its traditional otherworldly connotation. Second, no other term has the evocative power of the word *sacred*. Other terms, such as "special," "extraordinary," "unusual," or "incredible" do not have the same power. "Venerable," "sacrosanct," or "hallowed" might be used in some contexts, perhaps to supplement the word "sacred," but are more cumbersome. The word "worth" could be used in some other contexts, but again it does not have the evocative power of "sacred." "Dignity" is often restricted to persons involved in slower activity. Sometimes "cool," sometimes and often "awesome," in current English can be used in place of "sacred," but only when a more colloquial word is appropriate. Note should be made that this second justification for using this broader sense of "sacred" in this book is that it has evocative power. Evocative power, of course, can be dangerous. It can lead to obfuscation and fuzzy thinking. It can be used to persuade someone to adopt an attitude of reverence without thinking. In other words, evocative terms, such as "sacred," can be used to shortcut thinking. But, the potential abuse of this term should not prevent its use. Evocative language need not and should not be eliminated entirely. Rather, emotionally loaded terms should be used cautiously, balanced by rational, thoughtful language.

Karl Peters has a similar naturalistic definition of "sacred." For him, "sacred" refers to whatever is the center of our being, that around which our lives revolve, very likely the source of our existence, what "brought us into being and nurtures our growth and development" (Peters, 2002, 22). I would modify that definition by noting that the sacred is what we recognize as or hold to be the center of our being, a point that Peters grants in the rest of his chapter. Also, I am using the term in a broader sense, to include things and events that we hold to be very important, not exclusively to what we regard as the source of our existence. I believe that Peters' definition is more closely related to its monotheistic ancestor than mine.

What are the experiences of sacred events or things?

The first starting point, then, is reflection on immediate experiences of the sacred or what I have also called "minimal experiences of transcendence" (Stone, 1992). I learned how to use the word "sacred" by attending services in a liberal Protestant church. When we used this term, it always meant that we were treating an event or object with respect. We *held* something sacred by treating it with respect. Later, through graduate study in the many religions of the world, I became familiar with the major texts and theorists concerning sacred things.[1]

Now I wish to describe certain events in my life that I have learned to call sacred. What I wish to stress is their overriding importance for me. When my son had finished his first year of college, I drove to bring him home for the summer.

We worked hard together to pack the car. Ready to start home, my son turned and said to me, "Come on Dad, I'll buy you a beer." A simple gesture, yet filled with significance. From that moment on, we were to treat each other as equals. The beer tasted good, but not just because we were thirsty.

After Martin Luther King was murdered, some residents, both Black and White, of the city of Evanston, Illinois, organized marches to put pressure on the city council to pass an open housing ordinance. At that time, it was perfectly legal to refuse to rent or sell a house to anyone, including Blacks and Jews, because of their race or ethnic origin. Now, I was quite busy as a father, breadwinner, and graduate student. Yet, my wife and I felt that this was the right moment to pressure the city council. Also, we felt that this was a way to educate our two children by direct participation in values that we held dear.

One summer evening walking in a park after dinner, my wife and I heard a noise just over our heads and looked up to see a kestrel catch a junco in midair and carry it in its bloody claws to eat on a nearby telephone pole. It gave us both a thrill at the excellence of the hunter and a vivid realization that this struggle so close to us was yet quite other than our concerns.

These events have been paradigms, that is, events that have clearly illuminated things for me. They are examples of what I call experiences of the sacred. Reflection on them has helped shape my philosophy of life. An early religious training provided a set of ideas that helped me reflect upon some very personal experiences, ideas that were transformed in the process of interaction with these events. *Inherited language and lived experience have always been in transaction.* I have described these three events also *to call forth analogous events for the reader*, events that will be quite different, and yet, perhaps, may share some features with my experience.

Gradually I have developed a technical theory of sacredness. It goes something like this. The word "sacred" is a word we use to describe events, things, processes that are of overriding importance and also are not under our control or within our power to manipulate. In this sense, these events and others are sacred. To acknowledge anything as sacred is to move beyond the narrow boundaries of the self.

This sense of overriding importance is similar to Goodenough's notion of "horizontal transcendence" (Stone, 1998, 163). It is also parallel to the view in Carol Wayne White's *Black Lives and Sacred Humanity*: "Sacrality is a specific affirmation and appreciation of that which is fundamentally important in life, or that which is ultimately valued: relational nature." The major difference between us is that she includes nature in her notion of sacrality: "our sacrality is a given part of nature's richness, spectacular complexity, and beauty" (White, 2016, 33). I have developed the notion of the sacred and then said that nature is sacred. I take it that this difference is not significant. J. Ronald Engel, in his *Sacred Sands*, has described the struggle to save part of the Indiana dunes lakeshore from industrial development as a struggle to save an ecosystem held to be sacred (Engel, 1983). Donald Crosby, in Chapter 7 of his *Nature as Sacred Ground*, has developed a theory of nature as a whole as sacred (Crosby, 2015). Our theories are complementary, in that my starting point is the experience of sacred events and processes, rather than nature as a whole.

The stance for living that flows from this emphasis on the sacred is essentially that of openness, of readiness for the appearance of sacred events. Disciplined preparation and loyal commitment to the sacred are called for, but need to be balanced by a recognition that the sacred is essentially unmanipulable. Thus, Confucian focusing of heart and mind needs to be balanced by a Taoist openness to the spontaneous play of the sacred.

There are further implications of this notion of the sacred.

1. Given my commitment to a philosophy of naturalism, sacred events are not understood as manifestations of something deeper, such as a God. Rather, the overriding importance *is* the "depth" or "height." All of the world religions, as I understand them, speak of going beyond the surface understanding of life. My naturalistic outlook suggests to me that the deeper vision we seek to attain is not of another realm or of invisible spirits, but rather a revised insight into importance of things. There is a "depth," not apart from, but right in the midst of things. I am indebted to Paul Tillich's notion of the "depth" dimension and even more to John Dewey's adjectival "religious quality of experience" in *A Common Faith* (Dewey, 1934). As Ursula Goodenough likes to say, rather than "Hosanna in the highest!," it's "Hosanna, right here, right now, this."
2. There are no clear boundaries around the sacred. Some events are clearly sacred. Others are perhaps boundary-line cases. My experience at Horicon Marsh was not as deeply ecstatic as my first glimpse of bald eagles hunting on the Wisconsin River in January. Nevertheless, I would call my visits to Horicon Marsh sacred moments. Even sharing a beer can be sacred. It is not always possible to know whether some events or places are sacred. Perhaps, this means that all things are sacred, although I am not sure that we are capable of sustaining such a sense or even that we should.
3. The sacred is not a separate sphere of life. It is not to be found separate from the pursuits of truth, justice, beauty and selfhood, and so on. It is more like the caffeine in the coffee than like a cherry on top of a sundae. Here, I have been influenced by both Paul Tillich and John Dewey.
4. Religion could be thought of as a self-conscious acknowledgment of the sacred. In that case, there is no clear separation of the sacred and the secular, yet there is still a role for the deliberate recognition of the presence of sacred things. Religious communities and their traditions, what we sometimes disparagingly call "organized religions," are attempts to nurture and pass on the sense of the sacred. That is what they are at their best. All of these communities are in danger of being at their worst, for in representing the sacred, they are in continual danger of claiming to be sacred, to be of overriding importance themselves.

Besides thinking of religion as the self-conscious acknowledgement of the sacred, sometimes, I have another way of speaking about religion. "*One way* of getting at what we mean by religion is that it is our attempt to make sense of our lives and behave appropriately within the total scheme of things" (Stone, 2008, 226, emphasis in original). In other words, it is our attempt to live in the light of the big picture.

5. Spirituality can be thought of as the attempt to cultivate an awareness of the sacredness of things and an attempt to live out the revised sense of the importance of things that sacredness brings. Like organized religion, spirituality has its perversions, including self-importance, lukewarmness, and lack of discipline. These may be corrected or worsened through organized religion. (For a fuller discussion of naturalistic spirituality, see Chapter 4.)

6. It seems that almost always sacred things have a dual aspect. They both challenge and support the people who acknowledge their sacredness. For illustration of this from the world's larger religions, see my *The Minimalist Vision of Transcendence*, 1992, pages 22–23.

7. My own vision is that the sacred is plural in nature. As I sense it, sacred events and processes are just that—plural. I am among the most radically pluralistic of religious naturalists. This recognition of the possible plurality of the divine opens the door to a new appreciation of polytheistic sensitivities. Although there are both monotheistic and enlightenment sensibilities, which would discourage this, I find that this opens up exciting new possibilities. It may turn out that religious naturalism has very old roots and is indeed quite conservative after all! In fact, I have become a polytheist at heart, although this is in tension with the two roots of my religious heritage: the enlightenment and biblical monotheism.

8. Sacred things are plural, but they have enough similarity that we can apply the same adjective, "sacred," to them. There are no trees that exist apart from particular trees. There is enough similarity between the ash and the sycamore and even the swamp cypresses near the Cache River in southern Illinois that we may apply the abstract term "tree" to them. Thus, all trees are analogous. Likewise, there is enough analogy to all instances of the sacred that we may call them all, in English, "sacred." This, of course, indicates that the term "sacred" will have boundary-line examples, gradations, and all the vagaries, vagueness, ambiguity, and historical contingency of human terms.

It may be that at times of devotion, we will imaginatively unify the sacred, just as we may think about "trees" in general or "snow" or "water." But, these general terms, useful as they are, are abstract and are never instantiated apart from the particularities and contingencies of very specific trees. Joyce Kilmer may have written that he "may never see a poem lovely as a tree," (Kilmer, 1913), but it would be a very specific maple or pinyon pine or other tree that he would see when he saw a tree.

Now it is possible that there is an interconnectedness among sacred things that is not captured in my pluralistic language. It may be that all or most instances of sacred processes make up a web or matrix. I am agnostic about this possibility, although I feel sympathetic toward the notion as conveying

something of the plurality of the sacred. Indeed, the sacred may be a patchwork or mosaic.
9. This version of religious naturalism, like all versions, must speak to issues of social justice. It can speak to them, and it can speak as well or better than traditional theism. The sacred is found in the human and the non-human others and its overriding importance undermines all the idols that our minds create. On the whole, religious naturalism has not grown out of the struggle for caste, gender, or class emancipation. Nevertheless, it does have emancipatory significance in at least two respects. First, it helps in the dismantling of the oppressive aspects of traditional theism. It also elaborates a religious stance which is both fulfilling and definitely more empowering than traditional religion. Second, by being more in tune with the approaches and results of scientific inquiry, it challenges the authoritative stance of some of the more religiously oriented conservative social and political movements. Also, many religious naturalists have been especially focused on social justice.

A short statement of this minimalist theory of the sacred, which I now favor for its brevity, is that *sacred things are things of overriding importance.* I usually add: *and which are beyond our control.*

I have stressed the importance of particular experiences of the sacred. As a general rule, the child has specific experiences of the overriding significance of the world before having a sense of the importance of the whole, of everything. Even as an adolescent or adult, one generally moves from the flight of brown pelicans, a hug in the midst of grief, a bird on one's shoulder to an awestruck sense of the grandeur of the universe.

This sense of the whole needs further elucidation. It is something like Spinoza's intellectual love of God, a third level of knowledge above sense perception and rational knowledge (Spinoza, *The Ethics*, Props. XXXII-XXXVI, 1968, 157–159). In my reading of Spinoza, rather than referring to a "superempirical" form of cognition, he was speaking of a form of insight or appreciation of the whole system of nature. Unfortunately, Spinoza overemphasized the similarity of the universe to a complete mathematical system. Samuel Alexander, the early twentieth-century British philosopher and a pioneer religious naturalist, wrote in helpful terms about this third level of knowledge in his essay "Spinoza and Time" (Alexander, 1939, 374–378). This sense of the whole is something like the use of imagination for John Dewey in grasping the whole. We cannot perceive the entire universe. It is not an empirical datum, which is why it is not a superempirical form of cognition, but we can think about or imagine it.

The scientific big picture

The second starting point for our exploration of religious naturalism is the big picture, a narrative built upon scientific account of our universe as an experimental process. We shall summarize how four thinkers, Ursula Goodenough, Connie

Barlow, Thomas Berry, and Brian Swimme reflect on the process of finding meaning in this scientific account.

Ursula Goodenough

Professor of Biology at Washington University and past-president of the American Society of Cell Biology, Ursula Goodenough is the author of a best-selling textbook on genetics. Her major writing as a religious naturalist is *The Sacred Depths of Nature*, which made the *New York Times* best-seller list (Goodenough, 1998). She adopts a completely naturalistic outlook and is often explicitly non-theist in orientation. [This section is adapted from Stone, 2008.]

Her method is a three-step process: (1) scientific inquiry giving rise to (2) disciplined deliberation on her deeply felt responses to it culminating in (3) an artistically crafted expression incorporating gems from the world's cultures all wrought in her own crafting of religious material. She articulates a response to the universe as a whole and our existence within it, her "covenant with Mystery," and also develops a rich set of "Reflections" at the end of each chapter on specific stages in evolution, such as the development of enzyme cascades, speciation, or the regulation of gene expression. These reflections are combined with carefully chosen selections from poems, hymns, and meditations from a variety of cultures and religious traditions.

She conceives of her task as exploring the religious potential of the scientific understanding of nature, a task made easier by the emergence in recent decades of a coherent scientific cosmology and account of evolution. Such a task is what she calls a poiesis, a making or crafting of religious material. No one person, of course, constructs a religion. But, unless individuals "offer contributions, there will be no 'stuff' available to cohere into new religious orientations in future times" (Goodenough, 2000, 562). Our uneasiness about engaging in this project can be alleviated by recognizing its collective nature.

A viable religious orientation, she claims, will come from the integration of theology and spirituality. Scientific cosmology does not inherently call for belief. When we accept the findings of science, we have a "capacity to walk humbly and with gratitude in their presence. . . . Religiopoiesis, in the end, is centrally engaged in telling the scientific story in ways that convey meanings and motivations" (Goodenough, 2000, 565).

For Goodenough, religions address two basic concerns: "How Things Are and Which Things Matter." These become articulated as a cosmology and a morality. "The role of religion is to integrate the Cosmology and the Morality, to render the cosmological narrative so rich and compelling that it elicits our allegiance and our commitment to its emergent moral understandings" (Goodenough, 1998, 14). Today, we need a planetary ethics, a shared cosmology, and a shared morality to orient our global projects, to mitigate the fear and greed that presently operate. Her agenda "is to outline the foundations for such a planetary ethic, an ethic that would make no claim to supplant existing traditions but would seek to coexist with them." Such a global tradition needs to start "with a shared world view—a culture-independent, globally accepted consensus as to how things are" (Goodenough, 1998, 15–16). For her, our scientific account of nature, the epic of evolution, is the one story that has the potential to unite us, because it happens to be true. The scientific account of how things are and came to be is likely, at first encounter, to elicit alienation, anomie, and nihilism. A cosmology works as a religious cosmology only if it resonates, if it makes the listener feel religious. She tries to show how the scientific account can elicit gratitude and reverence and help us acknowledge an "imperative that life continue" (Goodenough, 1998, 17).

She affirms that the opportunity to develop personal beliefs in response to ultimate questions, such as "why is there anything at all," is important for humans. She does not dismiss these questions as meaningless nor treat them as simply scientific questions. Her own response is "to articulate a covenant with Mystery." She speaks of responses of gratitude that our planet is "perfect for human habitation" and "astonishingly beautiful" and of reverence in the face of the vast lengths of time, the enormous improbability, and the splendid diversity of it all. Her naturalism is explicit in her profession that this "complexity and awareness and intent and beauty" plus her ability to apprehend it serve as the source of ultimate meaning and value, requiring no further justification, no Creator (Goodenough, 1998, 167–168, 171). These attitudes give rise to action to further the continuance of life, including human life.

Goodenough also has a series of reflections on the religious significance of the stages in evolution. For example, "it was the invention of death, the invention of the germ/soma dichotomy, that made possible the existence of our brains," which can face the prospect of our own death (Goodenough, 1998, 149). The topics of these reflections include, among others, meditation on deference toward diversity of species and on the nature of human distinctiveness.

As a brief digression, I add that the physicist Stanley Klein of Berkeley thinks that religious naturalists miss the boat by ignoring quantum mechanics and starting their reflections on biology. He tells me that "QM is totally crazy whereas biology is totally awesome, but not crazy. Also biology doesn't deal with consciousness that could maybe be relevant to religious naturalism." As he stated many times at the summer 2016 meeting of the Institute on Religion in an Age of Science, "Quantum mechanics is weird" (Stanley Klein, personal correspondence, July 17, 2016). I do note that Bernard Meland, University of Chicago theologian, insisted that the problem with much nineteenth- and twentieth-century liberal Protestant theology was that it employed an old-fashioned Newtonian view of matter, and hence, had to introduce a concept of "spirit" or purpose to supplement this dead, lifeless matter. [See my article, "Bernard Meland on the Formative Imagery of our Time," in Zygon (Stone, 1995).]

Connie Barlow

In her book, *Green Space, Green Time*, writer Connie Barlow explores issues in relating science to what could be called an "eco-religious vision of the sacred"

(Barlow, 1997). There are various ways to infuse ecological concern with a vision of the sacred, such as a revision of monotheism, the way of the primal traditions, the way of transcendence (Daoism and Buddhism), and immersion through direct contact with nature. Barlow suggests that familiarity with science can enrich these other ways. Her method is to explore these issues with four biologists in the fields of evolutionary biology, conservation biology, ecology, and geophysiology.

Her concern is to reach an understanding of the meanings we can draw from these sciences, how they can affect our moods, our commitments, and our sense of the roles we play on earth and in the cosmos. Science may not be able to give us meanings directly, but it can be a base of meaning-making. The meanings that we draw from science are not part of science, but they are informed by science. These meanings are constructed by each person, but they are not arbitrary products of the imagination. Despite the subjectivity, meaning-making is not fabrication. "It is a response to, a declaration of relationship with, Earth and the cosmos" (Barlow, 1997, 17). To find meaning in the universe is as legitimate as finding beauty in a landscape. To be fully human is to have some sort of response to the scientific picture.

The meanings that Barlow finds in the results of science she has rendered in an epic narrative of cosmological and biological evolution. This epic is not identical with the findings of science, but is based upon it and attempts to be faithful to it. "The epic that dances in my soul is a retelling of the strictly scientific story." It is on a par with the mythic narratives that motivate cultures. "It is poetic, awesome, inspiring, accessible to my level of understanding, and deeply meaningful" (Barlow, 1997, 237). This epic highlights four great achievements of evolution: 1) the pageant of life, 2) the diversity of life, 3) bioregions, and 4) our self-renewing planet that can be called Gaia (Barlow, 1997, 236–237). Commitment to the protection and enhancement of these achievements are the four ultimate values of this outlook. This self-enriching cosmos is the source of these ultimate values. These values function in a manner that is analogous to what is normally called religious. In short, these are sources of overriding trust and gratitude and call for overriding responsibility and obligation.

A crucial question is how to find meaning in science when the results of science are constantly being revised. Barlow says that we must learn to live "with a book of revelation that comes with the promise of errata sheets" (Barlow, 1997, 281). Barlow's ease with this answer rests in part on her confidence that when old scientific paradigms die, they are replaced by fresh ones. A second issue is raised by John Maynard Smith, an evolutionary biologist, who warns against using science to develop myths, for fear that this would lead to bad science. Barlow asserts that we have not only a changing universe, but also changing human minds. There is not only an evolution of the universe, but also an evolution of science. We need to celebrate, in personal devotion and public ritual, the story of the changing story of the universe.

Thomas Berry and Brian Swimme

World religions scholar Thomas Berry and physicist Brian Swimme start with the major results of scientific cosmology, including astrophysics and quantum theory, evolutionary biology, archaeology, and human history. The first step in their method is to realize that there is an evolving, but relatively consistent, scientific picture, which indicates that the universe has a history, a narrative. Once this realization occurs, this history is articulated. The second step in their method is to meld precisely worded empirical generalizations with poetic metaphor. An example of this self-conscious use of emotionally charged language is their assertion that "instant by instant the universe creates itself as a bonded community" or their reference to carbon as "the element of life" or the "thinking element," using analogical in place of univocal language (Swimme and Berry, 1992, 35–36; see also Swimme, 1984, 64–66, 77–79).

Berry and Swimme reach coherence between religious insights and scientific discoveries by combining empirical generalizations and poetic metaphor in an overarching narrative. The cosmic scale of this grand narrative is a means of uniting contemporary people with the mythic stance of primal peoples while its scientific underpinnings constitute a new element in the history of worldviews and helps to prevent a naive romanticism. This narrative, cosmic yet also inclusive of each particular person, helps to form a bridge between the pursuit of scientific truths and the wisdom of the world religions. Indeed, this cosmic creative process is sacred, and if for some people the divine is held to be transcendent, then the universe is the primary revelation of the divine.

They reach the conclusion that we can restore, in a contemporary fashion, some degree of intimacy between humans and the rest of the world. This idea is part of their larger conclusion that affirms the interconnectedness, with varying degrees of relevance, of all parts of the universe. This interconnectedness is combined with the sense of history and narrative. The grasp of the significance of this irreversible, temporal dimension is the new element in human understanding, even though it is rooted in the Abrahamic traditions.

What is perhaps the key point in their tapestry is formed at a point where the threads of interconnectedness are woven together. This nodal point is that humans are an integral part of the ongoing universe-process, indeed that humans are this universe-process become self-conscious. Hence, "the mathematical formulations of the scientists are the way in which the multiform universe deepens its self-understanding" (Swimme and Berry, 1992, 400). These themes of interconnectedness, of cosmic narrative, and the immersion of humans in the universe-process result in a transformation of the modern Western outlook, an understanding able to meet the ecological crisis. (Berry's *Evening Thoughts* is a brief summary of his ideas with a helpful intellectual biography by Mary Evelyn Tucker. Berry, 2006; see also Berry, 1988; "Cosmogenesis" by Swimme, 1994).

Science and meanings

We need now to draw together the themes that Goodenough, Barlow, and Berry and Swimme have been setting forth. All of these writers suggest, in different words, four principal ideas: 1) the meanings we find in science are not a part of science, yet they should be informed by science, 2) the meanings we find have a temporal or narrative character, 3) while the meanings that individuals may find in this narrative may differ somewhat, this narrative is something that can be a human universal, held in common across cultures, and 4) one aspect of this meaningful narrative is that humans are immersed, indeed at home, in a universe that is not always nice. I agree with these four points with two qualifications.

The first of these is that we should remember that a variety of meanings could be loosely derived from science, including Social Darwinism (the view that the people in poverty are there because they have lost out in the battle for survival and should not be given any assistance or safety net) and Hitler's worldview. "In Hitler's world ... [p]eople were to suppress any inclination to be merciful and were to be as rapacious as they could." Struggle was the meaning of the scientific picture, "a tangible and total truth. The weak were to be dominated by the strong, since 'the world is not there for the cowardly peoples'" (Snyder, 2015, 6). In my optimistic moments, I think that the solution is to be found in more science, or at least better science education. Social Darwinism and the Nazi's "blood and soil" are, I believe, scientifically misguided. But, we must also remember the real possibilities of using science and pseudo-science as support for ideology. Science will not give us our ethics, but it can inform them.

My second qualification is that I am not so hopeful concerning intercultural agreement on a global scale about what we learn from science. When we realize how many of the American electorate, indeed of formally educated politicians, reject the findings of evolutionary biology and climate science, we must temper our optimism about agreement on a worldwide scale. Nevertheless, those postmoderns who dismiss science as only one of the stories that we can tell ourselves are wrong. For the type of story that it tells (empirically verifiable and quantitatively precise when possible), it is the best thing going so far. This does not mean that we should automatically dismiss the detailed and hard-won knowledge of people who might not be able to pass a graduate chemistry exam, yet who know how to grow corn, beans, and squash under arid conditions or people whose ancestors bred maize or navigated vast stretches of the Pacific Ocean without GPS.

It is also helpful to bear in mind the wide variety of scientific methods, including many that have been pursued in the past. The methods of geology and microbiology, of exobiology and quantum physics, of field biology and nuclear medicine are remarkably different. To be sure, there are family resemblances, and the constant need to refine and corroborate with evidence are crucial to science. But, the line of demarcation between science and non-science is not as easy to discern as the positivists and Karl Popper once hoped. Nevertheless, there is a large core of well-established theories with wide-ranging support, and we would be foolish to reject the main outlines of the evolutionary theory. Or, refuse to vaccinate our children (as of the time of this writing). This is not being closed-minded. It is using the best available science that we have.

We need science, the best science we have. Science is not our only way of engaging with the universe. There are other *daos*. To write a poem is another way of engaging the world. To lie on one's back and watch the clouds, to make the earth speak beans with Thoreau, to climb a tree in a storm with John Muir are not science, but are valid ways of engaging with the world.

The awe at the big bang, our visceral responses to data coming back from an inter-planetary probe, or discovering new life forms are not themselves science, but they are intimately connected with it. Science cannot tell us how to react to the universe, but it can offer suggestions and clues. There is a loose connection between science and meaning, between fact and value, and we should not be dissuaded from exploring this connection by having someone warn that we are about to commit the naturalist fallacy.

To relate our spiritual responses (whatever that means) to the world as scientifically informed, we do need errata sheets, but healthy religion has always made room for maturation. And, we do need to be careful lest our responses to the universe distort our scientific inquiry. But, organized religion is not the only way we humans have of letting our prejudices and colonial master-mentality and ego defenses distort our science. Empirical inquiry must always be on guard against the idols of the tribe, the cave, the marketplace, and the theatre.

As I point out in my *The Minimalist Vision of Transcendence*, there are at least five needs of science, which influence the type of data that we look for in science.

These include: "(1) the testing of particular hypotheses, resulting in directed observation . . .; (2) isolated systems with soluble problems . . .; (3) quantified or at least precise language . . .; (4) the search for manipulable or at least isolable variables; and, (5) . . . the search for publically repeatable data observable by any competent, unbiased observers" (Stone, 1992, 112).

Thus, the type of things we look for in science are not meanings in the sense that we refer to when we speak of the meaning of life. [For further comments about science, see Chapter 4, "A Generous Empiricism" of my *The Minimalist Vision of Transcendence* (Stone, 1992, 111–168).]

Conclusion

We need to alternate between two perspectives: experiences of the sacred, of events of overriding importance and the scientifically informed big picture, the epic of creation. The key thing is to keep alternating between immediate experience and reflection on the big picture. Whichever way you start, the important point is to alternate between one foot and the other. The value of speaking of alternate starting points is that it alerts us to the value of complementing each one with the other.

Lisa Sideris has critiqued advocates of what she calls "New Genesis," what I have referred to as the "epic of evolution," or "everybody's story," or "the universe story." These are people who use the narrative of cosmic, biological and human evolution as the basis of a new orienting myth. She has in mind Thomas Berry and Brian Swimme, Loyal Rue, Ursula Goodenough, Connie Barlow, and Michael Dowd. She also includes E.O. Wilson, Richard Dawkins, Neil DeGrasse Tyson, and advocates of Big History, especially David Christian.

Part of her critique is that these writers conflate science as method, science as a body of knowledge, and science woven into story form. Her critique here is important although, perhaps, somewhat overstated. Most writers of this type do distinguish between these three senses of science. But, she is correct that they are not always careful in distinguishing them.

She is also correct that a variety of narratives can be derived from the sciences. For example, paleobiologists can emphasize the oneness of the human species, while from a microbiologist's perspective each human organism seems to be a conglomerate of species (Sideris, 2016, 208).

Of most relevance for our concern here is her contention that the approach of the Universe Story and related narratives can "discourage sensory, experience-infused forms of engagement with nature that are less dependent upon and mediated by expert knowledge" (Sideris, 2015a, 136). It is for this reason that I stress two starting points for the environmental concerns of religious naturalism: an appreciative awareness of particulars and a knowledge of the scientific big picture.

Sideris has other criticisms of the New Genesis. Some of its advocates borrow their scientific materials in a selective fashion, for example, choosing the data that sees the universe as groping toward purpose and direction (Sideris, 2015b, 237). Another criticism is that "the scaled-up *species* vision of humanity obscures important differences among human cultures and their varied contributions to the global crisis in terms of fossil fuel consumption; it also downplays the critical role played by capitalism" (Sideris, 2016, 208, italics in original). Sideris is also concerned that the tendency of some advocates of the New Genesis celebrate "a shift to human domination of the planet ... in an inadvisable—even delusional—strategy" (Sideris, 2015b, 236).

My major point of agreement with Sideris is that the use of the big picture, the narrative derived from (not identical with) the sciences, needs to be melded with appreciative perception of particular places at particular times. However, I am more willing than her to balance this appreciation of particulars with the use of the scientific grand narrative, revisable though it is.

It is helpful to remember that Bertrand Russell was and Stuart Kauffman is well informed about science. Russell drew a sense of alienation from the universe, Kauffman a sense of being at home. A lesson I draw from this is that science by itself does not automatically lead to religious naturalism, to a response that the universe or any part of it is sacred. But, the best science that we have will inform our responses. To assume that either science will tell us how to feel about the universe or else to assume that we should ignore the results of scientific inquiry is a false dichotomy (Russell, 1903; Kauffman, 1995; Kauffman, 2008). I hope that this chapter helps to respond to her critique.

The world is not always full of vistas, of green pastures, and still waters. There are times when parts of it are red in tooth and claw. But, it is our home, and with lots of luck and some ingenuity and hard work, we can survive for a while, if we do not destroy it first.

Note

1 This section is adapted from my "What is Religious Naturalism?," *Journal of Liberal Religion*, Vol. 2, www.Meadville.edu; republished with addendum in *Religious Humanism*, XXXV (Winter/Spring 2001).

Bibliography

Alexander, Samuel. 1939. *Philosophical and Literary Pieces*. Edited by John Laird. London: Macmillan & Co., Ltd. (Reprinted Westport, CT: Greenwood Press Publishers, 1970).
Barlow, Connie. 1997. *Green Space, Green Time: The Way of Science*. New York: Springer-Verlag.
Berry, Thomas. 1988. *The Dream of Earth*. San Francisco: Sierra Club Books.
Berry, Thomas. 2006. *Evening Thoughts: Reflections on Earth as Sacred Community*. Edited by Mary Evelyn Tucker. San Francisco: Sierra Club Books and University of California Press.
Crosby, Donald A. 2014. *More than Discourse: Symbolic Expressions of Naturalistic Faith*. Albany: State University of New York Press.
Crosby, Donald A. 2015. *Nature as Sacred Ground: A Metaphysics of Religious Naturalism*. Albany: State University of New York Press.
Dewey, John. 1934. *A Common Faith*. New Haven: Yale University Press.
Engel, J. Ronald. 1983. *Sacred Sands: The Struggle for Community in the Indiana Dunes*. Middletown, CT: Wesleyan University Press.
Goodenough, Ursula. 1998. *The Sacred Depths of Nature*. New York: Oxford University Press.
Goodenough, Ursula. 2000. "Religiopoiesis," *Zygon: Journal of Religion and Science*. 35, 561–566.
Kaplan, Mordecai M. 1948. *The Future of the American Jew*. New York: Macmillan Company, Reprinted by Reconstructionist Press, 1981.
Kaplan, Mordecai M. 1985. *Dynamic Judaism: The Essential Writings of Mordecai M. Kaplan*. Edited by Emanuel S. Goldsmith and Mel Scult. New York: Fordham University Press.
Kauffman, Stuart. 1995. *At Home in the Universe: The Search for the Laws of Self-Organization and Complexity*. New York: Oxford University Press.
Kauffman, Stuart. 2008. *Reinventing the Sacred: A New View of Science, Reason, and Religion*. New York: Basic Books.
Kilmer, Joyce. 1913. *Poetry*.
Peters, Karl. 2002. *Dancing with the Sacred: Evolution, Ecology, and God*. Harrisburg, PA: Trinity Press International.
Russell, Bertrand. 1903. "A Free Man's Worship," reprinted in *Mysticism and Logic*. Lanham, MD: Rowman and Littlefield Publishers, 1988; reprinted also in *Collected Papers of Bertrand Russell*, Vol. 12 *Contemplation and Action, 1902–14*. London, UK: Routledge, 1985.
Sideris, Lisa H. 2015a. "Science as Sacred Myth?: Ecospirituality in the Anthropene Age," *Journal for the Study of Religion, Nature, and Culture*, 9, 136–153.
Sideris, Lisa H. 2015b. "Forum Response: The Confines of Consecration: A Reply to Critics," *Journal for the Study of Religion, Nature and Culture*, 9, 221–239.

Sideris, Lisa H. 2017. *Consecrating Science: Wonder, Knowledge, and the Natural World*. University of California Press.

Snyder, Timothy. 2015. "Hitler's World" *New York Review of Books*, Volume LXII, Number 14, 6.

Spinoza, Baruch. 1968. *The Ethics*. In Edited by Walter Kaufmann, *Philosophic Classics: Volume II: Bacon to Kant*. 2nd ed. Englewood Cliffs, NJ: Prentice-Hall.

Stone, Jerome A. 1992. *The Minimalist Vision of Transcendence: A Naturalist Philosophy of Religion*. Albany: State University of New York Press.

Stone, Jerome A. 1995. "Bernard Meland on the Formative Imagery of Our Time," *Zygon: Journal of Religion and Science*, XXX, 3.

Stone, Jerome A. 1998. "The Resacralization of Nature: A Religious Naturalist's Contribution." Paper delivered at the Highlands Institute for American Religous Thought, Bad Boll, Germany, August (unpublished).

Stone, Jerome A. 2000. "What is Religious Naturalism?," *Journal of Liberal Religion* (Fall). www.meadville.edu. [Reprinted with addendum, *Religious Humanism*, Winter/Spring 2001, 60–74.]

Stone, Jerome A. 2008. *Religious Naturalism Today: The Rebirth of a Forgotten Alternative*. Albany: State University of New York Press.

Swimme, Brian. 1984. *The Universe Is a Green Dragon: A Cosmic Creation Story*. Santa Fe: Bear & Company.

Swimme, Brian. 1994. "Cosmogenesis," in Edited by Mary Evelyn Tucker and John A. Grim *Worldview and Ecology: Religion, Philosophy, and the Environment*. Maryknoll, New York: Orbis Books.

Swimme, Brian and Thomas Berry. 1992. *The Universe Story: From the Primordial Flaring Forth to the Ecozoic Era—A Celebration of the Unfolding of the Cosmos*. San Francisco, CA: Harper Collins Publishers.

White, Carol Wayne. 2016. *Black Lives and Sacred Humanity: Toward an African American Religious Naturalism*. New York: Fordham University Press.

3

APPRECIATIVE PERCEPTION

This chapter will be about a kind of awareness, which we can call "appreciative perception." The practice of appreciative perception is a doorway to a sense of importance. Because, as we have seen, anything that is sacred is something of great importance, it follows that the practice of appreciative perception is one of the best doorways to a sense of the sacred, to the re-enchantment of the world. To state this in terms of the previous chapter, appreciative perception is one of the best ways to open oneself to specific experiences of the sacred.

In the late 1980s, the head of the Philosophy Department at the U.S. Military Academy at West Point offered an elective course in Environmental Ethics to the cadets. As the most helpful way to start the course, Colonel Paul led his classes in an overnight hike up Mount Katahdin in Maine. After setting up a camp near the top, the assignment for the students was to observe, write in a journal, and read from the journal around the campfire that night. Discussing this a few years later over breakfast one morning, Colonel Paul told me that he had decided to start the class that way so that the cadets would have some idea of what they were talking and reading about in the class. The colonel was generally pleased with the experience and was sharing this with me as a helpful learning tool. The colonel and I were at a conference designed to help teachers create courses in Environmental Philosophy. The conference was sponsored by the Center for Environmental Philosophy at the University of North Texas run by Eugene Hargrove, editor of *Environmental Ethics*.

Please note some things about the incident on Mount Katahdin. First, the teacher chose this as the best way to start the class, somehow fitting the trip into the crowded schedule of life at West Point. In short, he was deliberately nurturing what I shall call appreciative perception or sensitive discernment. Second, notice how the experience was felt as different from the normal life of the cadets. I suggest that the structured, instrumentally oriented life of the cadet can be seen as an intensification of the daily life of the industrialized world. Note in the third place the interplay between language and experience. The philosophy instructor had read Thoreau's account of his trip up Mount Ktaadn (the native's spelling in English) and knew that Thoreau wrote journals. The teacher came from a culture, indeed a written tradition. Further, he had his students *focus* and *share* their experiences by writing and speaking. Thus, language focuses and structures experience, while experience enriches and anchors language. Probably, there is little, if any, pure of immediate experience or isolated language for humans, once they learn to listen and talk. But, there certainly is language deficient in experience and experience deficient in language.

A second incident illustrates part of what I mean by *training appreciation*. I once taught an adult education class on the American Environmental Movement. I talked a lot about training appreciation, but my talk did not seem to get anywhere. Then, a student came to the rescue. She told about how she had taken a course in Nature Photography. Her assignment was to take pictures, of publishable quality if possible, of the same subject every week for 8 weeks. She chose a particular polar bear in the zoo. She said that it was the most difficult assignment she ever had, but also one from which she learned more about photography than any other course she had taken. Most of all, she said, she learned a great deal about that particular polar bear and how it differed from the other bears in the exhibit. On the last day of the class, she delighted us with an exhibit of her photos.

It is of utmost significance that appreciation is fostered by focusing on particulars. To generalize is to abstract. To focus may be to narrow attention, but it is also to overcome the thinness of abstraction. Possibly, this will work best for those capable of generalizing already. But, definitely, re-immersion in detail is superior to the thin pablum of abstract generality. In fact, it is not too far off the mark to say that abstraction, whether from reading, from Platonism, or from industrial and post-industrial civilization, may be what is really alienating us from our natural world, allowing us to destroy it without caring, indeed without even knowing we are doing it. Note that this immersion in the particular takes time. Note also that photography is a type of language, in the broad sense. Finally, there is a union, or at least an overlap, of knowledge and valuation. This is a knowledge with some degree of intimacy, not of alienation or distance.

A third illustration of appreciation and its nurture comes from my use of a journal in teaching Environmental Ethics. Students were to select an outdoor place near their home, preferably within walking distance, a place they enjoyed visiting. They were to make at least ten visits a week apart. For each visit, they were to make a journal entry about what they thought and felt. At least once in the journal, they were to reflect on past geological history and human land use, describe sounds and smells, record some ecologically significant measurements, write about some ecological relationships, identify some species of both plants and fauna, and make recommendations for the future. I encouraged some poetry, even prayers, or other creative writing if they chose. Finally, near the end, they were to comment on any changes they noted in their perception or appreciation.

Many students commented that the assignment was very enjoyable or meaningful. Some recalled earlier pleasant childhood association with the place. Many students thanked me for making them find the time to stop and look at the world. Many wrote about how they found it recuperative. Many spoke of plans to continue the practice. Clearly, the written assignment motivates, and perhaps, focuses appreciation. Some excellent students have said that it was one of the most difficult assignments they ever had. These were students, I suspect, who were not used to an assignment with such a major non-linguistic dimension.

In class, I used the assignment to talk about what I call the experiential anchor of environmental moral judgments. Most moral judgments require such an experiential anchor. Even rationally based ethical approaches such as Kant requires, it seems, an appreciative element, at least an appreciation of the importance of rational consistency and also of other persons as worthy of receiving consistent treatment.

In a related matter, when morality is taught in the form of commandments, it easily leads to rebellion or submission. But, when morality is taught as appreciation, it is joyfully embraced. How much of our violence is due to the fact that we have not supported parents in raising children, have schooled children in huge factories, use the entertainment media to stimulate wants rather than nurture appreciation, and form characters motivated by instant gratification? It is not just the criminally insane who are sick. Our culture is as well. Many in it believe that the Emperor's clothes are gorgeous. This is one of the reasons for the selective withdrawal from our culture that I urge for consideration. What we need is not to teach values, but to point to things and happenings with value.

There is one final reflection on the journal assignment. This requirement forced students from the shopping-mall generation to swim against the cultural tide in at least two ways. They were on foot. Also, they learned the value of solitude. Today, I would ask them to turn off their cell phones when visiting their places.

I have described a climb up Ktaadn, the photographing of one polar bear, and a journal assignment involving several visits to the same locale. I use these three illustrations to point to an appreciative perception of the natural world. Elsewhere I have called it a "sensitive discernment," which is a key component of a "generous empiricism" (Stone, 1992, 112–114). My teacher Bernard Meland, who helped shape my approach to these issues and who spent a lifetime encouraging a "radical empiricist" approach to the spiritual life, called it "appreciative" or "sensitive perception." I have learned much from my comrade "radical empiricists" in developing these insights of Meland, especially William Dean.[1] To use the language of William Dean, we need to develop an affectional sensibility as a way into the full dimensions of the valueful nature-history process (Dean, 1986, 83).

My best teacher in the practice of appreciation has been my wife who spots birds from the front seat of the car, with whom I have enjoyed countless hikes, and who keeps the binoculars ready beside the dining-room window.

My trepidation in writing this chapter eased when I realized that my task here is not primarily theoretical or referential, but evocative. I need to evoke in my readers a memory and anticipation of their own appreciation of the world that surrounds, delights, sometimes surprises, nourishes, and occasionally crushes or just plain disgusts or bores us. It seems that the best way to evoke such memories of appreciation is to tell stories such as those about Mount Ktaadn, a polar bear, and student journals. I do theorize in this chapter, but the theory is rooted in, even if it does not rest on a foundation of, the soil of experience.

There is probably no "pure" or "immediate" or "pre-linguistic" perception. All of the incidents mentioned in this chapter were motivated, directed, and interpreted by language. Also, let us not be misled by the word "evoke" into thinking that we are dealing with "merely subjective" feelings. As I understand it, most experience is transactional. It consists of experiences of real things, the result of interaction between experience and the experienced. It is not only language all the way down. There surely is more than language. When the mosquito bites me, it is surely not just my language that itches. We may not be in touch with the world by observations that can provide an indubitable empirical foundation for our knowledge, but we are not the sole authors of our experience. Instead of using a mirror, eye, or blank tablet as our basic epistemological image, it makes sense to use the image of dancing with a partner (See Karl Peters' image of dancing with the sacred. Peters, 2002, esp. pages 45–51).

Let us conclude these experiential evocations with a negative example of a lack of experiential anchor. In my freshman year of college, I was fortunate to take a Humanities course taught by Harold Haydon, painter and later art critic for a Chicago newspaper. One day, he asked the class what color the sky is. Like a fool, I raised my hand and blurted out, "Blue!" With an expression more full of pity than of scorn, he asked, "Did you ever look at the sky?" As a child, I had used a blue crayon to color the sky, but *not because I had looked at it, but because "they" told me what color to use.* Thus, painfully did I begin to learn how much culture can cut us off from the world, sometimes even from the plain, visible truth. May the reader look, listen, and smell.

In developing the notion of the perception of worth in the natural world, it will help to follow the lead of some observers who have opened their ears and eyes, and by doing so, have marked trails for us to follow. We shall focus on two well-known observers, Henry David Thoreau and Aldo Leopold. Then, we shall see where two recent writers on perception go, Delores LaChapelle and Gary Snyder.

Henry David Thoreau

In the early 1850s, Thoreau's journals became filled with detailed observations from his walks. His reading of scientists and naturalists became more intensive. He began to "look at Nature with new eyes." His *Journals* of 1851 and 1852, especially, are a rich mine of observations and reflections on observations. Much help is given in understanding Thoreau's reflections on observation by Laura Dassow Walls in her *Seeing New Worlds* (Walls, 1995).

Thoreau practiced noticing. For years, he walked daily around Concord, Massachusetts, making and recording observations. He structured his life and responsibilities so that his economic needs allowed him leisure to walk and have time to stop and poke around. Perhaps, most of us could not emulate him to that degree, but we do have some time, although many of us have two jobs, making it difficult. Perhaps, we need a selective withdrawal from the money economy. This would require thought on how to "make do," and similar to Gary Snyder, we would need to do more repairs. Note that sauntering slows us down enough to notice, to listen.

Thoreau visited many places in different seasons and in successive years. Recording his observations gave him a sense of the irregularities in the world and motivated him to ask for the reasons. He carried equipment: a spyglass, a notebook, and often, a botany book, and his walking stick was notched in inches. We are reminded what a difference botany books made to the youthful John Muir. Today, we might add a magnifying glass, a pH meter, perhaps, a laptop or tablet.

Thoreau often worked over his notebook jottings in the evening. The use of a notebook required the observer to focus, to decide what to observe, which aspects of the processes to focus on, and which words to use. To focus is to relegate something else to be out of focus. The choice of what to observe and how to describe is a choice not to observe something and not to describe in a certain way. Observation is a very active process, except perhaps for occasional moments of receptivity. The very anatomy of our sense organs requires action in their use. Even sound and smell sometimes require turning the head, cupping the ear, or following the trace of an odor. There is no blank tablet on which sensations write, as the early British empiricist John Locke thought. John Dewey was correct to describe old-fashioned empiricism as naive. The very data we start with are *takings* as well as *givings*, not givens, a reciprocity between us and what the world affords to us. Observation is an interaction, a transaction, in Dewey's term. This is why I can use the image of a dance as an image for observing or knowing.

Thoreau's practiced paying attention to particulars, much like the painter Monet paid attention to the coast of France or the rugged Massif Central or Winslow Homer observed Prout's Neck in Maine. Although Thoreau continued to call himself a transcendentalist, he was a very embodied transcendentalist who studied lichens, looked at grass under ice, followed snails across meadows, and watched ice melt. He did generalize, but while Emerson wrote an essay entitled *Nature*, Thoreau's famous book took the title of a very specific pond. Thoreau's vocation, as he matured, could be described as a love of particulars in action and reflection. His journal entry of November 22, 1851, where he recommends turning over a stone in midwinter to see the crickets and ants and their many little galleries or his reference to the beauty of the decay of stumps can be read as standing transcendentalism on its head, an inversion of the hierarchy of beings or Plato's allegory of the cave.[2] This concern for specifics is carried into appreciation of the despised and rejected. Swamps pleased him. His knowledge of birds is indicated by the index for the 1851 and 1852 volume of his *Journals*, which lists around seventy species of birds, depending on how generic listings are counted. Although he concentrated on the area around Concord, Thoreau's focus on particulars broadened into the study of accounts written by others. He studied local histories, guidebooks, and oral histories. One intrepid reader documented a minimum of 172 separate travel accounts, many in multiple volumes, which Thoreau read carefully (John Aldrich Christie, 1965, cited in Walls, 1995, 135).

Thoreau's interest in noticing and recording details is manifested in several notebooks, a "Fact Book," twelve Indian notebooks, a Canadian notebook, more than a thousand pressed plants, a collection of bird's eggs and nests, and Indian antiquities. He drew up hundreds of tables and charts, which still await analysis and which some critics, mistakenly I believe, take as a sign of diminished creativity (Walls, 1995, 140).

His attention to particulars was given impetus and shape at the beginning of the 1850s by his reading of Alexander von Humboldt. Laura Dassow Walls makes a strong case for Humboldt's influence on Thoreau. Humboldt, the German explorer and naturalist, was a culture hero before the Civil War in America. The state of Nevada was almost named after him. The Humboldtian program in science, according to Walls, was to explore, collect, measure, and connect. Susan Faye Cannon, in *Science in Culture* (1978), suggests that Humboldtians were easy to spot because of two characteristics. One was a tendency to fiddle with instruments, such as the barometer and sextant, in a search for accuracy. The other was a concern, new at the time, for the visual display of numerical results in maps and graphs (Walls, 1995, 100–101). Humboldt himself invented isothermal lines, maps of "vegetable coverings," and diagrams of cross-sections of mountains showing "zones of habitation" arranged according to altitude. The purpose of the detail and the visual displays was to help discover and exhibit patterns in the data that were not obvious at first.

The world view behind the procedure was what Walls terms "empirical holism." A chief principle in this approach was that a whole can be known only through a detached and patient study of its parts. Further, any details that did not fit into a pattern or theory were not to be dismissed as an anomaly, but rather as an indicator that the pattern or theory needed revision. In short, rather than contingent facts approximating to the laws of nature, contingent theories approximated to the patterns of nature. Some of this may seem obvious to us, but when we contrast this with the views of Coleridge, Emerson, or German *Naturphilosophie* and remember that scientists frequently correct observations to fit their theory, this concern for details takes on significance. Thoreau's walks, constant measurements, and detailed charts and notebooks do not represent the fall of a romantic poet who is losing his creativity into a compulsive attention to details. Rather, these were the practice of a self-conscious empirical holist who sought unsuspected patterns and connections through the study of the details.

By 1851, according to Walls, Thoreau is copying long extracts from Darwin's "Voyages of a Naturalist Around the World" and from Humboldt. Walls suggests that the move made by Darwin and Humboldt from the vision of the whole to the details to a fuller vision of the whole probably inspired Thoreau in his observations.

Thoreau was not a passive observer. Observation was activity. It was not a spectator sport. His trip to Cape Cod finds him exploring with his finger the cut in a whale's carcass. We find him making a quadrant to measure the heights of a riverbank (Thoreau, 1988, 112–118). In his *Journals*, we find him tearing apart in order to explore a hornet's nest, a moss ball, a muskrat's nest. He interacted with, stroked, and occasionally took home to release later an owl and a flying squirrel.

Thoreau did not pretend to practice innocent, pristine observation. His perceptions were shaped and focused by his reading. On the other hand, he would on occasion employ the painter's trick of putting his head upside down to get a fresher view of a landscape. The previous study that he brought with him to his observation and that he used in reporting the observations was important. He had a large color vocabulary that enriched his perception and description of clouds and skies.

The interplay of his observations and reading is indicated by his books in botany. He frequently took a botany book with him on his walks. In his *Journals* of 1851 and 1852, he refers to some thirteen books on plants, including volumes by Linnaeus, Asa Gray, and Agassiz. According to Walls, he began to read widely in science: in 1851 alone, he read, in addition to Darwin's *Journal of Researches* (1846), *The Earth and Man* (1849) by Humboldt's disciple Arnold Guyot, Cuvier's *Animal Kingdom*, Robert Hunt's *Poetry of Science* (1850), and the controversial books on evolution by Robert Chambers and Hugh Miller, engaging heatedly, at least in his *Journal*, in the wider debate they had ignited (Walls, 1995, 130).

As Walls puts it, Thoreau's readings, especially in botany, "give him *new words to see by*, and new words to see with." Thoreau can write later in his *Journal*:

> How much of beauty—of color, as well as form, on which our eyes daily rest goes unperceived by us! No one but a botanist is likely to distinguish nicely the different shades of green with which the open surface of the earth is clothed—not even a landscape-painter if he does not know the species of sedges and grasses which paint it.
>
> (Thoreau, XIV, 1906)

That his observations were shaped by his reading is further indicated by his concern to find a picturesque curve in a book or by his specific recommendations on how to make a landscape more picturesque. These are found in his journal entries from April 1 to April 7, 1852, which were occasioned in part by his experiments in applying William Gilpin's *Remarks on Forest Scenery* and which reveal a self-conscious awareness influenced by then-current trends in aesthetics. On the other hand, Thoreau knew that terminology can sometimes interfere with our observations if we focus on it and think that identifying a bird or plant is the main purpose of field study.

Whatever aid is to be derived from the use of a scientific term, we can never begin to see anything as it is so long as we focus on the scientific term, which our ignorance has imposed on it. Natural objects and phenomena are in this sense forever wild and unnamed by us (Thoreau, *Journal*, Volume XIII, 141).

In his observations, Thoreau played back and forth between what Walls calls familiarizing and defamiliarizing. He wished to become familiar enough to build on his observations and to be able to explore further. At the same time, he saw the need to defamiliarize the familiar, to overcome preconceptions, and to look with the "impartial eye" of a traveler who "may see what the oldest inhabitant has not observed." But, the traveler has the advantage of being unfamiliar with the territory. "It takes a man of genius to travel in his own country—in his native village" (Thoreau, *Journal*, Volume III, 356–357).

This alternation between familiarization and defamiliarization is paralleled by his wishing an intimate sympathy with the natural and a keen recognition that he should preserve its otherness and mystery. His journal is full of moments when Thoreau finds himself the object of an animal's gaze. Certain experiences especially brought home to him the otherness of nature, events such as the shipwreck off Cape Cod, his trip up Mount Ktaadn, or his trip to Fire Island to attempt to recover the shipwrecked remains of Margaret Fuller Ossoli and her family.

Another strategy employed by Thoreau was an alternation between directed and wandering perception, between what he called intentionality of the eye and the sauntering of the eye. Intentionality refers to focusing your attention. You cannot examine everything at once; therefore, you must learn to refocus your attention from rushes to oaks.

You are a little bewildered by the variety of objects. There must be a certain meagerness of details and nakedness for a wide view. A man sees only what concerns him. A botanist absorbed in the pursuit of grasses does not distinguish the grandest pasture oaks. He, as it were, tramples down oaks unwittingly in his walks (Thoreau, *Journal*, Volume XI, 153).

Likewise, one can refocus one's mind and alternate between being a naturalist and a poet. So, one can change the intentionality of the mind and eye and attend to different departments of knowledge. The problem with intentionality is that it can overlook whatever you do not look for. "The more you look the less you observe," Thoreau wrote. "Go not to the object; let it come to you. . . . What is needed is a true sauntering of the eye." He also calls this seeing with the side of the eye (Thoreau, *Journal*, Volume IV, 351; Volume V, 45).

As Walls puts it, the twin strategies we should alternate between are intentionality and a side of the eye approach, paralleling the alternation between familiarization and defamiliarization. We should learn science and then forget it. In the words of Walls: "Knowledge guides the eye, but limits it to what it already knows; ignorance informed by knowledge defamiliarizes the known and prepares the mind for the novel, the unanticipatable" (Walls, 1995, 174).

In a late essay, "Autumnal Tints," Thoreau suggests that it is the mind, not the eye, that sees. If we do not look with our minds, we will lose much. If we see only what concerns us, if we are not prepared, we will think that autumnal woods are sere and barren. The scarlet oak, seen unsympathetically, is dull and dark. However, if we are alert, we will see a burning red in the setting sun (Walls, 1995, 215).

Finally, Thoreau treats nature as speaking. The idea of nature as a book is old. The "book of nature" normally referred to its author, the Creator, who is separate from nature. But, for Thoreau, if I read him rightly, nature has its own voice, indeed several voices. As Thoreau put it in his memorable phrase, "all nature will *fable*" (Thoreau, *Journal*, Volume V, 135).

This means that we must listen and also that we may fail to do so.

"The great tragedy is man's refusal to *listen*: when the Billerica dam destroys shad returning to spawn, he asks, 'Who hears the fishes when they cry?'" (Thoreau, 1983, 37).

I take it this means that there is information that needs deciphering. There is also a certain animism here that the more positivist among us are likely to dismiss or at least treat condescendingly as a matter of mere poetic license. However, I wish to assert that referring to nature as speaking does force us to consider the moral status of nature. My cat communicates with me with noises. And, part of his moral standing, egocentric as I still am, is that he communicates to me, with clear intentionality.

If nature speaks, then someone can be a poet or scribe on nature's behalf. This was part of Thoreau's vocation. Thoreau spoke for nature. If the rest of us have ears less attuned to her, he hopes to lead us to listen.

Aldo Leopold

One of the most influential writers in the American environmental movement, Aldo Leopold was a U.S. Forest Service ranger, then Associate Director of the Forest Products Laboratory in Madison, Wisconsin, and finally, Professor of Game Management at the University of Wisconsin.

In the Preface to *Round River*, a collection of extracts from Leopold's journals, his son Luna wrote of his father's "lifetime of developing perception." In this Preface, Luna Leopold includes a number of points. One is that perception can grow. Another is that perception "is not acquired by formal education, nor is it necessarily vouchsafed to those who are learned in the arts or sciences." Rather, Luna refers to his father's "camp and field experience from which perception gradually emerged." Note that this reverses the view of a naive empiricism, which bases experience simply on ordinary perception. Rather, in becoming experienced, one can become better at perceiving. Finally, Luna clearly affirms that values are not mere projections, but are resident in things. For perception is "a recognition of ethical and aesthetic values to be found in natural things" (Luna Leopold, 1991, VIII-IX).

Leopold thought frequently about what it takes to motivate people. An ethics for the environment is all very well, but why would people want to follow it? He was quite clear that worry about shortages or fear of impending doom were not strong motivators. In a talk given to a university Farm and Home Week in 1939, he said: "Prudence never kindled a fire in the human mind; I have no hope for a conservation born of fear" (Leopold, 1991b, 255). He also said that fear and indignation, the two vehicles that conservation propagandists have most relied on, need to be disqualified as motives. To be sure, a knowledge of trends of environmental degradation entitles a person to fear and indignation, but as motivators, they do not work.

One possible motivator Leopold did place some stock in was curiosity and the pride of understanding something. Referring to a farm boy tending his tractor or building his own radio, he wrote:

> In a surprising number of men there burns a curiosity about mechanism and a loving care about their construction, maintenance, and use. . . . [W]hat few realize that an equal bent for the mechanisms of nature is a possible earmark of some future generations. . . . Soil, water, plants, and animals are an engine, subject, like any other, to derangement.
>
> Our present skills in the care of mechanical engineers did not arise from fear lest they fail to do their work. Rather, it was born of curiosity and pride of understanding.
>
> (Leopold, 1991b, 257–258)

The suggestion that adolescents or adults can be motivated by curiosity and the pride of knowing is intriguing. There are many questions to raise. How much of it is gender-specific or a gender tendency? How much of it is encouraged or stifled by today's different world? Does electronic visual or audio stimulation make for people with less curiosity? Are video games, TV, and electronic tablets easier forms of fun, and do they stifle curiosity? Does the fact that gadgets are miniaturized and not easy to take apart and put back together mean that people grow up with less interactive curiosity? Or, do computers increase our interest in the investigation of complex processes? I do not know the answers. I do suspect that some of these changes are difficult to perceive, let alone to study with any accuracy.

Besides curiosity and pride of knowing as motivators, Leopold refers to enthusiasm and affection. To really get a farmer involved skillfully in a conservation program and to get any of us involved in sustainable environmental living and working takes enthusiasm and affection.

This emphasis on "enthusiasm and affection" shows Leopold pointing out the need for a passionate involvement. This is akin to what we have called "appreciative perception," and it clearly involves active searching, an appreciative discernment arising from involvement, even manipulation, knowledge, and appreciation arising from doing and pride in understanding.

Later in the same talk, Leopold turns to another type of motivation: self-expression. The landscape of any farm is a portrait of the farmer. Conservation implies self-expression in the landscape, rather than compliance with economic dogma. "The future farmer would not more mutilate his creek than his own face. If he has inherited a straightened creek, it will be 'explained' to visitors, like a pock-mark or a wooden leg" (Leopold, 1991b, 263).

If perchance the creek fails

> to yield an owl-hoot . . . or a bunch of sweet william . . . the matter will be cause for wounded pride and family scrutiny, like a check marked "no funds". . . . On the parlor wall, where the embroidered "God Bless Our Home" used to hang, in exploitation days, hangs a chart of the farm's soil analyses. The farmer is proud that all his soil graphs point upward. . . . Around the farmstead are historic oaks which are cherished with both pride and skill. . . . It is a matter of neighborhood debate whose oaks are most clearly relics of oak-opening days, whether the healed scars on the base of one tree is the result of a prairie fire or a pioneer's trash pile. . . . The bird list for the farm is 161 species. One neighbor claims 165, but there is reason to suspect he is fudging. . . . His pond is our farmer's special badge of distinction. This farmer will tell you of the mad decade when they taught economics in the local kindergarten, but the college president couldn't tell a bluebird from a blue cohosh. Everybody worried about getting his share; nobody worried about doing his bit.
>
> (Leopold, 1991b, 263–265)

Leopold writes for three pages with sly humor about his hope for a time when down to earth, practical people will have a wide set of appreciations, scientifically informed, bound in local detail, involving learned skills of conservation, and all motivated by pride in values perceived and appreciated.

Thus it is that Aldo Leopold could formulate a new ethic and cast it in the form of a declaration: "A thing is right when it tends to preserve the integrity, stability, and beauty of the biotic community," and yet, know that for it to be practiced, we need more than a sense of duty. Hence, with Leopold, I urge that all ethicists reflect on the wellsprings of human motivation. Note that beauty is a key concept for Leopold. His famous maxim just quoted about when a thing is right ends with "and *beauty* of the biotic community." This sentence is preceded by "Examine each question in terms of what is ethically and *esthetically* right, as well as what is economically expedient" [emphasis added; Leopold, 1966, 262; see also "Land Esthetics," (Kinsey, 1999, 279–295)].

Another aspect of Leopold's thought is that he urges us to move beyond our culturally formed desire for beautiful scenery. J. Baird Callicott sets Leopold's views in illuminating contrast with the Western tradition. "Natural aesthetics is a pitifully underworked topic within the Western philosophical and critical literature." Much has been written on aesthetics, but most of it centers on humanly produced art, on the artefactual.

In sharp contrast to Far Eastern cultures, in the West, an aesthetic response to nature actually appears to be a lately acquired taste. Indeed, it seems that in Western civilization prior to the seventeenth century, nature was simply not a source of aesthetic experience (Callicott, 1987, 159. See also Leopold, 1991b, 8–12, and Callicott, 1989, 239–248).

Christopher Hussey suggests that the appreciation of natural beauty depended on the development of landscape painting by Claude Lorraine, Salvatore Rosa, and the Dutch. This meant that natural beauty was judged in terms of how suitable it was as a subject for a landscape painting. Indeed, "the picturesque" was a key category in late eighteenth and early nineteenth art criticism, particularly in the writings of William Gilpin and Uvedale Price. We found Thoreau dabbling in this, and one suspects that John Muir's writings on mountain scenery were influenced by it.

There is a great tradition of American landscape painting from the early nineteenth century until shortly after the Civil War, of whom Frederic Church, the Hudson River School, Albert Bierstadt, and Thomas Moran are some of the key representatives. American landscape painting helped generate a nationalistic pride in American natural beauty. It helped in the legislative struggle to set aside the earliest national parks. (Later, the photographs of Ansel Adams were to play a similar role.) Even some railroad owners commissioned painters to portray Western scenes to stimulate a tourist market.

Unfortunately, this concern for "vistas" and "scenic splendors" focused attention away from the less obviously picturesque elements of our world. We need to appreciate decomposition and decay. Swamps were long a symbol for despair or the home of demons. Perhaps, more original prairie would have been preserved if a Bierstadt of the plains had painted them. And, is it too far-fetched to say that the ecologically destructive monocultures we call lawns and corporate campuses are a love for the scenic or picturesque gone ignorantly haywire?

Aldo Leopold directly challenges the "scenic" tradition, not to overthrow but to expand it. "Our ability to perceive quality in nature begins, as in art, with the pretty. It expands through successive stages of the beautiful to values as yet uncaptured by language" (Leopold, 1966, 102).

This quotation is from an essay in which Leopold seeks to suggest aesthetic qualities of a scene, which, as Callicott points out, "the conventional picturesque natural aesthetic finds plain, if not odious—a crane marsh" (Callicott, 1987, 161).

For Callicott, the informed mind could direct attention and also increase appreciation. Callicott points out that, for Leopold, the appreciation of natural beauty can involve all of the senses. "Most of all it can invoke the mind, the faculty of cognition" (Callicott, 1987, 161). Vision had "become the predominant sensory modality for experiencing natural beauty in the conventional Western esthetic, and natural beauty was judged by esthetic criteria originally developed for the evaluation of painting." For Aldo Leopold, all of the senses are used in appreciation of natural objects and "esthetic experience is as cerebral as it is perceptual" (Leopold, 1991b, 9. See also Eugene C. Hargrove, 1989, 77–88).

To read Leopold is to read someone who constantly notices ecological relationships. This is an informed perception often including measurement, always appreciative, concerned for the long-range importance of what appears to be trivial, an ability to spot the drama in the small setting.

One pictures Leopold getting up before dawn in south central Wisconsin with his coffee, his watch, and notebook at hand, sitting on a stump to time the first calls of various birds. I think of him in his adult life taking notes on a hunting trip in New Mexico, noting the behavior of pintail ducks in a hailstorm and seeking for an explanation. Flader and Callicott stress the significance of this by publishing a facsimile of Leopold's field notes on this occasion, together with a reworked version for *The Condor*, journal of the Cooper Ornithological Society. I read of Leopold recording his observations of the feeding habits of pigs in southeastern Missouri and of what he learned hunting in the American Midwest and Southwest. We can see Leopold learning the optimum distances between food and cover for various types of game birds. We can see him with his children banding chickadees and note his appreciation of Number 65,290, a hardy survivor of several winters. Finally, we can hear him telling his students that "the purpose of this class is to learn how to read a landscape."

Scattered throughout Leopold's writings are references to his ecological observations. Some are derived from a desire either to hunt game birds and animals or to increase populations of game animals. (Leopold was a hunter for much of his life. However, as his attitudes toward the environment changed, he abandoned hunting and took up photographing animals.)

On hunting trips, he observed and made notes on what kind of foliage birds were in at what time of day, on the sleeping and feeding habits of ducks and does relative to the time of day, whether a deer startled by light tended to go uphill, into the wind, around a point, or toward cover, and what a deer startled by scent will do. As a game bird manager, he noted optimum distances between cover, feeding, and sunning areas.

As part of this emphasis on studying ecological relationships, Leopold wished to encourage the revival of the amateur naturalist. Partly, this was because he decried the denigration of field studies that he saw in the biological studies of his time. Laboratory studies are important, he thought, but only field studies will show us live ecological relationships, only field studies will suggest fruitful laboratory experiments, only real-life situations will confirm the conclusions of laboratory studies. However, in order to do field studies, we will need trained amateurs. There are not enough professional biologists to study all of the field locations. Field studies are also a key component in the development of ecological citizenship. The amateur naturalist may have a poor reputation. However,

> laboratory biology came into existence about the time when amateur natural history was of the dickey-bird variety, and when professional natural history consisted of labeling species and amassing facts about food habitats without interpreting them. In short, a growing and vital laboratory technique was at that time placed in competition with a stagnated outdoor technique. It was quite natural that laboratory biology soon came to be regarded as the superior form of science.

> In the interim, field studies have developed techniques and ideas quite as scientific as those of the laboratory. The amateur scientist is no longer confined to pleasant ambles in the country, resulting merely in lists of species, lists of migration dates, and lists of rarities. Bird banding, feather marking, censusing, and experimental manipulation of behavior and environment are techniques available to all, and they are quantitative science.
>
> (Leopold, 1991a, 96–98)

Leopold knew that it takes time and money to change curricula. Thus, "the average college student who inclines toward natural history avocations" is taught to carve dead cats instead of "being taught to see his native countryside with appreciation and intelligence" (Leopold, 1991a, 98).

A related reason to develop skilled amateurs is that he felt that specialization focuses on parts of whatever system it studies, but tends to overlook the system as a whole. We must "examine the collective behavior of biotic materials. This calls for a reversal of specialization; instead of learning more and more about less and less, we must learn more and more about the whole biotic landscape" (Leopold, 1991a, 96–98, 229).

His concern was not to displace the professional biologist, but to urge that the amateur be educated to do genuine research, not merely to repeat what the professional has already discovered.

Leopold was familiar with and cited the work of such amateurs as: homemaker Margaret Morse Nice whose backyard study led her to become a world authority on the social organization of birds, banker Charles Broley who discovered migration patterns of eagles, wheat ranchers Norman and Stuart Criddle who were authorities on wild life cycles, cowman Elliott Barker who wrote one of the best books on mountain lions, and an unnamed chemist who reconstructed the history of the passenger pigeon.

> [T]he whole structure of biological education (including education in wildlife) is aimed to perpetuate the professional monopoly on research. To the amateur are allotted only make-believe voyages of discovery, to verify what the professional authority already knows.
>
> (Leopold, 1991a, 94–95. On Margaret M. Nice, see Ehrlich, Dobkin, and Wheye, 1988, 579–581)

Leopold is very clear. He concludes his *A Sand County Almanac* with a penultimate note on the importance of nurturing perception. "To promote perception is the only truly creative part of recreational engineering." A page later, he repeats the point. "The only true development in American recreational resources is the development of the perceptive faculty in Americans" (Leopold, 1966, 290–291).

The final note in *A Sand County Almanac* is the importance of a sense of husbandry. In part, the importance derives from the accomplishment of actual care for the land derived from such a sense. In part, it comes from the pleasure to be derived, in part, from the increase in perception which active involvement brings (Leopold, 1966, 292–293).

Thus, Leopold urges the development of perception, husbandry, and also sufficient social isolation to allow a person to focus on the biotic neighbors. The final sentence of the *Almanac* is a plea to build "receptivity into the still unlovely human mind."

Leopold is quite clear that perception is to be scientifically informed. He refers to "the perception of the natural processes by which the land and the living things upon it have achieved these characteristic forms (evolution) and by which they maintain their existence (ecology)." The swoop of a hawk, for instance, can be perceived as the drama of evolution.

> The incredible intricacies of the plant and animal community—the intrinsic beauty of the organism called America . . . were as invisible and incomprehensible to Daniel Boone as they are today to Babbitt.
>
> (Leopold, 1966, 291)

To be ecologically informed does not mean to be merely academically trained. "[T]he Ph.D. may become as callous as an undertaker to the mysteries at which he officiates" (Leopold, 1966, 290–291).

"The Marshland Elegy" is a beautiful essay depicting such an ecologically informed, aesthetically aware perception. So also is "Wilderness," reflections on his very important visit to the apparently beautiful, but actually ecologically pathological forests of Germany (Leopold, 1966, 101–108; Leopold, 1991b, 226–229).

Leopold himself studied the writings of the ecologist Charles S. Elton and summarized the results of Elton's theories in the images of a stream of energy or round river and the land pyramid. As an educator, both inside and outside of the classroom, he stressed the importance of a good mental image.

This environmentally informed perception has its cost. One of the penalties of an ecological education is that one lives alone in a world of wounds. Much of the damage inflicted on land is quite invisible to laymen. An ecologist must either harden his skull and make believe that the consequences of science are none of his business, or he must be the doctor who sees the marks of death in a community that believes itself well and does not want to be told otherwise (Leopold, 1966, 197. For Leopold on the value of mental images, see pages 111-118, 188–202, 251–258).

Leopold liked to call this ecologically informed perception "reading a landscape." Indeed, the purpose of the class in ecology he taught to liberal arts students, he said, was to learn how to read a landscape. Outstanding examples of such reading may be found in "The Virgin Southwest." To be able to read an environment includes being able to read the signs of its history. He speaks of fence rows and thickets as being like the letters of a tragic history. He reads a Wisconsin woodlot in January. He ends his elegy on the marshland with the environmental history of the crane (Leopold, 1991b, 162, 172-180, 274-275; Leopold, 1966, 102-108).

In "Natural History," he makes fun of a bright student who has a biological education that stresses the anatomy and physiology of the individual organism.

He suggests that we visualize the sterility of such education by imagining that we take the student into the field.

> We are driving down a country road in northern Missouri. Here is a farmstead. Look at the trees in the yard and the soil in the field and tell us whether the original settler carved his farm out of prairie or woods. Did he eat prairie chicken or wild turkey for his Thanksgiving? What plants grew here originally, which do not grow here now? Why did they disappear? What did the prairie plants have to do with creating the corn yielding capacity of this soil? Why does this soil erode now, but not then?
> (Leopold, 1991a, 98)

Could our bright student begin to answer these questions?

Leopold is also clear that perception involves attention, and that attention on one set of things involves overlooking other things. In a delightfully written couple of pages ("The Deer Swath"), he tells about watching his weekend guests when he sits them where they can see deer. He finds four types of outdoorsmen, representing four different habits of human eyes. "The deer hunter habitually watches the next bend; the duck hunter watches the skyline; the bird hunter watches the dog; the non-hunter does not watch." He then depicts other habits, those of birders, botanists, foresters, and an elusive skill known as reading signs. The ecologist, finally, is someone who tries to do all of these. Naturally, he cannot, but to compensate, he tries to alternate his modes of perception. In a passage reminiscent of Thoreau's speaking of changing the intentionality of the eye, Leopold wrote that he found that when hunting plants, he could only pay minimal attention to animals (Leopold, 1991a, 186–189).

From his ecological training, Aldo Leopold learned to notice the small and unobtrusive, the small cogs and wheels, which a tinkerer should always take care to preserve. In particular, his attention included the bacteria, molds, and fungi under trees and plants. About this microflora, he was convinced that science knew very little, and despite slash cutting policies of much of the logging industry, but that science did know that in a complex forest, "it is best to let well enough alone" (Leopold, 1991b, 293).

This interest in the small and unobtrusive supported his concern for the specialist citizen-naturalist. The weeds in a city lot convey a great lesson; the farmer may learn more from his cow-pasture than a scientist traveling in the South Seas.

One of Leopold's most elegantly understated paeans to one of the unobtrusive creatures is a small entry in *A Sand County Almanac*. The draba is a tiny flower, one that you must search for on your knees in the mud. It plucks no heartstrings. But it does its small ecological job quickly and well. No poet sings its praises, but Leopold has given it relative immortality in a half page of rhapsodic irony (Leopold, 1966, 28).

Leopold writes in another place of the importance of the inconspicuous, uninteresting dog bush. Again, his purpose is to stress the difference between what is apparently uninteresting and its importance and capacity to generate interest when its ecological significance is stressed. Here, his term is "drama." There is drama in every bush, if you can see it, if you can learn enough of the language. This interest in the drama will be the basis of true conservation, of concern for the welfare of the land. Notice the melding of ecological and aesthetic concerns and language, which so often occurs in his writing (Leopold, 1991b, 261–265).

We have mentioned Leopold's essay "The Deer Swath." It is interesting how he closes this essay by using an image in which the hunter stands for any human exploring the world with camera, notebook, or naked curiosity. "Every ground is a hunting ground," even if "it lies between you and the curbstone." He concludes the essay with the aphorism, "The final test of the hunter is whether he is keen to go hunting in a vacant lot" (Leopold, 1991a, 189).

Paradoxically, although he calls attention to the small and unobtrusive, he also focuses on species that, while perhaps not often seen, are spectacular when seen. Without such a species, the whole of an ecosystem is diminished, ecologically and aesthetically. He calls such a species the *noumenon*, or we might say, essence of the system.

One source for this is his essay "Guacamaja" in *A Sand County Almanac*. The ruffled grouse is only a millionth part of the mass or energy of the autumn landscape in the northern woods, yet without the grouse, the whole thing seems dead. It is not just a loss in our minds. It is an ecological death, the significance of which is unstateable in terms of contemporary science. This is the importance of the thick-billed parrot or Guacamaja, which is the *noumenon* or "imponderable essence" of the Sierra Madre. A wolf is the *noumenon* in "Thinking Like a Mountain" (Leopold, 1966, 146–149, 137–141). Both of these are powerful laments for the ecological and aesthetic loss of the killing of the last of the *noumena* in these places, killings done for what seemed at the time like scientifically and economically wise policies, only to be shown with time to be disastrous. Perhaps, some wisdom can be gained in realizing that this was a crucial point in Leopold's advance in ecological thinking.

Leopold refers to these ecologically and aesthetically important species with the Kantian term *noumenon* or "imponderable essence." To be sure that this is a departure from how Kant used the term, as for Kant, a *noumenon* would not be empirical. Yet, to call a species that constitutes the inexpressible, often hidden, essence of a landscape, the *noumenon* of the landscape is remarkably in the spirit of Kant. Leopold was fond of these *noumena* and could specify many of them. "The grouse is the noumenon (sic) of the north woods, the blue jay of the hickory groves, the whiskey-jack of the muskegs, the piñonero of the juniper foothills" (Leopold, 1966, 147; see also 141–149; Callicott, 1987, 77–78, 166–167).

In J. Baird Callicott's felicitous phrase, these are "aesthetic indicator species" and also species that reflect the wholeness and integrity of the ecosystem, once again indicating how closely Leopold has merged ecological understanding and aesthetic appreciation. Thus, says Callicott, "he prefers the bobwhite quail in 'Grand-Opera Game' (1932) to the bigger and flashier, but artificially propagated and foreign pheasant, because the quail is a wild, native member of the American land community." These *noumena* are often birds and animals of prey: grizzly, great owls, and even ordinary hawks. In short, the *noumenon* is a special member of an ecosystem, of major ecological and aesthetic significance. Without it, the land would be diminished. "Is a wolfless northwoods any northwoods at all?" (Leopold, 1991b, 10, 228; 1991a, 217; Callicott, 1987, 167. It should be noted that Callicott's interpretation of Leopold here is open to debate).

It is clear for Leopold that an ecologically informed perception requires an ability to perceive the effects of human exploitation. Every time we substitute a tame species for a wild one or build a new waterway, we need to think about the effects. Will the new order maintain fertility? Will it promote or diminish diversity? What do we see in the way of erosion, of gullies, of dustclouds? (Leopold, 1991a, 235–236).

Thus, Aldo Leopold practiced through his speeches, writings, conversation, and teaching an acquired, ecologically informed perception. He notes that in the American Southwest, the Apache were confined on reservations, while in Mexico, they were for decades allowed freedom of movement. He notes a connection between this and the erosion of the Sierra Madre north of the border and the virgin stability and beauty of the mountains south of the border. The causal connection between these facts will seem absurd only to those who still think that the relationship between facts must be obvious. His paper "Conservationist in Mexico" is an explanation of the connection. He further notes that the places in the American Southwest are so badly damaged that "only tourists and others ecologically color-blind can look upon them without a feeling of sadness and regret" (Leopold, 1991b, 239).

Before leaving Leopold's reflections on appreciation, we should note that he found that when we appreciate the valuable gifts, which the world affords us, we have a new set of values and new motives. For one thing, we acquire "a refined taste in natural objects," which appreciates more than economic value. Hawks and owls compete with game and poultry, but we must ask "whether a hawkless, owlless countryside is a livable countryside." White cedar has been purged from what was once the northwoods in the lake states because of its economic inefficiency. White cedar grows too slowly. For a similar reason, beech has been eliminated from the timber forests of the southeast.

Leopold calls the refined state that can appreciate the beauty of the white cedar and beech an aesthetic taste. At times, he says, aesthetic values can trump economic values. He also realizes that the distinction between economic and aesthetic values is not so clear, as eliminating a species may have a deleterious effect on the health of the forest (Leopold, 1991b, 239).

A farmer can devote land to woods, marsh, or pond that have both utility and non-economic benefits. A farmer can also set aside land as fence rows and leave tree snags for raccoons and owls. Furthermore, a farmer can set aside fence rows for native wildflowers, prairie remnants, or just plain scenery. All of these things Leopold advocated.

Just as aesthetic values are different from economic values, sometimes competing, sometimes overriding, sometimes complementing, so also appreciative awareness must be combined in principle and often in actuality with critical awareness. This critical awareness is not just being critical or making critical comments. Leopold can refer to it as "the critical eye," an informed eye, almost as if in paying attention a person becomes aware of a lack, of something gone wrong. Leopold used the term "the critical eye" in writing about the forests that he examined during his crucial 1935 3-months trip to Germany to study forestry and wildlife.

In analyzing his sense of foreboding in the German forests, Leopold found two things wrong. One was a geometric layout. Creeks and rivulets were often "straight as a dead snake" in masonry channels. The trees were in straight rows, all of one kind, and often in parallelograms of ascending age groups. The boundaries between wood and field were sharp and straight. To be sure, by the mid-1930s, the German foresters were aware of the ecological danger of such geometrical precision, but Leopold could lampoon it as "cubist." The second thing a critical eye found was an almost total lack of birds and of animals of prey. To notice this, Leopold commented, would require an informed perception, for it is imperceptible to the average tourist (Leopold, 1991b, 226–228).

Taking our cue from Aldo Leopold, we may say that appreciative awareness should be combined with critical awareness. What we need to develop is both an appreciative and a critical eye.

There are a number of other writers who have reflected on attention or appreciation of the world: Annie Dillard, Barry Lopez, and others. For lack of space, we shall limit ourselves to sketches of the views of two thinkers: Delores LaChapelle and Gary Snyder.

Delores LaChapelle

Rock climber, deep powder skier, mountain guide, a recoverer of Neolithic, Daoist, and American Indian earth rituals, American deep ecologist, student of D.H. Lawrence, and public intellectual, Delores LaChapelle was one of the most imaginative people of our time. She was a pioneer in breaking down old ways of thinking. We cannot do justice to her multi-faceted reflections here, but we can summarize part of the fruit of her work on seeing nature (LaChapelle, 1988, 102–109).

She claimed that much of our common sense and scientific understanding of vision are based on Renaissance painting, which emphasizes linear perspective from a single point of view. Central to this understanding of vision are two assumptions, often unarticulated. One is that the observer occupies one single motionless place at one instant of time. Second, that the observer stands apart from the world at some distance from it. Drawing on her own experience as rock climber and skier, LaChapelle challenged both assumptions. [She drew on the work of psychologist James Gibson (Gibson, 1979).]

First, the way we actually observe the world normally involves motion of two sorts. The first is our own movement. Our eyes are attached to our bodies, and our bodies, when awake, are normally moving. This seems obvious, but we often fail to notice how this challenges the Renaissance paradigm. Instead of vision being the end product of light transmissions from object through eye and optic nerve to brain, each of these is a mid-point in a process of continual feedback, in which we move to improve, verify, and change our point of view. Vision is not physically passive, it is part of a process of exploration. In short, observation involves movement. Few would want to deny this, yet, we seldom realize how the implications of this challenges the Renaissance paradigm of a fixed point of view. From a linear perspective alone, you cannot tell whether you are confronting a tall mountain in the distance or a shorter hill up close. Aerial perspective, and perhaps, experience with vegetation zones may help, but the definitive test is to move laterally or toward the mountain. LaChapelle was a rock climber and skier and spoke from her experience in this. She also practiced tai chi in the mountains of Colorado and spoke of suddenly seeing a peak, during or after doing a tai chi form, which she had not noticed before.

The second sort of motion involved in seeing is the movement of the sun during the day, a movement that brings out a different aspect of the object. As a rock climber, LaChapelle spoke of watching a mountain several times in a day, as the changing shadows disclose surface features, which might reveal a path up to the summit.

While the first implication of the Renaissance way of seeing is that the observer occupies one single motionless place at one instant of time, the second is that even though it shows us a great deal of the world and its structure, paradoxically, it can tend to alienate us from this world. If we look at the world from one standpoint, this viewpoint becomes distinct from the rest of the world. Also, the motionless viewpoint helps us forget that we move *within* the world we are viewing. As Gibson said, when we look at the world, we always see the tip of our noses, but we usually ignore it (quoted in LaChapelle, 1988, 107). When did the tip of the artist's nose appear in a Renaissance painting? Yet, the tip of our nose reminds us that we are not distinct from the world, but immersed in it.

Thus, contrary to the Renaissance way of seeing, LaChapelle stresses our immersion in the world we observe and the significance of our motion and the sun's motion for observation. What movies, television, video, and cyberspace are doing to our vision has been the subject of some speculation. Inevitably, we can do little controlled observation and experiment in this area. This is a large subject to which we cannot devote much space. LaChapelle claims that Renaissance modes of perception may rest on outmoded historiography and an artificial homogenization of both Renaissance and post-Renaissance way of seeing. However, LaChapelle's notion that much of our view of vision, indeed of the knower of the world, has been profoundly affected by Renaissance linear perspective that ignores the importance of motion and that separates us from the world is important and needs further exploration. The new electronic media (and we are in the medium of these media) restore motion, but they tend to change, rather than remove, our alienation from the world. Even nature films present a distorted, if somewhat helpful, view of the non-human world.

Another major point in LaChapelle's writing on seeing is contained in her reflections on *affordance*, or what the world affords to us. This is a very pregnant word that she borrows from Gibson. It is not just that we look at the world, *take* a peek or glance at it. It is that the world *gives* us something to view. This has wide implications. It is not that the world has resources that we take. It is that the world gives us, affords us, things, events, and prospects, which sustain and delight us. It affords them because it can afford to. This play of words reminds us that the gifts, which are afforded to us, are budgeted. If we take too much, the world will not be able to give as much.

"Affordance" also helps us to remember that we do not have to figure out how to get everything or that we have discovered everything. It reminds us that many valuable and meaningful things are given to us; thus, values and meaningful things are not just our addition to a meaningless, value-free world. Furthermore, nature affords different things to different species or individuals. Thus, there is a reciprocal interaction between ourselves and nature. In elaborating this point, she quotes Gibson that affordances are the way specific regions of the environment directly address themselves to particular species or individuals. Thus, to a human, a maple tree may afford "looking at" or "sitting under," while to a sparrow, it affords "perching," and to a squirrel, it affords "climbing." But, these values are not found inside the minds of the animals. Rather, they are a reciprocal interaction between the living intentions of any animal and the dynamic affordances of its world (Gibson, 1979, 129, quoted in LaChapelle, 1988, 108).

A full treatment of LaChapelle's treatment of appreciative awareness would include further elements, which we can only sketch here. She is/was a student of ancient rituals and is attempting to revive their practice. A couple of characteristics of her appreciative perception stem from her practices of these rituals. The first is her emphasis on the changing seasons. Ancient Celtic ritual, developed in the temperate zone, emphasizes solstices and equinoxes as well as the approximate mid-points or cross-quarter days. Many of these times became significant holy days in European Christendom. By sacralizing these times, she directs attention to the seasonal changes of plants, landforms, and weather.

Some of her rituals involve walks, which can be seen as miniature pilgrimages. In her description of conducting several ritual journeys on foot, based partly on the Pawnee "hako" ceremony, she tells of leading people to places of great meaning. Part of the ritual involves recognizing especially impressive places, rocks, trees, vistas, and also birds. She clearly assimilates these moving experiences with the experience of the sacred, marking them with appropriate ritual action (LaChapelle, 1988, 202–215).

Finally, for LaChapelle, there is an overlap between heightened awareness of natural beauty, the sacred, and the erotic. The overlap between the natural and the erotic seems plausible as does to overlap between the natural and the sacred. But, the monotheistic culture has had a deep bias against blurring the distinction between the sacred and the erotic, a distinction that goes back at least to the struggle between the ancient Hebrews and the Canaanite fertility cults. This may have something to do with the excess which the sexual plays in our psychic and cultural life. We should not identify the erotic and the sacred, but neither should we keep a fence between them.

LaChapelle found a kindred spirit in D.H. Lawrence, which she brought out in her book-length study of him (LaChapelle, 1996). For both LaChapelle and Lawrence, the planet Venus is especially evocative of the overlap between the natural, the erotic, and the sacred. As I write these lines, I have a vivid recollection of a bright starry night in the Chama river valley in New Mexico, away from lights and pollution, overwhelmed by the almost forgotten brightness and number of the stars, outside an adobe casita midway between Espanola and Abiquiu. There, some years ago, my wife and I watched the bright evening star and saw how as it neared the horizon it almost plunged out of sight. Perhaps, my excitement came in part from having read LaChapelle. Or, perhaps, she opened my eyes to one of the affordances of the night sky.

Gary Snyder

Gary Snyder has had a profound effect on parts of the American environmental movement. He grew up in the rural northwest and worked in the logging industry as a young man. For a period, he was a poet in San Francisco during the period of the Beat writers. Several years were spent in Japan as a student of Zen and Chinese poetry. More recently, he has been learning with his family how to live lightly on the land in the Sierra foothills of northern California. A Pulitzer Prize winning poet, he taught creative writing part time at the University of California at Davis. He is a strong advocate of bioregionalism, which I define as the belief and practice of focusing on the ecological region as far more crucial than economic or political units.

Snyder has always been observant of the natural world.

> From a very early age, I found myself standing in awe before the natural world. I felt gratitude, wonder, and a sense of protection, especially as I began to see the hills being bulldozed for roads, and the forest of the Pacific Northwest magically float away on logging trucks.
>
> (Snyder, 1995, 126-127)

His poetry often draws attention to his natural setting.

Snyder writes of carefully observing changes in the landscape as he travels by car. For example, driving in northern California from Yuba River canyon to Crescent City, he notes passing through four bioregions. This type of observation may seem obvious, but Snyder is a careful observer of these changes and what they indicate of bioregional transitions (Snyder, 1995, 219–221). Yet, even for a careful observer like Snyder, it may take years before he notices a certain tree (Snyder, 1995, 263).

One of Snyder's contributions to our discussion is his view of language as both an avenue to the world and a filter shaping our perception of the world. These reflections are contained in a little essay, "Language Goes Two Ways" (Snyder, 1995, 173–180). Language "enables us to have a small window on to an independently existing world, but it also shapes . . . how we see that world" (Snyder, 1995, 174). In this sense, Snyder denies that there is nothing, but language. There is a real sense in which there is a transaction between language and world. Furthermore, language both helps us to see and shapes our seeing.

This far Snyder is in agreement with many American writers who see a transaction between language and world. What is different in Snyder is that he sees wildness in both world and language. His definition of "wildness" is crucial. It "alludes to a process of self-organization that generates systems and organisms. ... Wildness can be said to be the essential nature of nature" (Snyder, 1995, 174). Part of the wildness of these self-organizing systems is their complexity, and thus, unpredictability. There is an aspect of order in this wildness, which is crucial, for it gives stability and room necessary for the innovation that is found in wildness.

The human mind shares this self-organizing wildness. Consequently, it is not that language imposes order on chaos, as many literary theorists assert, but that language reflects the wildness of the universe back onto it. The implication of this is that instead of dismissing language in the name of unspeakable truths, we must turn back to language. We must know mind and language extremely well and to play with its possibilities. Then language will yield up surprises and can lead us back to direct experience (Snyder, 1995, 174–175). Contrary to romantic aesthetics, creativity is not a unique, godlike act. It comes from being immersed in what is and seeing the overlooked (Snyder, 1995, 176).

The usual idea of "Good Language" or "Correct Language" is based on the language of power and position. Another kind of "Good Language" is the technical sort that is dedicated to clarity and argument and is part of the toolkit of a successful person. This kind of writing is boring, but has "the usefulness of a tractor. It plows straight rows" and produces "scholarly essays, grant proposals, and final reports."

> Ordinary Good Writing is like a garden that is producing exactly what you want. ... But *really* good writing is both inside and outside the garden fence. It can be a few beans, but also some wild poppies, vetches ... and some juncos and yellow jackets thrown in. It is more diverse, more interesting. ... Its connection to the wildness of language and imagination helps give it power.
> (Snyder, 1995, 176–177)

Snyder summarizes his view of language by contrasting it with the more common view of language in some short propositions. The usual view is, first, "Language is uniquely human and primarily cultural." His contrary proposition is: "Language is basically biological; it becomes semi-cultural as it is learned and practiced." The truth of Snyder's view can be supported by pointing out the neurophysiological basis of speech, signing, or writing. The significance of his point is that language is often referred to indicate human superiority over animals. However, as all plants and animals differ biologically yet have some generic processes in common, Snyder's point indicates that while language differentiates us from animals, it is a discontinuity within a generic continuity. All species are different. Difference need not indicate superiority. Hence, the import of Snyder's term "semi-cultural."

The second part of the common view of language is that "Intelligence is framed and developed by language." On the contrary, Snyder suggests, "Intelligence is framed and developed by all kinds of interactions with this world." Hence, the view of some post-modernists that language does not hook up to the world is bypassed by Snyder. We have all sorts of ways of interacting with the world. We may not be able to represent it without interpretation, but we are *in touch* with it, and it does support and can destroy us.

The relationship between chaos and order is clarified in the third set of contrasting propositions. The usual view is that, "The world is chaotic, but language organizes and criticizes it." Snyder's contrasting view is that, "The world (and mind) is orderly in its own fashion, and linguistic order reflects and condenses that order."

From this comes the fourth contrast. The familiar view is that, "The more cultivated the language—the more elevated and precise and clear—the better it will tame the unruly world of nature and feeling." Snyder's view is that "The more completely the world is allowed to come forward and instruct us (without the interference of ego and opinion), the better we can see our place in the interconnected world of nature." This is Snyder's concise statement of what, in this chapter, we have been calling "appreciative perception" or similar phrases such as "appreciative awareness." It comes partly from his Buddhist training in mindfulness, being aware of the present moment in both meditation practice and in the practice of everyday life (Snyder, 1995, 178–179).

In a talk to a conference on the Rights of the Nonhuman, Snyder asked, how are we to treat the world better? To answer that we must ask how to know the non-human world. And, then, how do we communicate this to the human world (Snyder, 1995, 48)?

His answer is that there are three practices or styles of discourse. The first is the style of the philosopher, who speaks the language of reason, of public discourse, with the intention of being intelligible to anyone (Snyder, 1995, 48–49).

The second style is that of the yogin, an experimenter who creates a discourse of deep hearing and doing. The yogin has a specific set of exercises and disciplines by which to acquire a deeper understanding that the purely rational function will allow. A key difference between the literature of the yogic tradition and that of the philosopher is that the former makes special requirements of its reader that the philosopher does not. The yogin holds that certain ideas cannot be grasped except by proceeding through a set of disciplines. There is a Western counterculture that parallels this, the Pythagorean, alchemical, occult, Neoplatonic, and Gnostic traditions.

Some yogic-type practices express themselves in a certain type of poetry, forming a type he calls "the poet-yogin." Although he does not elaborate this in this conference talk, clues to the kind of poetry Snyder has in mind can be gleaned from Part Two of *A Place in Space* (1995) as well as his own poetry.

The third type of discourse, almost forgotten, is the shamanistic. This is an aspect of Snyder's re-appropriation of certain of the Old Ways, which are approaches to life antedating the Neolithic derailment of things. "The shaman speaks for wild animals, the spirits of plants, the spirits of mountains, of watersheds. . . . They sing through him" (Snyder, 1995, 49–51).

Closer to our times, the "pagan" battle of modern poetry shows that poetry has been a long, but not particularly successful defending action against state and church.

Summarizing the discussion

To summarize this chapter, we may divide these issues into five sections.

1. The first is to consider the topic of how to perceive. Thoreau and Leopold give us some very helpful suggestions on how to perceive. Perception takes practice. Perception can be trained. To some extent, it is a skill. Like any skill, the more we practice it on a regular basis, the better we become at it.

    Walking, sitting, or riding horseback provide a good time frame. Driving is too fast. Reading landscapes and landscape transitions, like Snyder exemplified in northern California, can be learned. Finding time is important, and this includes careful thought on not being engulfed in making a living, which is becoming harder these days. Equipment, such as binoculars, magnifying glass, microscope, field guide, and measuring stick, are helpful. Usually appreciative perception means being alone, although a good guide, a curious child, or a like-minded companion can help. All the senses should be employed.

    Perception requires *activity*. It is not a spectator sport. You need to interact with your surroundings, taking care to respect other creatures' space. Apart from this inter-species etiquette, you should peek, pry, and poke. Sketching and developing a color palette can help train appreciative awareness. This also means that we can move around to observe from different angles. This will also help us remember that the environment is not something different from us, but that we are an integral part of it and it of us. And, we can take the time to observe and listen at different times of the day, of the year, and in successive years.

    We can also develop *ecological perception*. As I write this section, I am in the midst of reading Aldo Leopold's *Game Management* (1933). This is the current part of my continuing effort to train my perception in an ecologically informed manner. Perhaps, I am not the amateur naturalist that Leopold wished. Nevertheless, as I study landscapes, I am starting more and more to look for food, cover, and resting areas and the distance between them, to notice predators and prey habits, and hunt for remnants of a previous period. Above all, I am slowly learning how to read the history of landscapes. This is not long-term geological time, rather this is mid-term landscape time, which, in my area at the southwest corner of Lake Michigan, is measured in decades, sometimes centuries, up to about 10,000 years ago. Perhaps, eventually, we will have more trained amateur naturalists. In any event, it definitely means a commitment to life-long ecological learning.

    We also need to both *familiarize and defamiliarize* our perception. We need to alternate between these two modes. We need to become familiar enough with what we are looking at to build on what we know. At the same time, we need to overcome our ongoing stereotypes. We need to alternate between sympathetic intimacy and a recognition of otherness and mystery.

We need both directed and wandering perception. That is, we need to employ both a focused, intentional perception and a sauntering, exploratory approach. There is a time to be attentive and absorbed in a narrow range of perception, and a time to let the eyes and the ears roam. Both are needed.

Habits of perception are useful, but we also need to develop new habits, lest we lose much. Whatever our basic way of looking, we also need to develop the skills of other types of outdoor people, so that we can, at least sometimes, perceive like a birder, a botanist, a forester, a tracker. Binoculars and dogs will help us, but we also need to learn not to be imprisoned by them. They can be as liberating and as confining as field guides and science texts.

2. The second major topic Thoreau, Leopold, LaChapelle, and Snyder coax us to consider is what to perceive. Attention should be given not only to how to perceive (the previous topic), but also to the education of our appreciative perception in terms of what we shall focus on. The study of *particulars* is important. The human ability to abstract and generalize is helpful in its place, but we have overdone it. We need to stand Plato's Divided Line on its head. Instead of talking about "Nature" and the "Environment," we need to concentrate on Pilgrim Creek, and Yosemite, the North Branch of the Chicago River, and the vacant lot down the block. Each of us must explore our own Walden. This perception in depth will surely lead to greater appreciation, which in turn will anchor environmental ethical judgment and supply the long-range passion to defend our Waldens. *And, it might even help evoke a sense of the sacred, of the very important, although there are no guarantees about that.*

We should also go beyond the scenic. The picturesque, the scenic, vistas, the pastoral, and the conventionally beautiful all have their place. But, we also need to explore and appreciate the less lovely. We need to see the beauty of the apparently boring, swamps, prairies, carrion, and the seemingly dreary mud season scenes. I once heard a TV personality say that there was nothing in Kansas. If only he had truly opened his eyes.

We also need to appreciate the smallest cogs and wheels, which a tinkerer should always carefully keep. We need to notice *the unobtrusive as well as the spectacular*. This especially includes the microflora and microfauna, the invertebrates and non-seed-bearing plants, nocturnal creatures, and the large communities within the soil. We concentrate so much on the Bambis and the large predators that we often overlook the crucial parts of the environmental community.

Leopold had much to teach us about the ecological drama of the apparently uninteresting, the tiny draba flower and the dog bush. Learning to see drama, to learn to read its language, will give us the interest, the concern, the appreciation for these crucial cogs and wheels. We need to learn with Leopold and Snyder that every ground, even between you and the curbstone, is hunting ground, "the final test of the hunter is whether he is keen to go hunting in a vacant lot" (Leopold, 1991a, 187). At the same time, we need not be embarrassed at enjoying the spectacular. These are often keystone species, crucial to the health or at least complexity of ecosystems. Also, they are often not seen frequently and the search for them teaches us patience. I am talking about Leopold's *noumena*, although to avoid unnecessary philosophical implications, I call them "spectacular species," what J. Baird Callicott calls "aesthetic indicator species" (Callicott, 1987, 67).

3. A key theme throughout this chapter, found in our four nature writers from climbing Mount Ktaadn to keeping nature journals, has been that *perception and language play an ongoing duet*, a continual transaction. It might be nice to have direct contact with "pristine" nature, uncontaminated with the trappings and baggage of the civilized world. But, that Robinson Crusoe fantasy is belied by Crusoe's own carrying of the cultural world of Defoe into his experience. There is little, if any, uninterpreted experience. On the other hand, it is not language all the way down. The world is more than just our social construction of it. We are born, and we usually die, not by our own choice. We do not construct the endpoints of our life. Nor do we create the fundamental environmental constraints upon our life, the need for optimum stressors intermittently applied (Van Rensselaer Potter, 1971). We may interpret and understand these endpoints, constraints, and needs with our cultural ideas, but we do not produce them. The fantasy of some post-moderns that the world is socially constructed overlooks the real constructive and deconstructive powers of the world. Such post-modernism continues the modernist dream of being in charge of the world.

The trick is to recognize that our experience is a transaction between our selves, our genetic, cultural and self-reflexive selves, and our environing systems. That, of course, puts it too simply, as the interaction shapes both poles of the transaction. The world affects us, shapes us and is in us, and vice versa. And, there is no self in the sense of a permanent, unchanging substratum. But, for simplicity's sake, we can refer to a mutual negotiation between ourselves and our world.

Once we recognize the transactional character of life, we can then move on to enriching our perception by our language and vice versa. It is neither pure experience nor merely language. It is a mutually enriching duet. By language, I mean not only writing and speech, but also the visual languages of painting, of film, of photography, of music, of dance, of Internet. I am an incurable book reader, but I do not wish to restrict discussion to my favorite medium.

4. We can have an *educated perception*. Whether it is through books, classes, Internet, or naturalists and park rangers, what we learn can increase what we perceive. As Laura Dassow Walls says of Thoreau, our education can give us new words to see by and new tools to see with. On the other hand, there is a time to put the books away and try to look afresh. Perhaps, putting our heads upside down or using a Claude glass is not a bad idea. Words can interfere with our observation, especially if we think that identification is the main

point of field study. Here, the truisms gain new point. Learning takes a lot of unlearning of our preconceptions, yet learned ignorance is superior to untutored ignorance.

5. Language is a two-way street. As Snyder says, language goes two ways. It both enables us to have an avenue or window on to an independently existing world, and it also shapes how we see that world. We do not have significant uninterpreted direct conscious contact with the world. On the other hand, it is not true that there is nothing, but language. There is a real sense, as we have stressed, that there is a transaction between world and language. Language both helps us to see and hear and also shapes our seeing and hearing.

There is a place for *wild language*. With Snyder, we can speak of the wildness in both language and world. "Wildness" is the process of self-organization, which generates complexity and unpredictability. This process involves both order and chaos, providing both stability and innovation.

Given this, truly excellent writing is more than conventional Good Usage, which ploughs straight rows, "*Really* good writing is both inside and outside the garden fence" (Snyder, 1995, 177). It tosses in some mariposa lilies with the beans and with them some juncos and yellow jackets to boot. If language does have the power to open the window on to the world, then it behooves us to pay attention to these language skills, to develop the rhetoric of appreciation. We are very good at conveying information, hype, and directives. Our skills at enhancing sensitive discernment, not with advertising slogans, but with authentic words, needs to be developed. We need to look to good nature writing.

A theory of appreciative perception

Building on this discussion, I would like to elaborate my own theory of appreciative perception.

Each of the guides to perception we have studied in this chapter, Thoreau, Leopold, Snyder, and LaChapelle, is very deliberate and experimental, in different ways, with their language. We could also look to good popular literary, music, or art criticism, when we can find it, perhaps even some good food or wine descriptions, good novels or poetry, even good prayers and sermons.

Reflection on Snyder's view of language is helpful here. "Language is basically biological; it becomes semi-cultural as it is learned and practiced" (Snyder, 1995, 178). Because it is biological, language is part of what unites us with all living and non-living processes. All species differ. Our language and our culture differentiate us, providing a discontinuity within a basic continuity.

Thus, we may employ and even celebrate our differences from other species, without pretending uniqueness or superiority. Or, to put it another way, *all* species are unique and relatively superior to the others in certain respects.

Furthermore, intelligence is developed not only by language, but by all kinds of interaction with our world. "Language plays a strong—but not the only—role in the refinement of thinking" (Snyder, 1995, 178). One of the best cures for the overemphasis on language (and on virtual reality) is to get down on one's knees, to get some soil on one's fingers, and even to sniff the earth. Whether off the wilderness trail, in the backyard garden, or the city park, we can vividly feel that we are in touch with our world (and that it is in touch with us) in ways that burst the bounds of language. Language and culture do not organize and civilize the world. Rather, the world has its partly chaotic order, which language and culture build on. Finally, the more the world is allowed to teach us, the better we can see our place in it.

We can even talk, in an extended yet genuine sense, of nature as speaking. Thus, we may speak of *the languages of nature*. This is not just the book of nature written by the Creator. It is rather that nature has its own voices, indeed a whole chorus, somewhat cacophonous. Some of us may wish to reject the apparent animism suggested here, and I do share strong sympathy for that view. However, to speak of nature's languages is not poetic license or mere metaphor. It may indeed be metaphor, but it is insightful, creative metaphor.

This means first of all that there is information out there that needs reading, deciphering, interpreting. It also means that we must pay attention, must actively listen. As Laura Dassow Walls puts it, the great tragedy is man's refusal to listen. When the Billerica dam destroys fish returning to spawn, Thoreau asks, "Who listens to the fish when they cry?" This also forces us to reconsider the moral status of nature. Definitely, mammals and birds communicate, often with clear intentionality. I am not as attuned to reptilian or amphibian communication, nor do I have the listening skills for insects of David Abram (Abram, 1996). Clearly, I must think about the moral status of whatever is communicating with me and even of whatever (whomever?) is communicating, even if not directly to me. Beyond this, it is only a short step to speak of plants as having a language, even if unintentional. Snyder talks of deciphering the language of nature's writing (Snyder, 1990, 66–77).

I do not wish to take this into an animistic direction, which would violate naturalism and move into supernaturalism. However, to think of nature as "speaking" to us, although it is an extended sense of the word, has some value. It urges us to pay attention to what needs deciphering. It forces us to consider the moral status of nature, both at large and in particular.

One further and obvious point needs mention. We, in the West, make much of our superiority to non-humans because we have language. To be sure, our language is subtle and complex. But, so is the dance of a ruffed grouse (dance *is* a language, is it not?) or the call of a mockingbird.

Finally, if nature speaks, then someone can be a scribe or poet or at least an interpreter. Nature fables. Who speaks for her?

Now, let us think for a moment about the relationship between *perception and values*. Throughout this chapter, we have been exploring perception, not value-free sensation, but appreciative awareness. Appreciation involves openness, a receptivity to the qualities, the values in a situation. Sometimes, this will be an active and disciplined receptivity, at others, a sauntering receptivity. At all times, it will be a discernment of worth, a cherishing a value.

Recognizing that we can have real appreciative perception, a discernment of worth, will help pull us out of the trap of subjectivism. In our time, we have created a dichotomy between facts and values, relegating the latter to the realm of the subjective and arbitrary. Value judgments are then mere opinion. However, when discernment of worth is taken as a guiding concept, we overcome the fact/value dichotomy. Events and objects have various types of worth, including triviality or baseness. To a major extent, these are objective characteristics of these events and objects. When we refer to something as gross, trashy, or evil, this is usually not arbitrary or misleading. There is some room for error, individual preference, and cultural difference. Such room, however, does not make these appraisals arbitrary or mere subjective opinion.

"Worth" involves transaction. It will always be the worth of something to some organism or group. On the other hand, the term "worth" focuses on the objective pole of the transaction. The term also encourages an attitude of openness to the object, the opposite of an attitude of manipulation or control. The term "worth" also suggests that the value of the object may be more than is presently discerned or articulated. The term has a heuristic thrust, calling for further openness to the exploration of the worthful object in its context. (For a fuller discussion of the use of the concept of "discernment of worth" and for its relation to John Dewey's notion of the "valuable," see my *The Minimalist Vision of Transcendence*, 1992, pages 83–87.)

In his post-modern metaphysics, *Being and Value*, Frederick Ferré has portrayed a major thread of modern philosophy, from the Renaissance on, as the expulsion of value from factual being. Pre-modern philosophy bound value intimately into the fabric of things. One of the emergent "post-modern" views of reality, which Ferré is trying to articulate, seeks to replace value back into factual being. He rightly focuses attention on beauty. Beauty is not merely the subjective product of human appreciation. Beauty is not just in the eye of the beholder. Rather, beauty, one of the particularly troublesome values, is an ingredient in the very structure of things (Ferré, 1996). My notion of discernment of worth is an independent attempt to say much of what Ferré is saying. I speak of a transaction between appreciation or discernment and value or worth. What I especially wish to say is that clearing the underbrush of outmoded ideas is helpful, but we need more. We need to perceive in order to appreciate and we need to appreciate in order to move our behavior. And—we, just perhaps, may be able to move from an appreciation of the beauty of the Grand Canyon and the draba flower to a sense of the sacredness of that place and that flower, and in doing so, will protect them.

Let us now ponder the relationship between *perception and motivation*. We need to reflect on the wellsprings of human behavior. Why should anyone be concerned about the environment? What motivates people to care about our sister creatures? About the slow violence afflicting the poor? (This term comes from Rob Nixon's *Slow Violence and the Environmentalism of the Poor*, Nixon, 2011.) We need more than the categorical imperative. Enlightened self-interest could help somewhat, but I worry about the possibility of enlightenment in this time of corporate labor and of market-induced narcissism. There is much to be said about human motivation and much that we do not know. There is a great deal of study to be done as well as intuitive hunches and guess work. Let me suggest that it is very important to stress the role of perception and appreciative awareness in motivating behavior. It is hard to protect the blue whale unless you love the blue whale, and it is hard to love the blue whale unless you have seen it. For most people, to see the blue whale is to love it and to love it is to protect it.

What about the things we have not seen? Even here, I believe, appreciative awareness has a crucial role to play. I myself have never seen a blue whale. But, I have seen the magnificent orca. It is my appreciative perception of the orcas that helps me to grasp the worth of the blue whale by appreciative analogy.

We should also consider that there are negative emotions that can accompany environmental awareness. Fear, depression, guilt can all come from an understanding of the eco-crisis and the human role in it. These feelings can give rise to denial, paralysis, or other dysfunctional reactions. Appreciative perception alone will not heal the damaging psychic effects of environmental disaster. However, there is a healing touch from some of the processes within the natural world. Sometimes, these have a restorative power to enable the discouraged eco-fighter to go on. We will not win all the victories we should. Yet, the little ecstasies, which the world affords us, often lift the flagging spirit.

Appreciative perception of the world's affordances is likely to give rise to a new set of values. We are more likely to acquire a refined taste in natural processes, a taste that appreciates more than economic or personal value.

I once stumbled upon a Sunday evening wine and cheese party at a nearby university, a party complete with good conversation and conviviality. Upon inquiry, I discovered that it was the final meeting of a non-credit wine tasting class. What a metaphor! If one's taste in wine can be educated and improved, how much more of our appreciative perception can be improved? Matters of taste, we discover, are not merely subjective. Perhaps, we *can* dispute about taste, but only if we jointly perceive. And, if appreciation is a skill, why must we suppose that everyone's taste is as good as everyone else's? Reading an x-ray or making a diagnosis is not a matter of unskilled perception such as reading a meter or looking at litmus paper. Perhaps, we have been misled by litmus paper readings to ask for simple operational definitions involving litmus paper tests.

I have learned, through contact with a variety of students and grass-roots movements, when I walk into some stores to ask "Where are all the people of color?" This remark, I hope, is not to be read as an anti-white people comment. Rather, it indicates a discomfort at housing patterns, which, for a variety of reasons, exclude people of color. I sense this as soon as I look around the store. It is hard to say whether this is perception or conscious thought. It probably indicates that there is no clear boundary between the two.

Is an all-white community a community of Americans? Likewise, is a wolfless northwoods any northwoods at all? When I explore the outdoors at twilight, I look and listen for the signs of my four-footed and feathered relatives. Many apparently lush places really seem lifeless. Is "a hawkless, owl-less countryside" a livable countryside for people "with eyes to see and ears to hear?" Leopold was right. "Poor land may be rich country and vice versa. In country, as in people, a plain exterior often conceals hidden values, to perceive which requires much living in and with" (Leopold, 1991a, 60). When you develop a good taste in wine, you learn to be dissatisfied with cheap grades. As appreciative awareness develops, so too will a critical ear and eye and nose. A critical awareness develops along with appreciative awareness. Of course, this easily results in snobbery or even misanthropy. As far as I know, this type of "greener-than-thou" attitude can be overcome by deep spiritual practice, including a compassion that realizes that we all are the oppressors and exploiters as well as the victims. We need some irony, some humor, some laughter and dancing, and even some good talk with the TV off, maybe around a good fire or overlooking a valley or river.

The development of appreciative perception will be aided by and will also stimulate changes in our ideas. We are likely to find ourselves *rethinking* some of our ideas. LaChapelle, in particular, suggests some of these shifts in our thinking.

We need to go *beyond the Renaissance*. LaChapelle is probably right. Much of our common sense and scientific understanding of perception is based on the Renaissance linear perspective from a single point of view. With this are the two assumptions 1) that visual observation, which we often privilege, involves an observer who occupies one single place and one instant of time, and 2) that the observer stands apart from the world. LaChapelle challenges both assumptions. Vision involves two motions: one is the motion of the perceiver, moving away or toward the object, weaving or bobbing to get "a better view," or, as this implies, a best viewpoint, to explore. The second is the motion of the sun during the day as well as the moon by night and the motion of the seasons. Spectating is not a spectator sport.

The second assumption underlying the Renaissance approach is that the fixed observer stands over against the world. But, a short stint of time outside of our houses will convince us, if we pay attention to our ears, eyes, and skin, that we are inside of the world. (And, of course, the environment is inside of us.) There is no environment that surrounds us on the outside. We are as surely immersed in it, and it is in us as any fish in the water. The environment is our medium and we are right smack dab in the middle of the medium. As the Latin phrase goes, we are *in medias res*.

What the new electronic media are doing to our perception no one knows. I do think that these media, in whose middle we are, will change our alienation from the natural world, not remove it. This is another reason to shut down the video game, turn off even the nature film, get out of the mall, put down the book, and get out of the skins of our buildings, out-of-doors, out-of-walls, even if it is just to the vacant lot, park, or berm. And, let us do this without our smartphones.

We need to be open to the world's *affordances*. LaChapelle is correct that we need to rethink what perception is. We do not just perceive the world. The world gives us something to perceive. It affords us glimpses, but real glimpses. It is not that the world has resources that we take. Rather, the world affords us prospects that sustain, delight, and terrify us. Our world affords then because it can afford to. These gifts afforded to us are budgeted. If we take too much, our world cannot afford to give as much.

These gifts remind us that we do not have to get or discover everything. The Faustian pact to know and control everything is a delusion. We need not, we cannot, master everything. Receiving gifts can sometimes be harder than giving. It may, indeed, be as much or more of a blessing to receive as to give. Who knows, perhaps the Lord loveth a cheerful recipient.

Values and meanings are not just our addition to a meaningless, value-free world. Values and meanings are afforded to us.

Our natural world affords different things to her children. The world literally looks different to the various species of feathered people, two-legged people, four-legged people, the people-who-swim, the people-who-burrow or creep, the flowering people, the upright people, and the people-who-grow-down-low. There are reciprocal transactions between all species and our natural matrix. As James Gibson wrote, an ash tree affords shade and beauty to us, perching to a sparrow, food to a nuthatch, and climbing to a squirrel. "Sitting under," "looking at," "perching," "eating," and "climbing" are species-specific. But, these values are *not* in the mind of the beholder. They are a transaction between the living animal and the gifts of our matrix.

For many of us, the appreciation of natural processes (love of the natural) and the erotic is an easy line to cross. For many also, there is an easy transition between the natural and the sacred. However, it is a difficult transition for many of us between *the sacred and the erotic.* This barrier goes deeply back in the history of monotheism to the struggle against the Canaanite fertility cults.

Crossing this barrier should not be forced. Most of us are very aware of the destructive excesses of the sexual in our individual and cultural life. However, most of us realize that the Puritanical guilt fostered by religion, especially in the West, has also often been very unhealthy.

The issues here are complex. Psychic health is usually hard-won and often fragile. Our current cultural life finds it hard to depict erotic health. Mediocrity and excess are marketable. And, most of this is inter-woven with gender and hetero- and homosexual power struggles. This writer cannot offer a panacea for our sexual and gender ills. I do urge that, on the one hand, we should not identify the erotic and the sacred. The erotic can often be destructive. The sacred is often near the demonic. On the other hand, we should not keep a fence between the erotic and the sacred. The erotic can often be a gateway to the divine. Sexual ecstasy, whether genital or polymorphous, can sometimes be also a religious ecstasy, a genuine theophany or epiphany.

LaChapelle is correct that the natural is often enabling, a catalytic third term between the erotic and the sacred. If truly naming the evening star with the name of the goddess of love is too erotic an act, then meditate on the marriage between Israel and her divine husband in the Book of Hosea, and remember that the Land was often the third term in the Covenant between Israel and God. Or, reflect thoughtfully on the Sabbath as the Bride and how love-making on the Sabbath is a *mitzvah*. All of this can easily justify patriarchal behavior, but let us remember that our cultural Romes are not dismantled (or deconstructed) in a generation.

This chapter has been about "appreciative perception." The practice of appreciative perception is a doorway to a sense of importance. And, because, according to our viewpoint, anything that is sacred is something of great importance, it follows that the practice of appreciative perception is one of the best entryways to a sense of the sacred. To state this in terms of Chapter 2, appreciative perception is one of the best ways to open oneself to specific experiences of the sacred.

If I were pressed to make a case for this approach to appreciative awareness, I would stress the need for motivation as we face the enormity of our environmental crises and catastrophes. To write with a touch of levity, if a fan of the Chicago Cubs is 90 percent scar tissue (for decades, they were known as the "lovable losers"), then certainly to be knowledgeable about environmental destruction is to become 90 percent scar tissue. Awareness and activism can be exhausting. Appreciation can renew the flagging spirit. This theory of appreciative perception is designed on a theoretical level to articulate the need to educate and train awareness of worth, perception of sacredness. On a practical level, it should help in emotional and spiritual renewal. To quote the Preface to Leopold's *Round River* again, "Prudence never kindled a fire in the human mind; I have no hope for a conservation born of fear."

In a sense, this chapter has been misleading. It has been focusing on appreciative awareness of the non-human world. However, as I have maintained throughout this book, the immanent sacred can appear in the human world also. (See my *The Minimalist Vision of Transcendence*, Stone, 1992, 33–40.)

For further discussion of appreciative awareness, see Bernard Meland, *Essays in Constructive Theology*, (1998, 209–300); *Higher Education and the Human Spirit* (1953, 48–75); Jerome A. Stone, *The Minimalist Vision of Transcendence*, (Stone, 1992, Chapter 4). Since finishing a draft of this chapter, I have been delighted by reading Kathleen Norris's description of life on the high plains of western South Dakota in *Dakota: A Spiritual Geography*. See especially her chapter on "Seeing" as well as the "Weather Reports" scattered throughout the book (Norris, 1993). Norris has obviously learned to love what the locals call West River. In such an area, the eye learns to appreciate slight variations in the landscape, the possibilities inherent in emptiness. Along with too much horizon and too much sky, the indifference of this land to the human can be unnerving. (So much for the pastoral nostalgia of The Little Brown Church in the Vale!) An eye that learns to appreciate often leads to the sense of the sacred. She compares seeing the Plains to seeing an icon: what seems stern and almost empty is a door into a simple and holy state (Norris, 1993, 156–157).

Finally, Jeremy Kidwell, currently a post-doctoral fellow at the University of Edinburgh, is doing important ethnographic work on nature conservation volunteers in Scottish religious communities. Building on Tim Ingold's work on the anthropology of landscapes and J.D. Dewsbury and Paul Cloke's concept of "spiritual landscapes," he is working on the affective dimension of the environmental knowledge of non-scientists and the importance of "lay knowledges" in creating awareness of climate change and motivating mitigation efforts (Tim Ingold, 2000; Dewsbury and Cloke, 2009; Brace and Geoghegan, 2010). This is important, as there is a disconnect between and understanding of climate change by the general public and that of climate experts.

Notes

1 See William Dean, *American Religious Empiricism* (Albany: State University of New York Press, 1986); Bernard E. Meland, *Higher Education and the Human Spirit* (Chicago: The University of Chicago Press, 1953) 48–50, 62–77; Bernard E. Meland, *Essays in Constructive Theology: A Process Perspective*. Edited by Perry LeFevre (Chicago: Exploration Press, 1988) 43, 73; Bernard E. Meland, "Can Empirical Theology Learn Something from Phenomenology?," in *The Future of Empirical Theology*, edited by Bernard E. Meland (Chicago: The University of Chicago Press, 1969) 292.
2 Parts of the following are based on my review of Volume 4: 1851–1852 of Thoreau's *Journals*, edited by Neufeldt and Simmons in the Princeton edition of Thoreau's Journals. This review is in *Newsletter* Number 68 of the Society for the Advancement of American Philosophy, June 1994, 32–34.

Bibliography

Abram, David. 1996. *The Spell of the Sensuous: Perception and Language in a More-Than-Human World*. New York: Vintage Books.
Brace, Catherine, and Hilary Geoghegan. 2010. "Human Geographies of Climate Change: Landscape, Temporality, and Lay Knowledges," *Progress in Human Geography*, 35, 284–302.
Callicott, J. Baird, editor. 1987. *Companion to a Sand County Almanac: Interpretive and Critical Essays*. Madison, WI: The University of Wisconsin Press.
Cannon, Susan Faye. 1978. *Science in Culture: The Early Victorian Period*. New York: Dawson and Natural History Publications.
Christie, John Aldrich. 1965. *Thoreau as World Traveler*. New York: Columbia University Press and American Geographical Society.
Dean, William. 1986. *American Religious Empiricism*. Albany: State University of New York Press.
Dewsbury, John-David, and Paul Cloke. 2009. "Spiritual Landscapes: Existence, Performance and Immanence," *Social and Cultural Geography*, 10, 695–711.
Ehrlich, Paul, David S. Dobkin, and Darryl Wheye, Eds. 1988. *The Birder's Handbook: A Field Guide to the Natural History of North American Birds*. New York: Simon and Schuster.
Ferré, Frederick. 1996. *Being and Value: Toward a Constructive Postmodern Metaphysics*. Albany: State University of New York Press.
Gibson, James. 1979. *The Ecological Approach to Visual Perception*. Boston, MA: Houghton Mifflin.
Gilpin, William. 1834. *Remarks on Forest Scenery*. Edinburgh, UK: Fraser & Co.
Hargrove, Eugene C. 1989. *Foundations of Environmental Ethics*. Englewood Cliffs, NJ: Prentice Hall.

Ingold, Tim. 2000. *The Perception of the Environment: Essays on Livelihood, Dwelling and Skill*. New York: Routledge.

Kinsey, Joni L. 1999. "Land Esthetics: Through Successive Stages of the Beautiful," in Curt Meine and Richard L. Knight, *The Essential Aldo Leopold: Quotations and Commentaries*. Madison, WI: The University of Wisconsin Press.

LaChapelle, Delores. 1988. *Sacred Land, Sacred Sex, Rapture of the Deep: Concerning Deep Ecology—-And Celebrating Life*. Durango, CO: Kivaki Press.

Leopold, Aldo. 1933. *Game Management*. Charles Scribner's Sons.

Leopold, Aldo. 1966. *A Sand County Almanac: With Essays on Conservation from Round River*. New York: Ballantine Books.

Leopold, Aldo. 1991a. *Round River: From the Journals of Aldo Leopold*. Minocqua, WI: Northwood Press.

Leopold, Aldo. 1991b. *The River of the Mother of God: and Other Essays*. Edited by Susan L. Flader and J. Baird Callicott. Madison, WI: The University of Wisconsin Press.

Leopold, Luna. 1991. "Preface," from Aldo Leopold, *Round River: From the Journals of Aldo Leopold*. Minocqua, WI: Northwood Press.

Meland, Bernard E. 1953. *Higher Education and the Human Spirit*. Chicago: The University of Chicago Press, 1953.

Meland, Bernard Eugene. 1988. *Essays in Constructive Theology: A Process Perspective*. Chicago: Exploration Press.

Nixon, Rob. 2011. *Slow Violence and the Environmentalism of the Poor*. Cambridge, MA: Harvard University Press.

Norris, Kathleen. 1993. *Dakota: A Spiritual Geography*. Boston, MA: Houghton Mifflin Company.

Peters, Karl E. 2002. *Dancing with the Sacred: Evolution, Ecology, and God*. Harrisburg, PA: Trinity Press International.

Potter, Van Rensselaer. 1971. *Bioethics: Bridge to the Future*. New York: Prentice-Hall.

Snyder, Gary. 1990. *The Practice of the Wild*. San Francisco: North Point Press.

Snyder, Gary. 1995. *A Place in Space: Ethics, Aesthetics, and Watersheds*. Washington, DC: Counterpoint.

Stone, Jerome A. 1992. *The Minimalist Vision of Transcendence: A Naturalist Philosophy of Religion*. Albany: State University of New York Press.

Thoreau, Henry David. 1906. *Journal, Volumes IV, V, IX, XIII, XIV*. Edited by Bradford Torrey and Francis Allen. Boston: Houghton Mifflin.

Thoreau, Henry David. 1980. *Natural History Essays*. Edited by Robert Sattelmeyer. Salt Lake City: Peregrine Smith.

Thoreau, Henry David. 1983. *A Week on the Concord and Merrimack Rivers*. Edited by Carl F. Hovde, William L. Howarth and Elizabeth Witherell. Princeton: Princeton University Press.

Thoreau, Henry David. 1988. *Cape Cod*. Edited by Joseph J. Maldenhauer. Princeton: Princeton University Press.

Thoreau, Henry David. 1990. *Journal. Vol. 3: 1848–1851*, edited by Robert Sattelmeyer, Mark Patterson and William Rossi. Princeton: Princeton University Press.

Walls, Laura Dassow. 1995. *Seeing New Worlds: Henry David Thoreau and Nineteenth-Century Science*. Madison, WI: The University of Wisconsin Press.

4
SPIRITUALITY FOR NATURALISTS

Naturalism, as I use the term, involves the assertion that there seems to be no superior realm, no God, soul or heaven, to explain, or give meaning to this world.[1] Like the spatial terms "left" and "right," "naturalism" is a term that derives its meaning in part from its opposite, "supernaturalism" (Stone, 2008, 1). A number of people discussing naturalism have suggested that proponents of naturalism need to stress what naturalism stands *for*, rather than *against*. In line with that, I add that, more positively, naturalism "affirms that attention should be focused on the events and processes of this world to provide what degree of explanation and meaning are possible to this life" (Stone, 2008, 1).

Recently, Mario De Caro and David Macarthur have published two collections of technical philosophical essays, *Naturalism in Question* and *Naturalism and Normativity* (De Caro and Macarthur, 2004; 2010). These are philosophically dense writings. In the "Introduction" to the former, the editors state that what they call "scientific naturalism" is the current orthodoxy in Anglo-American philosophy. They characterize this orthodoxy as having two themes: one ontological, a commitment to an exclusively scientific conception of nature, the other methodological, which conceives of philosophical inquiry as continuous with science (De Caro and Macarthur, 2004, 1–6).

De Caro and Macarthur, through these two collections, are nurturing an emergent "liberal" or "pluralistic" naturalism that challenges this orthodoxy. Liberal naturalism challenges scientific naturalism in part by questioning the latter's consistency (maintaining that the claims of scientific naturalism extend beyond the limited scope of scientific assertions). Liberal naturalism also challenges scientific naturalism by exploring its weaknesses in dealing with the topics of mind, agency, and normativity, especially ethical and aesthetic. According to De Caro and Macarthur, liberal or pluralistic naturalists share four features: 1) a shift in focus from non-human to human nature, conceived as a historically conditioned product of contingent forces, 2) a non-reductive attitude to normativity, 3) a view of philosophy as in some respects autonomous from scientific method, and 4) a pluralistic conception of the sciences, rejecting the ideal of the unity of the sciences as unrealizable and conceding that there is no clear demarcation around science.

A discussion of naturalized spirituality clearly is in sympathy with the liberal or pluralistic naturalism depicted by these authors. I suggest that a naturalized spirituality sidesteps the concerns of "scientific naturalism" as described above because spirituality is a different way of engaging the world (or being engaged by it) than science.

This chapter has two parts. The first presents some important, mostly recent, writers who are developing naturalist spirituality. The second will elaborate my own proposal for naturalized spirituality.

I must warn the reader that I am not an expert guide through the territory of spirituality. Some of these writers are. They have spent years undergoing the discipline of spiritual practice. They could be thought of as experts who have a first-hand acquaintance with what they write about. I do not have the experience that some of these people do. But, this may help me to achieve a critical distance, which is also useful in this inquiry.

Some theories of naturalized spirituality

The following theories are presented as examples of writers who have developed theories of spirituality within a naturalistic framework. The list of names is representative, but makes no attempt to be exhaustive. For example, Roy Wood Sellars has a brief theory of non-theistic or humanistic spirituality, but is treated elsewhere in this book. So also is Kenneth Patton.

Spinoza

I could start with Confucius, with the Hindu Carvaka, or with Epicurus, but I shall start with Grandfather Spinoza. (The following is adapted from Stone, 2008, 18.) Interpreters of Spinoza disagree, but surely his phrase "God or nature" indicates that he is a forerunner of contemporary naturalist spirituality. Now, perhaps, his use of the term "God" disqualifies him as a naturalist, but I suggest that he is at least an important pioneer explorer in this territory.

I would like to underline one important theme in Spinoza. His intellectual love of God is a third level of knowledge above sense perception and rational knowledge. I suggest that rather than a form of pseudo-cognition, Spinoza was driving at a form of insight or appreciation of the whole system of nature. (See the British philosopher Samuel Alexander's comments on Spinoza (Alexander, 1939, 346, 373–376; also Stone, 2008, 43.)

George Santayana

For Santayana, in *Reason in Religion*, religion is an imaginative symbol for the Life of Reason (Santayana, 1905; the following is adapted from Stone, 2008, 21–37). Part of his treatment of religion involves a discussion of religious sentiments. These sentiments are piety, spirituality, and charity.

> Spirituality is the higher side of religion, which imposes a direction and ideal on the forces of human life, in short, an aspiration. *We are spiritual when we live in the presence of an ideal.*
>
> However, spirituality can be pathological. It is subject to corruption. So, pedantry often displaces wisdom, tyranny replaces government, and superstition substitutes for piety and rhetoric for a reason. Further difficulties come with fanaticism or mysticism. Fanaticism aggressively narrows down concern to only one interest. The mystic passively either accepts all passions or rejects them all. Both represent arrested development of common sense.
>
> The rational person goes a step beyond spirituality and subjects it to the scrutiny of reason. So, the rational is a step beyond the spiritual.
>
> (Stone, 2008, 21–37)

Sam Harris

Harris, one of the so-called New Atheists, is a practitioner of various techniques of meditation and teachings of Tibetan Buddhism and the Advaita Vedanta. His extended discussion of spirituality is found in the last chapter of *The End of Faith*.

A range of human experiences can be called "spiritual/mystical" namely, "experiences of meaningfulness, selflessness, and heightened emotion that surpass our narrow identities as 'selves'" (Harris, 2004, 39). "Ordinary people can divest themselves of the feeling that they call 'I' and thereby relinquish the sense that they are separate from the rest of the universe" (Harris, 2004, 40).

Another description of spiritual practice is "investigating the nature of consciousness directly, through sustained introspection" (Harris, 2004, 209). If we can recognize that we are "the mere witness of appearances, we will realize that we stand perpetually free of the vicissitudes of experience" (Harris, 2004, 206). Almost all our problems are due to our feelings of *separateness*. A spirituality that undermined such dualism through the contemplation of consciousness would improve our situation (Harris, 2004, 214).

Introspection shows us that there is no subject of experience, no separation of knower and known. Spiritual life is a freeing of attention, so that the selflessness of consciousness can be recognized (Harris, 2004, 219).

Here is another definition. Meditation is paying close attention to the moment by moment experience of the world. This is not irrational. It is the only rational basis for making claims about subjectivity (Harris, 2004, 235). The goal of meditation is not to eliminate thought. It is not to get rid of thoughts, but to break our identification with these thoughts (Harris, 2004, 217).

One insight to be achieved by meditation is "that the feeling we call 'I'—the sense that we are the thinker of our thoughts, the experiencer of our experiences—can disappear when looked at in a rigorous way" (Harris, 2004, 235). Negative social emotions (hatred, envy, spite) proceed from this common dualistic perspective.

These experiences in which we divest ourselves of the feeling we call "I" are "spiritual" or "mystical" for want of better words. " 'Spirituality' and 'mysticism' have unfortunate connotations and neither word captures the reasonableness and profundity of the possibility . . . that there is a form of well-being that supersedes all others, indeed, that transcends the vagaries of experience itself" (Harris, 2004, 205). Harris uses the two terms spirituality and mysticism interchangeably, but in a cautious sense. After all, we are not dealing with "the healing powers of crystals and colonic irrigation" or "the ardors of alien abduction" (Harris, 2004, 205).

Owen Flanagan

Flanagan's discussion of spirituality appears in his book, *The Really Hard Problem*, particularly Chapter 6, "Spirituality Naturalized." Spirituality is "seeking to understand and develop a sense of connection to which is greater than and more comprehensive than [one's] self" (Flanagan, 2007, 199).

Spirituality is "having coherent beliefs about the higher purpose and meaning of the universe; knowing where one fits within the larger scheme; having beliefs about the meaning of life that shape conduct and provide comfort" (Flanagan, 2007, 201).

The healthy forms of spirituality involve "the degree to which they result in unselfish love of others." [Flanagan quotes this approvingly from Stephen Post. (Post, 2004; Flanagan, 2007, 207).] There are three major spiritual traditions that endorse such an unselfish love: Buddhism, "Jesusism," or the ethical teachings of Jesus and utilitarianism or consequentialism. These three can all be lived naturalistically. Buddhism and Jesusism do not need to be conceived supernaturalistically, while consequentialism is overtly secular.

The reason why one would want to live in such an ethically expansive manner is that it is one reliable way to human flourishing (Flanagan, 2007, 209). The path of universal love and compassion is the best strategy to find happiness; in addition, this strategy can be conceived naturalistically, which is the best philosophical view. Happiness, flourishing, and meaning come from having a goal beyond one's own personal desires, which is inclusive of all actual and potential persons (possibly of all sentient beings), as well as to the earth and the larger cosmos (Flanagan, 2007, 219).

The next question is how to be motivated to live in such an ethically expansive way. Perhaps, we can encourage the relevant human impulses through rational and emotional support and a method of moral education and socialization. Meditation is a very helpful strategy, for it transforms the mind-brain by "reconfiguring neural circuits" (Flanagan, 2007, 212).

Instead of merely wishing for no suffering for others, through meditation on such scenarios, as the Dalai Lama suggests, we can have more of the love that one usually has for one's loved ones for other people. The three traditions ask us to consider this. Such universal love takes lots of work and practice: meditation, concentration, rational arguments, and charismatic exemplars can do much. They are promising strategies. Supernatural foundation is not required (Flanagan, 2007, 218).

Robert C. Solomon

In *Spirituality for the Skeptic*, Solomon characterizes spirituality as the thoughtful love of life (Solomon, 2002). Along with most of these current writers, he sees spirituality as involving the transformation of the self in terms of an expansion of the self beyond selfishness. Spirituality takes us out of ourselves into community with a larger whole. As a naturalized spirituality, it is non-religious, non-exclusive, non-dogmatic, not based on belief, not anti-science, and not other-worldly. It embraces science because it seeks to know more about the world that it loves.

Interestingly, as a love of this life, naturalized spirituality embraces appetites, sex and sensuality, possibly even fast cars, money and luxury, all in their proper place. What counts is living well. But, Solomon is a little uneasy about this, because he admits that spirituality can be vulgarized into living luxuriously and simply enjoying oneself. As he phrases it, spirituality involves a *larger* sense of life. However, not any larger sense of life will do. Patriotism, for example, while it can have a spiritual dimension, can also be narrow and confining. So, although there are dangers of vulgarity and narrowness, love of this life, or better, thoughtful love of this life, is what a naturalized spirituality is about. Being in love, losing oneself in music, feeling at one with nature, are all ways of being spiritual.

Solomon is clear that spirituality involves thinking, feeling, and acting. It is rational, emotional, and active. Indeed, spirituality is a passion, and this involves Solomon's elaborate notion of a passion. Passions are investments of the self with life in a way that emotions are not. The erotic love in spirituality involves choice, engagement with life, including uncertainty about the future. Passions can be cultivated, and be it noted, are not out of control.

Solomon has analyzed spirituality in terms of three emotions: erotic love, reverence, and trust. The objects of these emotions are ultimately the world or life itself. And, when the world or life is specified as the object of love, reverence, and trust, the distinction between emotions and moods is dissolved.

Love of a lover, humanity, or the world, is exemplary of spirituality as an expansion of the self, a fusion or merger with the larger world. Now, of course, we cannot be passionately intimate with everyone, but we can expand our erotic world.

In spirituality, one *chooses* to see the world as beautiful, as an object of love or fascination, not just as a resource or challenge. So, spirituality is not disinterested, but involves appreciation as well as comprehension. But, this choice is steadfast, not fickle. Spirituality is resistant to change.

Now, eroticism can be dangerous, as in the eroticism of fascism. Erotic love needs *reverence* to be spiritual. [Solomon owes a great deal to Paul Woodruff here. (Woodruff, 2001).] Being spiritual means being reverential before the world, before other people, the law, and other social institutions worthy of reverence. Reverence has nothing to do with God or religion. Reverence means recognizing one's limits, even with regard to the most feeble creatures. It implies responsibility, not just humility. Reverence does not mean politeness, hyper-seriousness, or a lack of humor. Nor is reverence to be equated with awe. Awe is too passive. Reverence is active and responsible.

Solomon can also describe spirituality as cosmic trust. Trust is a determined stance toward the world, which implies dependence and vulnerability. Trust entails risk and also responsibility for our engagements in the world. Trust includes being prepared to accept life's many possibilities.

Authentic trust is not given, but "earned, and cultivated, and worked at" (Solomon, 2002, 46). It is something we do, and therefore, is something for which we take responsibility. In a nutshell, the problem is "How do we get past the cynical (aka 'realist') position that sees the utter contingency of life without falling into the naivete of philosophical optimism?" (Solomon, 2002, 47).

Thus, it seems that "spirituality is a synthesis of uncertainty and confidence, a sense of powerlessness combined with resoluteness and responsibility" (Solomon, 2002, 47). The trust in spirituality presupposes that matters are not wholly in one's hands, but also not totally out of one's hands.

Now, there are emotional poisons that hinder such trust: paranoia, envy, and resentment. Envy, for example,

> closes off any possibility of appreciating ourselves *for ourselves* or getting along with those we envy. . . . [Envy] closes off that larger view that allows us to be thankful for what we've got, accepting of what we do not have, and grateful for the very chance to be so alive at all.
> (Solomon, 2002, 54–55)

(At this point, Solomon confesses that the struggle against envy and resentment is why spirituality is such a challenge for him.)

The spiritual life is sometimes wrongly defined as life without the distractions of affections. On the contrary, for Solomon, the spiritual life is defined by the most passionate caring, and in fact, this *defines* its rationality. Reason and the passions are ultimately one and the same. "Spirituality is and must be both rational and passionate at once," although there are both irrational and dangerous forms of spirituality (Solomon, 2002, 61).

Rationality is "not just our ability to criticize and argue, but also the perspicacity and vision to appreciate complexity, to find (or make) meaning in disorder and confusion" (Solomon, 2002, 62). But, this is what passions do, too. The right passions bring perspicacity and vision, which are characteristics of rationality. Science is not the *only* kind of rationality.

Solomon turns now to the problem of suffering. Life is not fair. Bad things happen. Spirituality accepts that fact. But, that is not to say that life is meaningless nor does it justify dwelling on tragedies or overlooking the blessings and benefits of life. We need not opt for feeling victimized or for cynicism. Feeling victimized and cynicism are sometimes the products of our eagerness for blame and our extravagant sense of entitlement. We need a combination of gratitude and humor. We need to confront tragedy and engage passionately with the people and details of our life.

Life is a gift none of us deserves. The odds are that one would have been born impoverished, malnourished, and ignorant, in the midst of famine, war, or dictatorship. Thus, gratitude is the best approach to life. It implies an admission of limitation as well as appreciation.

Spirituality is the enlargement, not the negation of the self. It is not just an awareness of suffering, but also a sense of the joy of the world. Spirituality involves a compassionate ordinary self that has become enlarged and enhanced. To get locked into petty tasks and competitions is a distortion of ourselves. Selfishness turns out to be a constriction of our humanity. In fact, one can speak of "soul" as the full realization of our ordinary self. Thus, soul is both something natural and something to be striven for. Perhaps, soul is our better self.

The naturalized notion of spirituality is an arduous process, but well worth striving for. It is awareness not only of suffering, but of cosmic joy and humor as well.

Ursula Goodenough

We have already introduced Ursula Goodenough in Chapter 2 with her naturalistic covenant with mystery as her response to the ultimate question of why there is anything at all, her gratitude that the earth is beautiful and suitable for human habitation, and her reverence in the face of the vast lengths of time, the improbability and the diversity of it all. Since *The Sacred Depths of Nature*, Goodenough has been exploring several innovative lines of thought. [This and the next section are adapted from Stone, 2008.] She has come to distinguish between horizontal and vertical transcendence. The spirituality of horizontal transcendence requires identification not merely with the non-human living, but also with the inanimate, "the massive mysticism of stone," to use Robinson Jeffers' phrase (Kalton, 2000, 199). The reward of vertical transcendence is unification with a purposeful Creator. *The reward of horizontal transcendence is homecoming.* The ethics of vertical transcendence is fitting into an ideal scheme. *The ethics of horizontal transcendence is responding appropriately to our situation.* "An ethical approach to nature must be anchored both in deep attunement and deep knowledge" (Goodenough, 2001, 29). Our children must have a chance to play in the woods and to be taught, with wonder, gratitude, and respect, at their mother's knees, that the trees are genetically scripted.

Another line of thought Goodenough has been exploring is the concept of *mindful reverence*. In collaboration with philosopher Paul Woodruff, she explored reverence and other virtues (Goodenough and Woodruff, 2001; see Woodruff, 2001). To be mindful as developed here, is more than awareness in the classic Buddhist sense, it is scientifically informed consideration. But, it is also more than learning scientific facts. It is living in consideration of them. It is to be mindful of our place in the scheme of things. Reverence is a capacity, developed in the process of evolution, a capacity that can be cultivated.

Recently, Goodenough and Terrence Deacon, Professor of Biological Anthropology and Linguistics at Berkeley, have been attempting to specify the concept of evolutionary *emergence* in detail and to articulate its significance for spirituality (Goodenough and Deacon, 2006). In their formula, emergence refers to the generation of "something else from nothing but."

While recognizing that some physicists suggest that emergence starts at the subatomic level, Goodenough and Deacon begin their story at the molecular level. To condense the whole epic of evolution in a few sentences: with life genes encode proteins that fold into shapes that give rise to cell organization and behavior, metabolism, and energy transduction, and communication between cells. These are emergent properties. With the development of nervous systems, humans have new traits—symbolic languages, cultural transmission, and an autobiographical self—which are "something else" emergent from "nothing but" ancient protein families displayed in novel patterns and sequences. "Biologically we are just another ape; mentally we are a whole new phylum" (Deacon, 1998).

Goodenough and Deacon suggest that one *spiritual response* to the phenomenon of emergence would be a re-enchantment of the universe whenever we take its continuous coming into being into awareness and a re-enchantment of our lives when we realize that we also are continually transcending ourselves. Another spiritual response will be reverence, a deconstruction of hubris and a recognition that our context is vastly larger and more important than our selves. Further, the emergentist outlook can inspire our stammering gratitude for the creative universe, this astonishing whole to which we owe our lives.

Deacon centers his notion of spirituality, much like Goodenough's notion of "horizontal transcendence," on a sense of connectedness with the world. He also refers to an extended self beyond the space and time of our bodies, for the consequences of our lives ramify in all directions through all time. He suggests this as an improvement over the usual self-centered spirituality focusing on saving an immortal soul (Deacon, 2005, Answer to Questions 9 and 10).

Sharon Welch

Sharon Welch was treated in Chapter 1. Here, a summary of her treatment of spirituality is in order. Her thinking about the spiritual dimension of social action falls into two periods. In her earlier period, the divine is a characteristic of relationships or of the capacity to enter into right relationships with other people, with nature, and with ourselves. There is no separate divine entity. Rather than God-language, she uses "divine" as an adjective to refer to grace or the power of relations.

In her later writing, Welch speaks of the motivation of moral action as welling up from such things as gratitude, joy, mourning, and rage. Acts of persistence, resistance, and transformation come from gratitude and the affirmation of this life in which there is suffering and moral failure, and death. Spirituality has power and value, and yet is fraught with danger. We need an ironic spirituality that recognizes our limits and failures and finds joy in our successes. We need to be ironic *and* committed, suspicious *and* celebrative simultaneously [Welch, 1999a, 128 and 156 n. 25. See also her article "Spirituality without God," *Tikkun* Vol. 14, No. 3, May/June 1999. Her notion of spirituality can be amplified by Chapters 1, 2, 4–6 of *After Empire* (Welch, 2004), where she draws on engaged Buddhism and First Nations to describe democratic practices as forms of ceremony, of spiritual awareness and expression].

André Comte-Sponville

For Comte-Sponville, author of *The Little Book of Atheist Spirituality*, there are certain moments of experience or awareness of the all, the entire universe of being, when the ego vanishes (Comte-Sponville, 2007). These are moments of affirmation and of acceptance. These moments are rare, but powerful enough to be unforgettable, moments that can be characterized by such words as mystery, self-evidence, plenitude, eternity, serenity, and acceptance.

William R. Murry

Unitarian Universalist minister and former President of Meadville Lombard Theological Seminary, William R. Murry has been showing how religious humanism is an adequate approach to life in the twenty-first century. In *Becoming More Fully Human*, he develops a theory of virtues, including reverence and awareness (Murry, 2011, 87–89, 119–121). Both of these are often considered aspects of spirituality.

Drawing on Paul Woodruff, Murry articulates a non-theist approach to reverence. It involves awe and respect for what transcends humanity, particularly justice and nature. Surely, nature is transcendent to humans, and as an unrealized ideal, justice is also beyond us. Reverence, thus, can save us from the hubris that can destroy the good we have accomplished.

Awareness is paying attention. It is similar to Buddhist mindfulness. Awareness involves attention in the present moment, both to the world around us and to the total complex we call our minds and bodies.

This survey of the literature indicates that there is a great deal of current interest in spirituality without God or a metaphysical transcendent. These recent advocates of natural spirituality are saying three things about spirituality: we are spiritual, first, when our sense of connection is enlarged. Second, we are spiritual when we aspire to greater things, when we attempt to realize our ideals. Finally, we are spiritual when we ask the big questions. Note that these three: connection, aspiration, and reflection on profound questions are all forms of enlarging our selves, of breaking through the narrow walls of the ego. (John Tobin has questioned the use of the term ego here. I am using it in a loose sense to indicate an attention and concern with oneself.)

A theory of naturalized spirituality

In this part of the chapter, I propose a naturalistic theory of spirituality or what could be called "naturalized spirituality." By this, I mean a spirituality that is open to the treasures of this world, to its joys and even its heartaches, without escaping to a higher realm. If spirituality is supposed to be leaving this world behind, if spirituality means climbing up Jacob's ladder to the heavenly realm of Plato's ideas, that's not for me. It may be fine for some people, but I will take a pass. Spirituality in the past has often meant just that, withdrawing from this world and ascending by degrees to a heavenly vision. But, if spirituality means being more open to this world and its riches, then I am interested. Being open to the world and its riches is a way of enlarging ourselves, of breaking through the narrow walls of the ego.

Thoreau, in his *Journals*, wrote about turning over a slab of ice that formed on the grass in winter to examine the bits and pieces and crawly things on the underside. I take this to be a very significant action. Ever since Plato, we have been urged to climb up to the higher realms. Thoreau advocates digging down into the details, digging down both literally and metaphorically, to turn the whole Western tradition upside down. We need to develop what Ursula Goodenough calls "horizontal transcendence" (Goodenough, 2001).

I shall define spirituality in the primary sense as experiencing the extraordinary or the sacred, which I define as "which is of overriding significance." In the secondary sense, I shall define spirituality as the attempt to cultivate an awareness of the sacredness of at least some things and an attempt to live out the sense of the importance of things that sacredness brings.

So, spirituality is first of all an experiencing of the sacredness of some things (or possibly all things), and second, it is the cultivation of this experiencing and the living out of its implications. In the first sense, spirituality is the experiencing of the extraordinary or what is of overriding importance. In the second sense, it is the cultivation of this experiencing and the living in its light.

This requires a theory of the sacred, which I have introduced in Chapter 2, and shall discuss again shortly. But first, as I am a skeptic, although an appreciative skeptic, I must talk about the perversions of spirituality. Like organized religion, spirituality has its perversions, including self-importance, lukewarmness, and lack of discipline. Now, I want to say that these perversions of spirituality may be corrected through organized religion at its best. I also wish to say that organized religion may worsen these perversions.

In agreement with the other writers, my notion of spirituality includes both cognitive and affective dimensions and can become motivation for action. More than the other writers, I stress that these experiences of the sacred come with varying degrees of intensity from the ordinary to the ecstatic. With Harris and Flanagan, I note that spirituality can be an intentional practice requiring methodical discipline. However, with Comte-Sponville, I recognize that, sometimes, the experiences of the extraordinary can come unbidden. In other words, spirituality can vary from the spontaneous to the routine. And, routine is not always a bad thing. Routine can be related to method and discipline. Unlike the other writers, I stress that healthy spirituality can and perhaps should involve both an imaginative grasp of the totality of the universe, a sense of the big picture, and appreciative attention to the concrete particularities of life. In other words, I balance Spinoza and Comte-Sponville with Thoreau.

It must be stressed that healthy spirituality provides a motivation to pursue responsibility beyond the self. Spirituality is not a matter of navel gazing. There can and should be a sense of connection, an enlargement of concern. To be sure, zeal can harden into fanaticism. A strong spirituality, however, will provide enough flexibility and openness to prevent such excess. In short, a spiritual life without social concern is truncated and pathological. Indeed, a spiritual life can provide the motivation and psychological resources to persevere in the arduous tasks of social responsibility. Social, political, and environmental activism can be draining and exhausting. Spiritual practice can help provide strength and suppleness.

In short, spirituality can become pathological. Narrow chauvinism, racism, indeed any uncritical devotion can move us beyond narrow ego boundaries, which is why the prophetic strand in religion at its best has always spoken against the danger of idolatry. The severest critics of religion have often been religious.

At this point, I would like to ask, can you combine spirituality and skepticism? I am not sure that you can. What may occur is that you alternate between skepticism and engaged experiencing. It is something like kissing. If someone approaches with lips, you either are skeptical or you enjoy the kiss. Now, here is a dichotomy, skepticism or engagement. These two are distinct attitudes in what is probably a whole cluster of possible attitudes. Think of the difference between a kiss of greeting, a passionate kiss, a kiss on stage, and having to kiss Aunt Matilda. The philosopher William Hocking suggested an alternation between the mystical attitude and the ordinary attitude. I am following up on this by secularizing the spiritual. But, I am not sure that skepticism and spirituality are incompatible at one point in time. So, I am not certain that we have to alternate. Humans are capable of rather complex feelings.

Howard Radest, a leader of the Ethical Culture Society and former Dean of the Humanist Institute, reminded me that sacredness has connotations of unapproachability. (The following is adapted from Stone, 2000.) He is correct. I would like to make a distinction between behavioral and methodological restraint. When we speak of the sacredness of human beings, we hold up behavioral restraint as part of a proper attitude of respect. To call something sacred implies that we will not destroy or damage it. Indeed, that we will protect it. However, when we speak of the sacredness of scripture or prelates, we usually mean that we will not question their dicta. We mean methodological restraint. Now, I very much wish to shout from the housetops that the word "sacred," as it should be used, implies behavioral, not methodological restraint. Let us never put a bar to inquiry.

In Chapter 2, I described three events in my life, which I describe as sacred: the first beer my son bought me, open housing marches, and a kestrel catching its prey. I wish now to depict two other events from my experience, which I have learned to think of as sacred. Again, *what I wish to emphasize is their overriding importance in my life.*

First, I remember the day my father died. I was sitting in my apartment feeling rather sad when my daughter, at that time about 8 years old, came home from school. When I told her what had happened, she said, "Oh, Dad" and put her arm around me. It was one of the most comforting and supportive moments of my life.

Two, for over 60 years, my life has been entwined with that of my wife. Through shared joys and struggles, I have always felt that my life has been made real by her companionship. I have not deserved her, but I am very grateful for her. We both say that we have learned what "we" means.

These five events have been paradigms of sacred events for me. That is, they are of major importance and were not under my control. Reflection on them has helped shape my philosophy of life. An early religious training provided a set of ideas about the sacred, which helped me reflect upon some very personal experiences, ideas that were transformed in the process of interaction with these events. Inherited language and lived experience have always been in transaction. I have described these events also to call forth analogous events for you, events that will be quite different, and yet, perhaps, may share some features with my experience.

John Tobin has pointed out that I provide no criterion for when the use of the term "sacred" is appropriate. I do not think that a definite demarcation marker can be provided. It is an act of discernment, and subjective factors will come into play. It does not mean that the use of the term is arbitrary.

Let me say a few words about drawing on Hindu or Buddhist resources of spirituality. Some people say you need a guru. Well, maybe. A coach or a teacher, sure. But, do not surrender your hard-won intellectual and emotional maturity. Hinduism and Buddhism can take us beyond egotism. But, that can be carried too far. Whenever I taught Buddhism to my Unitarian Universalist pre-ministerial graduate students, I always asked them if the Buddhist notion of "no-self" is what you want to tell a battered woman or an abused altar boy. I think the Buddhist idea of no-self means, in part, that you are not trapped in your present self—and that can indeed be a liberating word, as one of my female students pointed out. I also want to ask, who is taking care of the children while you are meditating? Who is cleaning the latrine? Now the answer may be that the monks are taking turns with housework in between meditation—and that's fine. Finally, let us remember the great variety of Asian forms of philosophy and spirituality: Shankara's Advaita Vedanta is not the same as Ramanuja's bhakti-oriented Vedanta, and Zen no-mind seems rather different—at least at one level—from Tibetan projecting of various gods and goddesses into phenomenal existence. But, that would take us too far from our topic.

Here, we need to raise the following question. Can we still use traditional language? Can we still use words such as "spirituality" or "sacred," not to mention "religious" as in "religious humanism" or "religious naturalism?" At the simplest form of the discussion, there are two opposed views. One view says that traditional words such as "spirituality" or "sacred" are hopelessly outdated. The other view says that at least some of these words can be modified, revised, and updated. Some proponents of this view claim that many traditional words have emotive power to motivate us, while the other side is *worried* about this power.

For purposes of illustration, Roy Wood Sellars, a drafter of the first *Humanist Manifesto*, may be taken as one approach to these issues. He was opposed to liberal Protestant theology's reinterpretation of the term God. However, he allowed the term "religious humanism" conceived of as "religion adjusted to an intelligent naturalism," while "the spiritual is man at his best . . . loving, daring, creating, fighting loyally and courageously for causes dear to him" (Sellars, 1933, 10; 1947, 158). Also, John Dewey could speak in derogatory fashion of "a religion," and yet, seek to revise the concept of "religious" as an adjective applied to certain human attitudes ("a unification of ideal values that is essentially imaginative in origin" and "the *active* relation between ideal and actual"), and Dewey even tried to revise the concept of God (Dewey, 1934, 43, 51).

The choice of which words to keep, if any, I suggest, depends on at least two factors. One is a judgment call as to which words are still viable or else are hopelessly encumbered by too much baggage. The other factor is how much a person has been wounded, especially in childhood, by the oppressive use of these words.

It should be clear that I myself am willing to use the words "spirituality," "sacred," and "religious." Some people challenge the honesty of using traditional words, such as "spirituality," even in a revised sense. I wish to claim that there is no *a priori* reason to reject these old words. The decision needs to be made for each term and sometimes on a contextual basis. Scientists are allowed to modify the meanings of words such as "atom." I see no automatic reason not to allow traditional terms to be used with new meanings, although these meanings should be spelled out. Some skeptics do not like this modification of old terms. They prefer a stationary target. But, why should the privilege be accorded in the scientific domain and not in the area of personal philosophies of life?

In the space of this chapter, I have not been able to develop details of a spirituality that can nurture an appreciation for the sacredness of the non-human world. Persons are sacred, but we are not alone in our importance. That is why, I prefer to call myself a religious naturalist, rather than a humanist. Developing a spirituality oriented to the non-human environment is an important part of addressing our ecological vulnerability. I suggest that developing appreciative awareness, as developed in the previous chapter, is the key to extending spirituality beyond, while yet including, the human world. With Mary Oliver in "The Summer Day," we may say, "I don't know exactly what a prayer is / I do know how to pay attention" (Oliver, 2005).

When we hold something sacred, we will protect it. Such a spiritual practice will require us to shut off our phones, train our senses, be scientifically informed, and learn to appreciate our bioregions and local ecosystems. It is important to my personal spirituality to realize that all of us dwellers on earth are made of stardust, that indeed, we are an intimate part of the non-human world. If you want to know about the environment, put your hand upon your chest. The environment, the natural world, is within you, and likewise, you are within the natural world.

In conclusion, the survey of recent writers on naturalistic spirituality in the first part of this chapter found three modes of spirituality. Spirituality is a breaking of the ordinary bounds of the self or ego 1) through a sense of connectedness, 2) aspiration, or 3) reflection on profound questions. I propose my conception of sacredness as a designation for uncontrollable events of overriding significance as one way of understanding and of fostering such an expansion of the self.

Why bother about spirituality? Well, why bother about love or beauty? It is part of the richest flavor of life. Indeed, spirituality *can* come with an overriding insistence. But, you better go into it with your eyes wide open. Somehow combine or alternate between the engaged and the skeptical attitudes. As I said at the beginning of this chapter, a naturalized spirituality is one that is open to the treasures of this world, to its joys, and heartaches. Echoing Goodenough, we are a piece of evolved pre-Cambrian mud that everyday has a chance to sit up and look around and shout—"Hosanna, right here and now."

Note

1 Parts of this chapter are adapted from the September 2012 issue of *Zygon: Journal of Religion and Science*. An earlier version was given as a lecture at the Center for Inquiry, International in Amherst, NY.

Bibliography

Alexander, Samuel. 1939. *Philosophical and Literary Pieces*. Edited by John Laird. London: Macmillan and Co., Ltd. (Reprinted Westport, CT: Greenwood Press Publishers, 1970).
Comte-Sponville, André. 2007. *The Little Book of Atheist Spirituality*. New York, NY: Viking Press.
Deacon, Terrence W. 1998. *The Symbolic Species*. New York, NY: W.W. Norton.
Deacon, Terrence W. 2005. "Interview with Terry Deacon," *Science and Theology News*, (Fall).
De Caro, Mario and David Macarthur. 2004. *Naturalism in Question*. Cambridge, MA: Harvard University Press.
De Caro, Mario and David Macarthur. 2010. *Naturalism and Normativity*. New York, NY: Columbia University Press.
Dewey, John. 1934. *A Common Faith*. New Haven, CT: Yale University Press.
Flanagan, Owen. 2007. *The Really Hard Problem: Meaning in a Material World*. Cambridge, MA: The MIT Press.
Goodenough, Ursula. 1998. *The Sacred Depths of Nature*. New York: Oxford University Press.
Goodenough, Ursula. 2000. "Religiopoiesis," *Zygon: Journal of Religion and Science*, 35, 561–566.

Goodenough, Ursula. 2001. "Vertical and Horizontal Transcendence," *Zygon: Journal of Religion and Science*, 36, 21–31.

Goodenough, Ursula and Terrence W. Deacon. 2003. "From Biology to Consciousness to Morality," *Zygon: Journal of Religion and Science*, 38, 801–819.

Goodenough, Ursula and Terrence W. Deacon. 2005. "Religious Naturalism Defined," *Encyclopedia of Religion and Nature*. Edited by Bron Taylor. www.religionandnature.com/ern.

Goodenough, Ursula and Terrence W. Deacon. 2006. "The Sacred Emergence of Nature," in *Oxford Handbook of Science and Religion*. Edited by Philip Clayton. New York: Oxford University Press, 853–871.

Goodenough, Ursula and Paul Woodruff. 2001. "Mindful Virtue, Mindful Reverence," *Zygon: Journal of Religion and Science*, 36, 585–596.

Harris, Sam. 2004. *The End of Faith: Religion, Terror, and the Future of Religion*. New York, NY: W.W. Norton & Company.

Kalton, Michael. 2000. "Green Spirituality: Horizontal Transcendence," in *Paths of Integrity, Wisdom and Transcendence: Spiritual Development in the Mature Self*. Edited by Melvin E. Miller and P. Young-Eisendrath. London, UK: Routledge, 187–200.

Murry, William R. 2011. *Becoming More Fully Human: Religious Humanism as a Way of Life*. New Haven, CT: Religious Humanism Press.

Oliver, Mary. 2005. *New and Selected Poems, Volume One*. Boston, MA: Beacon Press.

Patton, Kenneth L. 1954. *Man's Hidden Search: An Inquiry in Naturalistic Mysticism*. Boston, MA: Meeting House Press.

Post, Stephen. 2004. "Religion & Spirituality and Human Flourishing: Field Analysis," www.metanexus.net/tarp.

Santayana, George. 1905. *Reason in Religion*, Vol. III of *The Life of Reason, or the Phases of Human Progress*. New York, NY: Charles Scribner's Sons.

Sellars, Roy Wood. 1933. "Religious Humanism," *The New Humanist* 6 (May-June), 7–12.

Sellars, Roy Wood. 1947. "Accept the Universe as a Going Concern!," in *Religious Liberals Reply*. Edited by Henry R, Nelson Wieman. Boston, MA: The Beacon Press.

Solomon, Robert C. 2002. *Spirituality for the Skeptic: The Thoughtful Love of Life*. New York: Oxford University Press.

Stone, Jerome A. 1992. *The Minimalist Vision of Transcendence: A Naturalist Philosophy of Religion*. Albany: State University of New York Press.

Stone, Jerome A. 2000. "What is Religious Naturalism?" *Journal of Liberal Religion*, Vol. 2. www.meadville.edu/journal. [Reprinted with addendum, *Religious Humanism*, XXXV Winter/Spring 2001, 60–74].

Stone, Jerome A. 2008. *Religious Naturalism Today: The Rebirth of a Forgotten Alternative*. Albany, NY: State University of New York Press.

Welch, Sharon D. 1999a. *Sweet Dreams in America: Making Ethics and Spirituality Work*. New York: Routledge.

Welch, Sharon D. 1999b. "Spirituality without God," *Tikkun*. Volume 14, No. 3 (May/June).

Welch, Sharon D. 2000. *A Feminist Ethic of Risk*, revised. ed. Minneapolis, MN: Fortress Press.

Welch, Sharon D. 2004. *After Empire: The Art and Ethos of Enduring Peace*. Minneapolis, MN: Fortress Press.

Woodruff, Paul. 2001. *Reverence: Renewing a Forgotten Virtue*. New York: Oxford University Press.

5
THE "G_D" WORD

"Some call it evolution, / And others call it God." Thus did the poet William Herbert Carruth assert in 1925. Can we dispense with the word "God"?[1] The reason for this question is that there are some religious naturalist writers who continue to use the term "God," but in a revised naturalistic sense. How can they talk about "God," if there is no God, as naturalists almost always claim? The answer is that they are not talking about the traditional notion of God. When they talk about "God," they are usually either trying to talk about the entire universe or else a part of it. In other words, they have a *naturalistic conception of God*. They can be called "naturalistic theists." For example, the seventeenth-century Dutch philosopher, Spinoza, spoke of "God or Nature" in such a way as to say that "God," rightly conceived, is the same as the entire inter-connected universe. In other words, in saying "God or Nature," the word "or" functions as an equal sign.

We started in Chapter 1 by saying that religious naturalism is the attempt to lead a religious or spiritual life without the *traditional* beliefs in God, afterlife, and a soul. Religious naturalists believe that this world, this universe is, (most likely) all there is. Now if, instead of the traditional belief in God (which normally means that God is somehow like a personal agent), we revise the concept of God, then some people think that perhaps we could use the old word in a new sense. Somewhat analogously, some people now accept the idea that a same-gender couple, with or without children, are a family. Thus, the word "family" has been revised. This boils down to a question of language or semantics. Is it appropriate to use the term God when referring to all or a part of the universe? Now, when we say, "It is a matter of semantics," many people shrug their shoulders as if the matter under discussion is not important. But, after all, if you are threatened with some of the crises of life and feel the urge to pray, matters of semantics can seem very real.

Naturalistic theism

Among the naturalists who continue to talk about God, there are a variety of positions, although they seem, to boil down to two main options. Some of these positions describe God as the totality of the universe considered religiously. Others depict God as the creative process within the universe. Thus, there tend to be two types of naturalistic theists. Among those who think of God as the totality of the universe considered religiously are a group of thinkers not as well known today, including the philosopher Samuel Alexander, and the theologians George Burman Foster, Edward Scribner Ames, Frederick May Eliot, William Bernhardt, the later Bernard Loomer, and Michael Dowd. Most well known of this first type of naturalistic theist was the seventeenth-century Dutch philosopher Baruch Spinoza and (probably) the scientist Albert Einstein. The second type of naturalistic theist, those who think of God as the creative process within the universe, include the theologians Shailer Mathews, Henry Nelson Wieman, and Ralph Wendell Burhoe. A case could also be made that the philosopher John Dewey falls within this group. Others such as the theologians Karl Peters, Gordon Kaufman, and Victor Anderson seem to bridge these two types. The naturalistic theists continue to use the term God in some radically revised sense and defend this usage.

Frederick May Eliot

For the Unitarian preacher Frederick May Eliot, later President of the American Unitarian Association, religion is found in depths that lie too deep for words. However, gestures, including gestures in words, can give expression to these depths. Eliot is quite explicit when it comes to the word "God." The word is "the simplest and most familiar of all the symbolic forms by which belief in the purposefulness of the universe can be expressed." He grants that some people are unwilling to use the word "because it has meant such very different things to different people, and they are afraid of being constantly misunderstood" (Eliot, 1928, 107).

When I use the term "God," Eliot wrote, "I am using a symbol for the reality that I believe exists behind the deepest convictions of my own mind and heart," convictions that he had spoken of as "the moral law, the rational nature of the universe, the kinship of my life with the universe, and the element of purposefulness." In addition, his conviction is that there is a reality behind these experiences, and the word "God" can be used to summarize and symbolize the validity of these convictions and "their authority over my life" (Eliot, 1928, 108). He grants that different words besides "God" can be used, such as Julian Huxley's term "sacred reality." However, "It is obviously cumbersome, and unfamiliar, and awkward. Furthermore, it lacks the connotations which grow up about a word through long use in certain definite circumstances, and for this reason it lacks the emotional quality which a religious symbol needs" (Eliot, 1928, 109–110).

Early Chicago naturalists

In the early decades of the twentieth century, there was a period of theological innovation at the University of Chicago. These scholars are often referred to as the "early Chicago school" (Stone, 2008, 59). Although known especially for their historical and psychological studies of religion, especially the Christian tradition, as they matured, they often engaged in theological reflections of a naturalistic kind. They are of great importance in the development of religious naturalism. Especially significant is that the explorations of these thinkers occurred at one of the major American graduate schools for training ministers.

George Burman Foster

George Burman Foster was a theologian at the Divinity School of the University of Chicago whose first two books *The Finality of the Christian Religion* (1906) and *The Function of Religion in Man's Struggle for Existence* (1909) both caused considerable comment pro and con, widely covered in the Chicago newspapers, with unsuccessful attempts to remove him from his teaching position. Foster was transferred out of the Divinity School into the Department of Comparative Religion at the University. The center of our attention will be *The Function of Religion in Man's Struggle for Existence*.

In this book, Foster has two ways of thinking about God. The first is that "The word God is a symbol to designate the universe in its ideal-achieving capacity."

> The content of our God-faith is the conviction that in spite of much that is dark and inharmonious in the world, reality is on the side of the achievement of values such as our. . . . Our vocation is to achieve ideal values; religion is the conviction that such values are by us achievable, in virtue of our constitution and of the constitution of that whole of which we are a part.
> (Foster, 1909, 108-110; Peden and Stone, 1996, I, 52)

The second way of thinking about God for Foster is that, just as modern people have learned to think about the mind as the body in one of its aspects or ways of behaving, rather than as a separate spirit-like substance, so also God is the universe in one of its aspects or ways of behaving, rather than a separate spirit. Just as we speak of the rising sun, even though we now know that it is really the rotation of the earth, so we can speak of the soul, even though we now know there is really only a single organism with intelligent features.

Likewise, we may talk about God even though there is only a single cosmos.

> There is no such thing as a self-dependent soul freely active or interactive with an organism which we call the body, just as similarly there is no self-dependent deity freely active or interactive with that larger body which we call the cosmos. All this is a survival of primitive animism.
> (Foster, 1909, 21; Peden and Stone, 1996, I, 45)

Edward Scribner Ames

Edward Scribner Ames, another Chicago theologian, taught in the philosophy department at the university from 1901 to 1935, was Dean of Disciples House from 1928 to 1945, and minister of the University Church of the Disciples of Christ for several years. He thought that the idea of God should be revised, just as we often revise the idea of mind.

> [T]he endeavor to locate the mind as a specific entity is relinquished. Mind is increasingly regarded as a term descriptive of the behavior of some organisms. When they behave in certain ways they are said to exhibit mentality.... [T]heir apparent deliberation before action, their ability to deal with novel situations effectively ... are evidences of mentality. Mind is not therefore something separable, so far as science knows, from the organism. ... An analogous procedure is taking place with reference to the conception of God.
>
> (Ames, 1929, 150–151)

When revised, God will be understood as the reality of the world in its aspects of orderliness, love, and intelligence (or order, beauty, and expansion). Ames should not be misread as meaning that God is only a projection of humanity's longings upon the cosmos. God is not a mere projection of human ideals, but refers to real aspects or functions of the cosmos. (See Ames, 1929, 154–156; Peden and Stone, I, 1996, 97–99.)

Ames also thought of God in terms of what he termed "the practical absolute." The practical absolute arises in any type of thinking or practical interest. "In reasoning men seek a procedure which validates their arguments. They appeal at last to the nature of reason, to the law of contradiction, or to the sufficient law of reason" (Ames, 1929, 180). Our moral life also has such a practical absolute. "Kant's dictum, 'So act that the maxim of our deed may become a universal law,' expresses this craving for the substantiation of individual conduct by a law or principle.... This is the way the religious man uses God. God is the judge, the umpire, the referee" (Ames, 1929, 180–181). Thus, for Ames, the idea of God may be reconceived both as the world in certain of its aspects and also as a standard of validity for our practical thinking.

Shailer Mathews

A third of the early Chicago theologians of interest to us is Shailer Mathews, who taught at the Divinity School from 1895 to 1933. Known basically as a socio-historical historian of the Biblical period and of Christian theology, in his later writings, he developed a naturalistic conception of God. "*For God is our conception, born of social experience, of the personality-evolving and personally responsive elements of our cosmic environment with which we are organically related*" (Mathews, 1931, 226, italics in original; for similar definitions, see also Mathews, 1940, 34; or Peden & Stone, I, 1996, 152. I have an analysis and critique of this definition in Stone, 1992, 52. Mathews has had a profound influence on me, even more than Ames or Eliot.)

Later Chicago naturalists

Henry Nelson Wieman

Henry Nelson Wieman was perhaps the most influential of the Chicago naturalists. Specifying the object of inquiry is a key phase of any investigation. Thus, much of his work was spent refining the definition of the object of religious inquiry. A typical definition went like this: "What transforms man as he cannot transform himself to save him from evil and lead him to the best that human life can ever attain, provided that he give himself over to it in religious faith and meet other required conditions" (Wieman, 1975, 273). In traditional religious language, this is God.

Wieman's worldview was naturalistic in which the only things that can exist or can do anything are events, relations and qualities (Wieman, 1946, 6). Now, within this world conceived naturalistically, the only thing that can transform us as we cannot transform ourselves is a single process, the process of integration in the world or what he later called "the creative event" ("creative process" might have been better) or "creative interchange."

His thinking went through stages. In *Normative Psychology of Religion* (Wieman and Wescott-Wieman, 1935) and *The Growth of Religion* (Wieman and Horton, 1938), the process of integration extended before the appearance of humans and included the history of the cosmos and biological evolution. In *The Source of Human Good* (Wieman, 1946), he focused almost entirely on creative interaction between human individuals and groups. By the time of *Man's Ultimate Commitment* (Wieman, 1958), reference to God has almost disappeared, and he referred to creative interchange on the human level as which transforms us as we cannot do so, and is thus, worthy of our highest dedication.

Bernard Loomer

Another theologian, Bernard Loomer, toward the end of his life identified God with the "concrete, interconnected totality of the world as a whole." This raised the question, "Why deify this interconnected web of existence by calling it 'God'? Why not simply refer to the world and to the processes of life?" As in this new usage, "God is not an enduring concrete individual with a sustained subjective life, what is gained by this perhaps confusing, semantic identification?" Loomer's answer is that:

> In our traditions the term "God" is the symbol of ultimate values and meanings in all of their dimensions. It connotes an absolute claim on our loyalty.

It bespeaks a primacy trust, and a priority within the ordering of our commitments. It points the direction of a greatness of fulfilment. It signifies a richness of resources for the living of life at its depths.

(Loomer, 1987, 41–42)[2]

Thus, we may say that the Chicago naturalists tended to use the word "God" either as the religiously important part of the total universe (Mathews' personality producing forces, Wieman's creative process of integration) or as the entire universe religiously considered (for Ames, the reality of the world in certain aspects such as perhaps order, beauty, and expansion as well as the practical absolute; for Foster, the world in its ideal-achieving capacity; and for the later, Loomer, the interconnected evolving web of all existence). Further discussion of the Chicago naturalists could include the later Gerald Birney Smith and Bernard Meland (See Stone, 2008, 64–66, 86–96; Stone, 2013, 705–707).

Recent theistic naturalists

Ralph Wendell Burhoe

Trained in the natural sciences, Ralph Wendell Burhoe used his position as the first Executive Officer of the American Academy of Arts and Sciences to form the Institute on Religion in an Age of Science (1954).[3] In 1964, he went to Meadville Theological School in Chicago to develop a course using modern science as the basic resource. In Chicago, he established the Center for Advanced Study in Religion and Science (now the Zygon Center for Religion and Science) and started *Zygon: Journal of Religion and Science*.

Burhoe thought that the wisdom of the ancient religious traditions about humans is desperately needed today, and that this wisdom can be reinterpreted and placed on a solid basis through modern science. His key idea is that the process of evolution is, in fact, what the ancient religions referred to as God, the selective process of evolution being the equivalent, in scientific terms, of the judgment of God. (See "The Concepts of God and Soul in a Scientific View of Human Purpose," in Burhoe, 1981, Chapter 5.) The religious traditions referred to a system or reality or power sovereign over humans. This sovereign system the sciences understand more fully as the process of evolutionary selection. That is, "god" is "the total sovereign system, which in scientific language may be said to be the total cosmic ecosystem, including the details of local systems on earth" (Burhoe, 1981, 24).

Gordon Kaufman

Harvard theologian Gordon Kaufman toward the end of his career moved into a religious naturalist position, although he preferred to speak of himself as a "biohistorical naturalist."[4] His naturalism comes out in *In Face of Mystery* and *In the Beginning . . . Creativity* (Kaufman, 1993; Kaufman, 2003. Kaufman 2007 is a good introduction).

For Kaufman, the word "God" refers to something that produces a fuller human existence, and at the same time, relativizes all our projects, accomplishments, and values. In brief, God is something that humanizes and relativizes (Kaufman, 1993, 316). Although this symbol is a construction of disciplined human imagination for which we are and need to assume responsibility, nevertheless, it refers to a reality that is

> neither a simple fantasy of ours nor something that we can manipulate or control, make or remake as we choose; God is a reality genuinely distinct from us and all our imaginings, that which—quite apart from our own doing—has given us our being as humans and continues to nurture and sustain us.
> (Kaufman, 1993, 317)

In place of the traditional personal-agential model of divine creativity, Kaufman utilizes a model based on the serendipity of the long cosmic, biological, and historical process. Serendipity refers to the unforeseen and unexpected results of a process, results that are not always happy or fortunate (Kaufman, 1993, 268, 274, 279). This long cosmic process has various "trajectories" or series of events, which, building on each other, seem in retrospect to take certain directions, humanity being one of them. "Thus the appearance of human modes of being in the world would be properly regarded not as a metaphysical surd but rather as grounded in the ultimate nature of things, in the ultimate mystery" (Kaufman, 1993, 284).

This complex notion of trajectories of serendipitous creativity provides a vision that gives meaningful, but not dominate, significance to human life within the universe. This can provide a basis for hope, though not certainty, to help motivate people to take responsible roles in creating a more humane world (Kaufman, 1993, 294). The word "God" is used to focus our attention and dedication to the serendipitous processes of creativity.

> On this view the symbol "God" refers us not to a particular existent being within or beyond the world, but rather to that trajectory of cosmic and historical forces which, having emerged out of the ultimate mystery of things, is moving us toward a more truly humane and ecologically responsible mode of existence: it is *that* to which I commitment myself; it is which I will serve with my life.
> (Kaufman, 1993, 347–348, italics in original)

Why should we continue to use the traditional word "God"? "Why not just speak of 'cosmic and historical forces' working toward humanization and ecological order?" The answer partly lies in the need to connect ourselves with the historical past in order to see our place in the trajectory moving into the future. This symbol focuses our devotion and makes clear that we do not think of ourselves as disconnected from our forebears, but instead as participants in an ongoing history and community.

> The idea of "cosmic and historical forces" working toward humanization and ecological responsibility . . . is much too abstract and intellectual to be able to generate universal interest and support. To commit ourselves to *God*, however, is to express just such a stance and loyalty by means of a symbol which is capable of drawing together and unifying persons of differing degrees of sophistication in all walks of life.
>
> (Kaufman, 1993, 348)

Furthermore, the word "God" helps us see the gradually increasing unity and directness of the specific cosmic trajectory toward humaneness. "'God,' as a proper name . . . focuses our minds so that they will grasp as significantly unified and of existential import to us what we might otherwise take to be simply diverse processes and powers" (Kaufman, 1993, 348). For Kaufman, the bottom line is that "The God-symbol is well worth keeping. Not only can it help keep us humble; thought of in the way I am proposing, it can continue to orient us to what is of greatest importance for us" (Kaufman, 2003, 99).

He writes, in an echo of George Burman Foster, that to use the term "God" does not commit us to the existence of additional entity in or beyond the world, any more than the word "self" refers to an additional something alongside the body. To use the word "God" is to attend to the import of the unity and direction which developed in this specific evolutionary historical trajectory.

This idea of serendipitous creativity includes a transcendent principle of criticism and prophetic protest that challenges our standards and dreams, like Ames' practical absolute.

> What is needed is a nonreified version of the normative, a version according to which it is never expected that life "on earth" will perfectly conform to the ideal—that there will always be room for criticism and further transformation . . . but at the same time it is not held that the perfect or ideal "exists" somehow or somewhere "outside" or "beyond" the world.
>
> (Kaufman, 1993, 327)

Serendipitous creativity on a cosmic scale gave rise to many trajectories, some in conflict with others. Thus, creativity in the abstract is not normative for us as humans. The creativity that is normative for humans is the trajectory that produced us, creativity on earth. In this particular trajectory, the attitude and behavior termed "love" becomes important, although we should not say without qualification that "God is love" without placing this phrase in a constellation of other terms including "power." Human actions, practices, and institutions that are destructive of the biohistorical conditions within which we must live are evil, while whatever nurtures and sustains the evolutionary and historical trajectory of which we are part and is compatible with earth's ecological order is good (Kaufman, 2004, 59–66).

It should be noted that Stuart Kauffman, biochemist and proponent of emergence theory, has a theory similar to that of Gordon Kaufman. In *Reinventing the Sacred*, he writes, "God, a fully natural God, is the very creativity of the universe" (Kauffman, 2008, 6).

Karl Peters

Serendipitous creativity is a term Karl Peters, co-editor of *Zygon: Journal of Religion and Science*, uses for the two-part process involving the occurrence of variations in cosmic, biological, and human history and the selection of some of these variations to continue (Peters, 2002, 53–58). Briefly put, God is the creative process, which is made up of a set of interactions that create variations plus a set of interactions that preserve some of them. Much like Burhoe whom Peters draws on, God is the two-fold process of innovation and selection in cosmic, cultural, and personal evolution. Selection is good from the viewpoint of the selected variations, and perhaps, by extension of the total process itself. However, from the viewpoint of anything left behind in the process, selection will appear evil. Cosmic and biological evolution and personal life can be thought of in Daoist fashion as a dance or conversation in which no one leads and each mutually influences the others. There is no goal, but the reward is participation in the dance itself.

This chapter's discussion of the theistic naturalists is far from complete, but to attempt anything like a complete survey would take up too much space for a volume of this size. Mention could be fruitfully made of the ideas of the philosopher Samuel Alexander, the Jewish theologians Mordecai Kaplan and Jack Cohen, the Protestant theologians William Dean and Charley Hardwick, the physicist Albert Einstein (discussed in Chapter 1), and two thinkers who might be classified as philosophers of religion: William Bernhardt and Philip Phenix. Analyses of their work can be found in my *Religious Naturalism Today* (Stone, 2008). Michael Dowd, in *Thank God for Evolution*, presents a view of God as the universe in its entirety (Dowd, 2008). Stressing the importance of the evolution of the universe, Dowd says that once we really realize that we are made of stardust and are on the cutting edge of the universe, that we will find meaning and purposefulness to our lives. Dowd, with his wife Connie Barlow, has been literally a travelling evangelist for the type of religious naturalism willing to use the traditional term "God" for the universe as a whole. Loyal Rue sees the process of moving toward a naturalized God in the following way: "God, we may say, is gradually being naturalized, while nature is gradually being divinized" (Rue, 2011, 125). In Alice Walker's *The Color Purple*, Shug declares "I believe God is everything . . . Everything that is or ever will be" (Walker, 1983, 178). Much earlier, Harriet Monroe, early editor of *Poetry* magazine, wrote: "Call the Force God and worship it at a million shrines, and it is no less sublime; call it nature, and worship it in scientific gropings and discoveries, and it is no less divine. It goes its own way, asking no homage, answering no questions" (Monroe, 1938, 454; see 450). A quotation from Edward Arlington Robinson's *King Jasper* indicates both an appropriate reticence of speech when talking about such matters and also the vector quality of our concrete experience as pointing us beyond ourselves:

I don't say what God is, but it's a name that sometimes answers us when we are driven to feel and think how little we have to do with what we are.
(Robinson, 1935, 91–92)

The God-question: five answers

At least five positions can be discerned among religious naturalists concerning the legitimacy of using the word "God." There are some, such as Frederick May Eliot and Bernard Loomer, who think that the concept of God is vitally important, at least in the Western tradition, provided that it is radically revised. Gordon Kaufman, for example, takes the relativizing and humanizing function of the concept to be of paramount importance. Spinoza and Karl Peters would also be included in this group.

Then there are those who allow for a devotional use of the term "God," but who understand that an analysis of the concept would reveal something so far removed from the traditional concept that it no longer has any theoretical use. The early writings of Bernard Meland, who we encountered in Chapter 3, are probably the clearest example of this. For Meland, as for Wieman, there must be an alternation between the languages of devotion and theoretical reflection (Meland, 1933; Wieman, 1968, 30, 32; Wieman, 1987, 99–100, 190; Stone, 1992, 157–167). The term "God" unifies the multiplex conditions on which we are dependent and gives them a cosmic import, but the language of critical reasoning recognizes the plurality of these conditions and instead uses carefully crafted rational and instrumental terminology designed for understanding, explanation, and practical adjustment.

In an exchange in *The Christian Century* in 1933 and 1934, Dewey stressed the plurality of these conditions on which we are dependent and Wieman stressed their unity. (For analyses of this exchange, see Stone, 2008, 126–128; Shaw, 1995, 80–85. The original texts can be found in Dewey, 1933a and 1933b; Wieman, 1933. In the Meland archives in the Special Collections at Regenstein Library at the University of Chicago, there is a letter from Dewey to Meland indicating that Meland's summary of the dispute was on target. (See Meland, 1933. I am not familiar enough with Dewey's treatment of younger scholars to know how much weight to attach to Dewey's letter. I am inclined to take it at face value.)

In the third place, there are those who think that God-language should be avoided, but for purposes of communication or joint celebration or repentance are willing to use a translation device. I myself am willing to invoke the deity when I take an oath in order to indicate the seriousness with which I undertake my obligation. When I was at the bedside of a patient wracked with pain and was asked to pray, I did so with fervor. It was not about me and my doubts. When I attended memorial services for my mother and later my sister, I knew there would be prayers, so rather than grumble, I used my own translation device: "God is the traditional term for the sum of the constructive and challenging aspects of the universe." Yet, when I see the demonic and destructive possibilities of religion in today's world, especially when mixed with political fervor, I wish to urge extreme caution in the use of the old term "God." And, I definitely wish to defend the rights of atheists and agnostics. If they are silenced, religious naturalists will be next.

In the fourth place, there are those who think that the concept of God is not helpful, but who accept, indeed often appreciate, its use by other people. Ursula Goodenough is a representative of this view.

Finally, there are those who think that the concept of God is so dangerous as to be beyond rehabilitation. A number of people could be mentioned, including those who self-identify as humanists, especially secular humanists and probably most religious humanists. We need not sort out the distinctions between these two types of humanism nor their various relationships to religious naturalism. (Those who call themselves "religious humanists" often fall under our label of religious naturalism, while secular humanists generally would reject the label. But, the boundaries are porous. For a fuller discussion, see my *Religious Naturalism Today*, Stone, 2008, 7–8). To illustrate this fifth group, those who believe that the term "God" is beyond repair, we may take the examples of William Jones and David Bumbaugh.

William Jones, former Professor of Religion Emeritus and Director of Black Studies at Florida State University, attempted to open a place for Black humanism by challenging Black theologians who equate Black religion in America with the Black church. Jones defines religion so as to include humanism (Jones, 1978, 227). He defined religion as the attempt to find the way to salvation and then asserts that humanism is a way of salvation. For Jones, the key principle for humanism is *the functional authority of wo/man*. This means that "choosing without absolute guides is the given condition of humankind" (Jones, 1998, 213). Jones uses the term "functional ultimacy" to refer to the liberation of Black people, indeed of all humans (Jones, 1998, 243, n. 2).

Another thinker who strongly rejects the use of the term "God" *is* David Bumbaugh, retired Unitarian Universalist minister and until recently Professor of Ministry at Meadville Lombard Theological School. He develops what he calls a humanist theology of reverence. According to him, we are called to reverence in the face of "this miraculous world of our everyday experience, . . . a world in which neither god nor humanity is at the center; in which the center is the void, the ever fecund matrix out of which being emerges." He refers to

> a deep reverent, mystical sense of being an integral part of a sacred and holy reality which is the interdependent web of being. . . . We are called to define the *religious* and *spiritual* dimensions of the ecological crisis confronting the world and to preach the gospel of a world in which each is part of all and every one is sacred, and every place is holy ground.
> (Bumbaugh, 1994, 37, italics in original)

A briefer statement of the sacredness of the universe could hardly be penned. The scientific picture of evolution and ecology is also a religious story "in that it calls us out of our little local universes." It is religious, in that it enlarges our sense of responsibility to include all living things and their habitats.

> Our existence, our struggles and our failures are lent moral significance by the fact that they occur within a larger context—within the largest context our imaginations can conceive. . . . This is a religious story; it invites us to awe; it demands a vocabulary of reverence.
>
> (Bumbaugh, 2001, 57–59)

My understanding of the term is that God is our social symbol for the set of very important creative and challenging aspects of our world. (See my *The Minimalist Vision of Transcendence*, Stone, 1992, 9–20.) This notion is a long way from the traditional notion of God. On the other hand, the relatively transcendent creative and challenging aspects of our world can function much like the traditional God. They are a real resource for living and a continuing challenge to growth. This is what the traditional notion does in a person's life. I speak from experience here.

I am reluctant to use the word "God." A simple "yes" or "no" to the question of its dispensability is not adequate, but vacillation and compromise are also dangers. It is partly a question of linguistic innovation or linguistic conservation. We allow physicists to redefine the term "atom," but many people feel it is troublesome to redefine the word "God." The issues are often momentous. Shall we redefine the term "family" to allow gay marriage? It is not just a conservative impulse that wishes to hold on to traditional meanings. Many skeptics dislike attempts to redefine "God." They prefer a stationary target to attack.

It is also partly a matter of whether we need both a theoretical language and a language of devotion, aspiration, or celebration. Thus, as is often the case, appropriate use of a term depends on the context. It may be that the term God is useless in careful reflection on the universe and the meaning of life. But, at times of personal and communal dedication, grieving, or gratitude, there may be no substitute, at least in societies with monotheistic roots. Of course, this vacillation opens the door to hypocrisy, evasion, and obfuscation. But, what else is new? When we learned to communicate with language, we improved our ability to deceive.

My answer to the question of whether it is legitimate to use the term "God" in a naturalized and attenuated sense is that it is a matter of choice and context, although I prefer not to use the word. It is close enough to the traditional concept of God that one could extend the concept to cover what I call the minimally transcendent (the sum of relatively transcendent resources and continually challenging resources in the world). Nevertheless, I think that the dangers of intellectual obscurantism and psychological and social repression are sufficiently real that the "G_d" word should generally be avoided.

For some family gatherings, such as a funeral, or making a promise to fulfill one's civic duty, as in taking an oath to serve on a jury, to insist on one's right to refuse God-language may be to interfere with the important matter at hand. Intellectual honesty, very occasionally, may be trumped by an overriding moral responsibility. My personal semantic decision is that the traditional word "God" can, reluctantly and cautiously, whenever it is appropriate, be used to refer to minimal experiences of transcendence. When so used, the term "God" will be a complex term designating some naturalized variant of the term, such as *natura naturans* (Spinoza, Loomer, Crosby) or the creative process within the universe (Wieman). In my own version, the word "God" will refer to the collection of relatively transcendent real resources and the lures of continually transcendent values, imaginatively entertained in a unified fashion as an ontological and religious ultimate. Having said this, I prefer to avoid or minimize the use of the traditional term "God."

Notes

1 Parts of this chapter are adapted from my articles, "Christian Naturalism," *The Routledge Companion to Modern Christian Thought*, edited by Chad Meister and James Beilby, New York: Routledge, 2013, 703–712 and "Is a 'Christian Naturalism' Possible?," *American Journal of Theology and Philosophy*, 32 (September 2011), 205–220 and from my *Religious Naturalism Today* (Stone, 2008, 59–68, 72–80, 84–100).
2 Bernard Loomer. 1987. *The Size of God: The Theology of Bernard Loomer in Context*, Eds. William Dean and Larry Axel. Macon, GA: Mercer University Press; also available in *American Journal of Theology and Philosophy* vol. 8, nos. 1&2 (January and May), 1987.
3 These pages on Burhoe are adapted from my *Religious Naturalism Today*, 2008, 100–101.
4 These pages on Kaufman and Peters are adapted from my *Religious Naturalism Today* (Stone, 2008, 165–167, 203–206).

Bibliography

Ames, Edward Scribner. 1929. *Religion*. New York: Henry Holt and Company.
Bumbaugh, David. 1994. "The Heart of a Faith for the Twenty-First Century," *Unitarian Universalist Selected Essays 1994*. Boston: Unitarian Universalist Ministers Association, 28–38.
Bumbaugh, David. 2001. "Toward a Humanist Vocabulary of Reverence," *Religious Humanism*, XXXV (Winter/Spring), 49–59.
Burhoe, Ralph Wendell. 1981. *Toward a Scientific Theology*. Belfast: Christian Journals Limited.
Carruth, William Herbert. 1925. *Each in His Own Tongue*. New York: Wise-Parslow Co.
Eliot, Frederick May. 1928. *Toward Belief in God*. St. Paul, MN: Unity Church.
Dewey, John. 1933a. "'A God or the God,' review of 'Is There a God?—A Conversation by Henry Nelson Wieman, Douglas Clyde Macintosh and Max Carl Otto'". *The Christian Century* (February 8), 193–196.
Dewey, John. 1933b. "Dr. Dewey Replies," *The Christian Century* (March 22), 394–395.
Dowd, Michael. 2008. *Thank God for Evolution: How the Marriage of Science and Religion Will Transform Your Life and Our World*. New York: Plume Books.
Foster, George Burman. 1906. *The Finality of the Christian Religion*. Chicago, IL: The University of Chicago Press.
Foster, George Burman. 1909. *The Function of Religion in Man's Struggle for Existence*. Chicago, IL: The University of Chicago Press.
Jones, William R. 1978. "The Case for Black Humanism," in *Black Theology II*. Edited by Calvin E. Bruce and William R. Jones. Lewisburg, PA: Bucknell University Press.
Jones, William R. 1998. *Is God a White Racist?: A Preamble to Black Theology*. Boston, MA: Beacon Press.

Kaufman, Gordon D. 1993. *In Face of Mystery: A Constructive Theology*. Cambridge, MA: Harvard University Press.

Kaufman, Gordon D. 2003. "Biohistorical Naturalism and the Symbol 'God,'" *Zygon: Journal of Religion and Science*. 38 (March), 95–100.

Kaufman, Gordon D. 2004. *In the Beginning. . . Creativity*. Minneapolis, MN: Fortress Press.

Kaufman, Gordon D. 2007. "A Religious Interpretation of Emergence: Creativity as God," *Zygon: Journal of Religion and Science*. 42 (December), 915–928.

Kauffman, Stuart. 2008. *Reinventing the Sacred: A New View of Science, Reason, and Religion*. New York: Basic Books.

Loomer, Bernard. 1987. *The Size of God: The Theology of Bernard Loomer in Context*. Edited by William Dean and Larry Axel. Macon, GA: Mercer University Press. Also available in *American Journal of Theology and Philosophy*. 8 (January and May).

Mathews, Shailer. 1931. *The Growth of the Idea of God*. New York: The Macmillan Company.

Mathews, Shailer. 1940. *Is God Emeritus?* New York: The Macmillan Company.

Meland, Bernard E. 1933. "Is God Many or One?" *The Christian Century*, 50, 725–726.

Monroe, Harriet. 1938. *A Poet's Life*. New York: The Macmillan Company.

Peden, W. Creighton and Jerome A. Stone. 1996. *The Chicago School of Theology—Pioneers in Religious Inquiry*. Volume One. Lewiston, NY: The Edwin Mellen Press.

Peters, Karl E. 2002. *Dancing with the Sacred: Evolution, Ecology, and God*. Harrisburg, PA: Trinity Press International.

Robinson, Edward Arlington. 1935. *King Jasper*. New York: The Macmillan Company.

Rue, Loyal. 2011. *Nature is Enough: Religious naturalism and the Meaning of Life*. Albany, NY: State University of New York Press.

Shaw, Marvin C. 1995. *Nature's Grace: Essays on H.N. Wieman's Finite Theism*. New York: Peter Lang.

Stone, Jerome A. 1992. *The Minimalist Vision of Transcendence: A Naturalist Philosophy of Religion*. Albany, NY: State University of New York Press.

Stone, Jerome A. 2008. *Religious Naturalism Today: The Rebirth of a Forgotten Alternative*. Albany, NY: State University of New York Press.

Stone, Jerome A. 2013. "Christian Naturalism," in *The Routledge Companion to Modern Christian Thought*. Edited by Chad Meister and James Beilby. New York: Routledge.

Walker, Alice. 1983. *The Color Purple*. New York: Washington Square.

Wieman, Henry Nelson. 1933. "Is God Many or One?," *The Christian Century*. Volume L (April 31), 726–727.

Wieman, Henry Nelson. 1946. *The Source of Human Good*. Carbondale, IL: Southern Illinois University Press.

Wieman, Henry Nelson. 1958. "Naturalism," in *A Handbook of Christian Theology*. Edited by Marvin Halverson and Arthur Cohen. New York: Meridian Books, 243–246.

Wieman, Henry Nelson. 1968. *Religious Inquiry: Some Explorations*. Boston, MA: Beacon Press.

Wieman, Henry Nelson. 1975. *Seeking a Faith for a New Age: Essays on the Interdependence of Religion, Science and Philosophy*. Edited by Cedric L. Hepler. Metuchen, NJ: Scarecrow Press.

Wieman, Henry Nelson. 1987. *Science Serving Faith*. Edited by Creighton Peden and Charles Willig. Atlanta, GA: Scholars Press.

Wieman, Henry Nelson and Walter Marshall Horton. 1938. *The Growth of Religion*. Chicago, IL: Willett, Clark & Co.

Wieman, Henry Nelson and Regina Westcott-Wieman. 1935. *Normative Psychology of Religion*. New York: Thomas Y. Crowell.

6
NEEDED PARADIGM SHIFTS

Resacralization of the earth

Let me start by defining "*holding sacred.*" We shall be drawing on our theory of the sacred developed in Chapter 2. We hold something sacred when we are overwhelmingly impressed by its worth or significance. To adopt a religious attitude toward something is to hold it sacred, to hold it of great significance, of overriding importance. This is neither a subjective nor an objective judgment. Rather, it is a *bridge judgment* anchored in both our attitude and the value residing in the object of our attitude. We could say it is a *transaction* between our judgment and the worth of the object. A *religious naturalist*, in my current approach, holds that the entire universe and potentially anything in it is sacred, certainly living things and their habitats are potentially sacred, that is of great significance or value.

I want to be very clear. I am not referring just to the non-human world. I am not only talking about backpacking in the forest, or watching a sunrise, although we may very well hold these sacred. I include inter-human interaction—including your reading this book—among things that *might* be held to be sacred.

Another caveat. The sacred is always dangerous. To hold something sacred may hinder inquiry and breed fanaticism. We are well aware that the Nazis spoke of the sacredness of "blood and soil." Sacredness has connotations of unapproachability. I would like to make a distinction between ethical and methodological restraint or unapproachability. When we speak of the sacredness of human beings, we normally hold up ethical restraint as a proper attitude of respect. We will not harm, indeed we may protect and care for what we hold sacred. However, when we speak of the sacredness of scripture or priests, we usually mean that we will not question their dicta. This is a methodological restraint. I very much wish to shout from the housetops that sacredness, as it should be used today, implies ethical, not methodological restraint. Let us never put a bar to inquiry. This is very important, for the notion of sacredness could easily foster intellectual complacency, dogmatism, and fanaticism.

Material spirits

Another needed paradigm shift is to reconceive the relation between matter and spirit. The long-standing dualism of spirit and body or spirit and matter should be re-thought, so that we can speak of "spirited matter" or "material spirits."

The split between spirit and matter is deeply rooted in the Christian tradition. Much of it traces back to the antagonism of flesh and spirit in the letters of Paul of Tarsus to early Christian churches (e.g., Galatians, 5:16–24). This split was reinforced by the Platonic dualism between the ideal forms and empirical objects or historical processes, which at best only approximated to the forms. This dichotomy was mirrored in the division between knowledge and opinion. It was Augustine especially who melded the Pauline and Platonic dualisms. In one variety or another, this dichotomy between the spiritual and the material is suffused throughout Christian civilization. It was aided by the ascetic practice of monks and the periodic dietary restrictions of Friday and Lent by laity. And, it was all oriented toward eternal life in which we finally shook off the burdens of this earthly body.

Religious naturalism knows of no spiritual realm apart from the physical. As Bernard Loomer claimed, there is a movement from an outlook that

> maintains that resources for salvation ultimately derive from a transcendent God to an outlook that suggests that the graces for the living of a creative life emerge within the depths and immediacies of concrete experience. It is a transition from the wisdom of the sojourner ... to the wisdom of the evolved earth-creature.
>
> (Loomer, 1987, 21)

In addition, this ancient dualism detracts from the very real environmental and other problems we face and detracts from the enjoyment of this physical world.

One approach would be to do away altogether with the notion of "spirit." The proposal here is to reconceive this notion. This is important for two reasons. For one thing, "spirit" is an imprecise, yet powerful image reminding us of our aspiration to *significance*. Furthermore, many people are not ready to jettison the concept of spirit. Both of these points are reflected in the popularity of the term "spiritual," as in the phrase, "I'm not religious, but I am spiritual."

The first thing to do in reconceiving the idea of "spirit" is to rethink the opposite term, which in many contexts is "matter." How we conceive of matter will shape how we think of "spirit." Many people have what Loyal Rue in *Nature is Enough* calls the "grunge" theory of matter. This is the view that the material world is so inert and valueless that nothing worthwhile can be found there. Rue contrasts this with the "glitz" theory of matter, which holds that wonderful things can develop out of matter, indeed, that life and things of beauty can arise out of matter (Rue, 2011, 52–53).

The second thing is to realize that spirit can be embodied. Indeed, a naturalist would say that spirit cannot exist without being embodied. It may help to realize that the word "spirit" came from the word for breath. Indeed, the Latin word is *anima*. When a body is animated, we can say that it is spirited. Or, we say that when the body is working creatively that a person is inspired or full of spirit.

Although the word "spirit" is very ambiguous, my claim is that it can be used by a naturalist, provided that appropriate mention is made of its naturalist restriction to the material. I am reminded of the Unitarian Universalist congregations where humanists sing "Spirit of Life, Come Unto Me" with gusto. Many of these humanists urge that our language be clear, precise, and unambiguous. Yet, they are perfectly willing to talk about the "Spirit of Life." Now, that is partly because they are singing, when we often allow ourselves a little leeway in our expressions. But, it is also because "spirit" is an ambiguous enough term that it can be used in a limited, naturalistic sense as well as referring to ghosts, fairies, and angels. Bernard Meland, for example, developed a naturalistic notion of "spirit." In his early writings, spirit is the next development beyond the average human, the possibilities of which are rooted in the psychophysical nature of the human organism (Meland, 1948, 75–78, 82–86).

In my usage, "spirit" refers both to (a) the human spirit and to (b) the divine spirit(s), a larger matrix of support and challenge. By human spirit, I mean that level or dimension in which our lives are inspired or animated. By divine spirit, I mean the human and non-human matrix that inspires and animates us. We can quite literally refer to "team spirit," the "*esprit de corps*," and the spirit of a nation. Note that by referring to the divine spirit(s), with a possible plural, I am recognizing that while the entire history of the universe is the largest context of our inspiration, there are degrees of relevance, and it is my cup of coffee or the Grand Canyon of the Yellowstone that is most significant for my inspiration. Thus, I wish to respect the insights of both the monotheists and the polytheists. God (if we can use that term) may be one, but the spirits are many.

Of course, the spirits are dangerous. They can get out of hand. The spirit blows where it will (John, 3: 8). That is why, in sociological terms, charismatic leadership and bureaucratic leadership are continually struggling. Spirits move us, but we must constantly test the spirits, lest we follow demonic powers.

Broadening care

A fourth paradigm shift that we need to undergo is to broaden our care beyond the human world to include other living beings, their species, and habitats. We need to dethrone the assumption that the rest of the world was made for our benefit (Stone, 1993, 194–203).

Aldo Leopold and J. Baird Callicott, among others, speak of the need to extend our moral concern to the land or the environmental community and to develop a land aesthetic. Indeed, Callicott has proposed that we go from a "land ethic" to an "Earth ethic" (Callicott, 2014). Religious naturalism can contribute to this. For example, see Donald Crosby's *The Thou of Nature* (Crosby, 2013).

To specify the divine or sacred character of events, we may note that the sacred is often portrayed in two aspects. These two aspects were expressed by Rudolph Otto in *The Idea of the Holy* when he referred to the numinous as both *fascinans* and *tremendum* (Otto, 1958). In Christianity, these aspects are often called gospel and law. Irenaeus, the second-century Christian theologian, referred to the "two hands of God." (For reference to the polarity of gift and blessing and obligation or demand in other traditions, see my *The Minimalist Vision of Transcendence*, Stone, 1992, 22–23.) It is important to affirm both aspects of the sacred, because naturalists often think of religion as the pursuit of ideals, overlooking the point that it is also a response to realities.

Thus, we may approximate a working definition. The "divine" or "sacred" aspects of events refer to surpassing realities and ideals, to relatively transcendent resources and challenges. More precisely, these words refer to the surpassingly creative quality of processes, which qualities we occasionally perceive (and thus "hold sacred" these processes), and also to the continually surpassing lure of ideals, which we occasionally acknowledge (and thus "hold sacred"). In language I have used elsewhere, the "divine" or "sacred" refers to the situationally transcendent character of some processes and to the continually transcendent lure of some ideals. (See my *The Minimalist Vision of Transcendence*, Stone, 1992, 9–21.) In short, the divine or sacred, what I sometimes call this-worldly, minimalist, or relative transcendence, is the surpassing or extraordinary quality of the resources and challenges of the universe.

We may speak of the real and the ideal aspects of the transcendent, the divine, or the sacred. The real aspect of the transcendent, defined minimally, is the collection of all unexpected and uncontrollable creative processes of the universe. Defined minimally, this real aspect or reality is a collection. It might be a unity or unified system, but we do not have enough evidence to assert that. There is some degree of unity, of course, because the universe hangs together somewhat. But, we cannot assert that this collection has any more unity than the generic property of creativity. "Web" or "matrix" may be helpful terms here, instead of collection. The plurality of this conception of a collection of resources was clearly stated by two Christian theologians Shailer Mathews and the early Bernard Meland, and by the philosopher John Dewey in his exchange with the philosopher of religion Henry Nelson Wieman (Meland, 1931, 1933; Dewey, 1933; Wieman, 1933). To quote Mathews: "For God is our conception, born of social experience, of the personality-evolving and personally responsive elements of the cosmic environment with which we are organically related" (Mathews, 1931, 226).

This is helpful, provided that we do not limit ourselves to the personality-evolving and personally responsive aspects of the cosmic environment. And, of course, we must remember that the cosmic environment is not always creative of *human* good. The universe is as destructive as it is creative. Indeed, it often creates by destroying. And, as I asserted in the previous chapter, I am reluctant to use the word "God."

The ideal aspect of transcendence or the sacred, defined minimally, is the set of ideals insofar as they challenge us. There are a number of these that people often recognize. The following are four examples. There is the challenge to universalize respect and care. This is the challenge to learn that all humans are members of one family, that all people are our sisters and brothers. But, it is also the challenge that we have moral obligations that extend even beyond the human community to other living things and their habitats. Then, there is the challenge to love more fully. There is always more giving and listening, more care and forgiving, and support that another person elicits from us. In the third place, we have the challenge to seek adequate information and understanding. We know that we do not have all the answers. When this is genuinely recognized, we accept the challenge to improve our knowledge. Finally, there is the challenge to develop strength and sensitivity of character.

All of these are continuing challenges to us. They are ever-elusive, ever-challenging ideals, which beckon us on to new attainments. Indeed, these challenges can be transformative of our established ways, even potentially revolutionary. We often are not satisfied in our pursuit of meaning and worth, but yet, find the quest worthwhile. This continually challenging by ideals is the ideal aspect of the transcendent. The ideal aspect of transcendence makes all of our projects questionable, all causes penultimate. Ideal transcendence gives us the power of negative thinking.

All of this calls for an attitude of openness, of willingness to grow, and even to be radically challenged. What makes this naturalism religious is not the use of quasi-traditional language, such as "the divine" or "the sacred," or honorific capital letters. This is a religious form of naturalism, in that it calls for and seeks to nurture openness to relatively transcendent or surpassing resources of growth, healing, and transformation, and to the continually lure of penultimate, but greater values. All of us, religious and non-religious people, are subject to the temptation to close ourselves off from superior resources and challenges.

Let us now explore the ramifications of this particluar variety of religious naturalism, what I call the minimalist vision of transcendence, for environmentally aware and active living. The basic moral principle of this naturalism is that we should be critically open to challenging ideals and critically open to transcendent resources. In short, "*we should adopt and continually nurture a stance of critical openness and commitment*" (Stone, 1992, 83. I have elaborated this principle in Chapter 3, *The Ethics of Openness*, in my *The Minimalist Vision of Transcendence*, Stone 1992, 83–110).

The first half of this moral principle is that we should adopt and nurture an orientation of critical commitment to challenging ideals. It is a short step from this to.the imperative that we should widen our loyalty and care to include the whole human community and beyond to include the universal community of all existence, and as far as possible, all of its members. This will be a recovery, on a naturalistic basis, of the prophetic principle of the ancient Hebrews.

In human life, we can sometimes see a movement toward reference to a universal community. The societies by which we are judged are often self-transcending, and sometimes the process of self-transcendence does not stop until the total community of being is reached. This process of transcendence is sometimes noticeable in our political life, for the transcendent reference groups in a democracy can be widened until they include humanity as a whole and beyond that the total community of all being. The imperative is to adopt and nurture the movement toward universal intent, to critically commit ourselves to this process of transcendence.

This is an appropriation, on naturalist grounds, of H. Richard Niebuhr's radical monotheism and its roots in George Herbert Mead, Josiah Royce, and Jonathan Edwards. Radical monotheism, as Niebuhr conceives it, accepts the value of whatever exists. The cause for which it lives and devotes itself is both the principle of being (God) and the realm of being (everything else).

Niebuhr sees analogies to this in certain areas of our secular life, including our political life in a democracy and scientific inquiry. I appropriate this, without the principle of being and without radical monotheism, in my minimalist naturalism through the notion of critical commitment to ideal transcendence and the consequent care for the total community of all beings.

In developing the notion of a generalized other, George Herbert Mead, the pioneer American social psychologist, hinted at the notion of a higher reference group in *Mind, Self, and Society*.

> The only way in which we react against the disapproval of the entire community is by setting up a higher sort of community which in a certain sense out-votes the one we find. A person may reach a point of going against the whole world with the voice of reason. . . . But to do so he has to speak with the voice of reason to himself. He has to comprehend the voices of the past and the future.
>
> (Mead, 1934, 167–168)

Josiah Royce developed a way of thinking about the possibility of going beyond or transcending limited loyalties through his notion of loyalty to loyalty (Royce, 1908, 118–119, 377; Royce, 1913, Volume I, 96–106; Lecture IV: ii-iv). This involves moving from loyalty to a specific cause to a loyalty that loves loyalty itself, including the loyalty of the stranger and the enemy, and from thence to the community of all loyal persons. Although this community is never realized historically, all persons ideally belong to it. The fact that it is not realized in history means that it transcends any particular community. As I put it in *The Minimalist Vision of Transcendence*, "From within our naturalistic orientation we use the concept of intention toward an ideal and transcendence and loyalty to the universal community as our analogue to Royce's concept of a universal community" (Stone, 1992, 95–96).

Drawing on Mead and Royce, H. Richard Niebuhr discovered a struggle between universal and partial intent in democracy. The patriot is loyal to his country, not just as a community, but as a community plus to which her co-patriots refer.

> A democratic patriot in the United States, for instance, will carry on his dialogue with current companions, but as one who is also in relation to what his companions refer to—representatives of the community such as Washingtons, Jeffersons, Madisons, Lincolns, etc. . . . But now the transcendent reference group . . . represent(s) not the community only but what the community stands for.

In Spain . . . the national-state . . . was believed in as the servant of the true Catholic religion. The United States and France came into being in their modern form as devoted exponents of democracy and the rights of men. Germany sought its unity as well as its power as the exponent of culture. . . . In all these nations the loyalty of citizens has therefore a double direction: on the one hand it has been claimed by the transcendent end, on the other, by the nation itself as representative of the cause.

(Niebuhr, 1963, 85; Niebuhr, 1960, 66–67)

In Niebuhr's analysis, the history of our political life is the history of a zstruggle between a partial loyalty, that is, loyalty to the nation as one among other nations, and a universal loyalty to which the nation refers. He illustrates the mingling of these two loyalties by reference to the dual roots of our democratic ideals. One root of religious freedom, for example, is the need to compromise between conflicting religious groups. This loyalty of partial intent struggles with a loyalty of universal intent, which recognizes that religious faith takes precedence over all other loyalties, that obligations to the universal commonwealth takes precedence over all duties to the state. These two loyalties are illustrated in the U.S. Supreme Court's *Macintosh* case. In his dissent, Chief Justice Hughes asserted that: "in the forum of conscience, duty to a moral power higher than the state has always been maintained." Justice Sutherland, for the majority, countered that "government must go forward upon the assumption . . . that unqualified allegiance to the nation . . . [is] not inconsistent with the will of God" (*U.S. v. Macintosh*, 283 U.S. 605, October term, 1930, quoted in Niebuhr, 1960, 71n.). Another example of the struggle between partial and universal loyalty is found in the belief in the equality of all persons. Sometimes, it expresses a universal belief that all people have worth because of the relation to a common source of value. But, sometimes, it is based on a nationalistic faith that does not accord equality to those who are not citizens.

The importance of Niebuhr here is his articulation of an obligation to universal loyalty, an obligation, which, if followed to the end, would result in loyalty to the universal community. This universal loyalty is appropriated within the religious naturalism elaborated in this book by the notion of ideal transcendence, which involves the lure of loyalty to the universal community.

It seems as if, for Niebuhr, the drive toward universality stops at the human community. But, this is largely because he is discussing our political life. He is quite clear that the universal community to which we owe loyalty is the community of all beings. In this, he explicitly draws upon *The Nature of True Virtue* by Jonathan Edwards, for whom "True Virtue most essentially consists in *benevolence to Being in general*" (Edwards, 1960, 3, italics in original). For Edwards, this benevolence is primarily love of God as the greatest and best of beings, but it is also a love for all beings, except for those who are enemies of being in general. Thus, benevolence to a person or private system is a private affection, and not benevolence to being in general, unless it is subordinate to a love of God and benevolence to being in general. Such a private affection is a partial loyalty and can set up enmity against the total system of being. (For a somewhat different use of Edwards and Royce, see Richard Hall's article in *The Pluralist* (Hall, 2016).)

Religious naturalism does not speak of the Lord of the community of beings. However, it can speak in naturalistic terms of care for the universal community of all beings, although the ontological reticence of naturalism suggests that this notion be treated as a regulative idea imaginatively entertained.

Aldo Leopold and J. Baird Callicott project the possibility and the desirability of extending the realm of moral consideration beyond the human community to include not only warm-blooded creatures, not only animals that can feel pain, but all living things and their systems and habitats. Naturalism by itself cannot decide whether species, communities, and systems can be objects of moral consideration, although its roots in process-relational thinking would affirm this. Beyond this, the practice of appreciative perception we discussed in Chapter 3 shows us that appreciation and discernment of worth can be extended past individual persons and living creatures to communities of living beings and ecosystems.

Religious naturalism, as I develop it, will not solve all environmental dilemmas. But, its concern for an appreciative empiricism and its recognition of the continuing lure of challenging ideals provides a general direction toward widening the sphere of moral consideration and toward including groups, networks, systems, and webs of relationships within this sphere. In particular, appreciative perception and holding nature sacred will not solve the knotty questions of cost/benefit analysis and contingent valuation, but it can provide a cautionary tale that the use of these approaches will not settle our environmental issues either. What religious naturalism can also do is to combine the abstraction of "the community of all being" with a particular affection for very specific ponds, crane marshes, and *calypso borealis* and draba flowers on this Turtle Island. As related above, one of my students reported that she learned to love nature by watching, studying, and photographing one polar bear for hours at a time over several weeks. We need to bring the thinness of essays on nature back to the thickness of essays on Walden grounded in woodchucks, hoeing beans, and thawing sandbanks.

Loyalty to the universal community involves a lifestyle of care, both in principle for the interconnected web of being and for particular beings. It will be a lifestyle of respect, defense, and nurture. It will be an orientation ready to accept both intrinsic worth and acquired merit, and ready to learn from all creatures in the universal community of being. It will be an orientation ready to protect or preserve, to nurture or restore any being and its context. This is an open-ended and indefinite responsibility to protect and nurture.

Re-imaging the divine feminine

We must learn to re-envision the feminine side of the divine. The struggle of Biblical monotheism against fertility religions has profound consequences for Western and Moslem civilizations. As one of my students said, "I need religious symbols to celebrate the fact that I am a woman." This might lead us to a closer relation to the natural world.

Of course, the divine transcends gender. But, on the other hand, we have a strong tendency to anthropomorphize. Supposedly, hard-headed, rational scientists in the space program referred to the "intrepid" spacecraft "braving" the dangers of interplanetary travel. "Don't anthropomorphize the spacecraft," said V*oyager* Project Manager John Casani, "they don't like it." [As recollected by imaging team member Terrence Johnson quoted in Jim Bell, *The Interstellar Age: Inside the Forty-year Mission of the* Voyager *Mission* (Bell, 2015, 20).] Perhaps, we have here another instance of the principle that in religious language we need to alternate between the theoretical and the devotional. [For an extended treatment of the relation between these two languages, see my *The Minimalist Vision of Transcendence* (Stone, 1992, 157–167).] And, if we anthropomorphize, we will be tempted by gender. Although I myself would rather dispense with the word "God," I was pleased when a friend of mine blessed a meal of strangers becoming friends by invoking "Father God, Mother God."

The idea of the feminine divine is not so strange. We refer to "Mother Nature." The Greek term "Sophia" or Wisdom is feminine. Feminist theologians from a wide spectrum of viewpoints from Elizabeth Johnson, Sally McFague, Rosemary Radford Ruether, Mary Daly, Carol Christ, and Judith Plaskow have been urging a recovery of the feminine divine.

Of course, re-imaging the feminine divine may not be of much help in our environmental struggles. If women are relegated to inferior positions in the household economy of cooking and cleaning lavatories while the men do the serious work, then re-envisioning the feminine divine may not be of much help. In that case, Mother Nature's job may be an imaginative way of conceiving of the environmental service of providing food and cleansing pollution while male humans get on with the serious work of science and industry. Nevertheless, re-imaging the feminine side of the divine, as long as it is understood to be symbolic, may be a paradigm shift worth taking.

A final paradigm shift in religion is that we need to learn from the wisdom of the older religions.

This is such a major topic that we will devote the entire next chapter to it.

Bibliography

Bell, Jim. 2015. *The Interstellar Age: Inside the Forty-year Mission of the* Voyager *Mission*. New York: Dutton.

Callicott, J. Baird. 2014. *Thinking Like a Planet: The Land Ethic and the Earth Ethic*. New York: Oxford University Press.

Crosby, Donald A. 2002. *A Religion of Nature*. Albany, NY: State University of New York Press.

Crosby, Donald A. 2013. *The Thou of Nature: Religious Naturalism and Reverence for Sentient Life*. Albany, NY: State University of New York Press.

Dewey, John. 1933a. "A God or The God," *The Christian Century*. Volume L (February 8), 193-196.
Dewey, John. 1933b. "Dr. Dewey Replies," *The Christian Century*. Volume L (March 22), 394–395.
Edwards, Jonathan. 1960. *The Nature of True Virtue*. Ann Arbor, MI: The University of Michigan Press.
Hall, Richard. 2016. "The Communitarian Ethic of Edwards and Royce," *The Pluralist*, 11(3), 72–94.
Loomer, Bernard. 1987. *The Size of God: The Theology of Bernard Loomer in Context*. Edited by William Dean and Larry Axel. Macon, GA: Mercer University Press; also available in *American Journal of Theology and Philosophy*. Volume 8, Nos. 1 & 2 (January and May).
Mathews, Shailer. 1931. *The Growth of the Idea of God*. New York: The Macmillan Company.
Mead, George Herbert. 1934. *Mind, Self and Society from the Standpoint of a Social Behaviorist*. Edited by Charles W. Morris. Chicago, IL: The University of Chicago Press.
Meland, Bernard E. 1931. "Toward a Valid View of God," *Harvard Theological Review*, 24, 197–208.
Meland, Bernard E. 1933. "Is God Many or One?," *The Christian Century*, 50, 725–726.
Meland, Bernard E. 1948. *America's Spiritual Culture*. New York: Harper & Brothers.
Niebuhr, H. Richard. 1960. *Radical Monotheism and Western Culture: With Supplementary Essays*. New York: Harper and Row, Publishers.
Niebuhr, H. Richard. 1963. *The Responsible Self: An Essay in Christian Moral Philosophy*. New York: Harper and Row, Publishers.
Otto, Rudolf. 1958. *The Idea of the Holy: An Inquiry into the Non-rational Factor in the Idea of the Divine and its Relation to the Rational*. Translated by John W. Harvey. New York: Oxford University Press.
Royce, Josiah. 1908. *The Philosophy of Loyalty*. New York: The Macmillan Company.
Royce, Josiah. 1913a. *The Problem of Christianity*. New York: The Macmillan Company.
Rue, Loyal. 2011. *Nature is Enough: Religious Naturalism and the Meaning of Life*. New York: State University of New York Press.
Stone, Jerome A. 1992. *The Minimalist Vision of Transcendence: A Naturalist Philosophy of Religion*. New York: State University of New York Press.
Stone, Jerome A. 1993. "Broadening Care, Discerning Worth," *Process Studies*, 22(4), 194–203.
Wieman, Henry Nelson. 1933. "Is God Many or One?" *The Christian Century*. Volume L, 31, 726–727.

7
LEARNING FROM INDIGENOUS PEOPLES

We shall start this chapter with a quotation from Kathleen Norris, a non-Indian who has learned to be modest when speaking of native American spirituality.

> "What makes an Indian an Indian," [Paula Gunn Allen (Laguna) said in an interview], is a deep connection to the land, built over generations, "that imbues their psychology and eventually their spirituality and makes them one with the spirit of the land." While this comment is vulnerable to a simplistic interpretation, and Dakotans grow weary of tourists claiming to be one with the land . . . [A]fter week-long camping trips in the Black Hills, Allen touches on a deep truth. The spirit of the land is not an abstraction in western Dakota, but a real presence. . . .
>
> I suspect that when modern Americans ask "what is sacred?" they are really asking "what place is mine? what community do I belong to?" I think this explains in part the appeal of Native American religions. . . . We are seeking the tribal, anything with strong communal values and traditions. But all too often we are trying to do it on our own, as individuals. [Indian writer Linda Hogan] sepaks eloquently of her discovery: "[T]hat many of (my) non-Indian students are desperately searching for spirits, for their own souls, that something in the contemporary world has left many Euro-Americans and Europeans without a source, has left them with a longing for something they believe existed in earlier times or in tribal people. What they want is their own life, their own love for the earth, but when they speak their own words about it, they don't believe them, so they look to Indians, forgetting that enlightenment can't be found in a weekend workshop, forgetting that most Indian people are living the crisis of American life, the toxins of chemical waste."
>
> (Norris, 1993, 128–130)

[The interview with Linda Hogan is from Laura Cotelli, *Winged Words: American Indian Writers Speak* (Cotelli, 1990). Norris, a New Yorker transplanted to the high plains of western South Dakota, knows something about this.]

I make an assumption in this chapter. The old traditions have much to teach us. To be sure, much ancient wisdom has been lost. But, not all. There is still much we can learn. Nor do the followers of the old ways have all the answers, but neither do the rest of us.[1]

Clara Sue Kidwell, Homer Noley, and George E. "Tink" Tinker, in their *A Native American Theology*, put it this way:

> Americans' continuing fascination with Indians has attracted many to Native "spirituality." . . . Native Americans . . . see appropriation as an attempt by Amer-Europeans, whose ancestors conquered this continent, to "own" the heritage of Natives as thoroughly as they claim to own the land and its resources. Russell Means put the matter starkly when he names it a problem "because spirituality is the basis of our culture; if it is stolen, our culture will be dissolved. If our culture is dissolved, Indian people as such will cease to exist."
>
> (Kidwell et al., 2001, 173–174)

My hope is that I will not be stealing Indian ways. Rather, my hope is that I will find inspiration and some general clues on how to develop a religious naturalist approach.

To set out what I think I have learned from indigenous peoples, I shall speak of a series of obstacles to learning from them and of how these obstacles can be lessened. The dominant ideas of Western culture have been a mix of themes derived from scientific–industrial modernism and from monotheism. Most of the obstacles from learning from indigenous peoples arise because these older ways challenge the major assumptions of scientific modernism and of monotheism.

One way of addressing these obstacles is to point out that the distinction between modern Western culture and the ways of indigenous peoples is often exaggerated. It is at this point that Thomas Norton-Smith challenged me to rethink my viewpoint. He argues that there is a deep gulf between indigenous and modern Western outlooks. For an extended discussion of this challenge, please see the second endnote at the end of this chapter.[2]

A second way is to rethink the superiority of humans. Third, the older ways are not simply pre-scientific. The issues are far more complex. Besides these three, we need to deepen our understanding of gender, of ritual, of what it means that we are embodied. And, we shall need to discover the value of multiple images of time.

Above all, we should drop the question of which religious tradition is true, or better, or superior. To be sure we are faced with the question of the coherence of specific religious symbols with the rest of our beliefs or with their moral adequacy, but it is time to set aside the question of whose religion is superior. Instead, we should ask what we can learn from each other, in this case, what religious naturalists can learn from the older religions or cultures. (I do *not* suppose that the reader is not from one of the indigenous peoples of the world. In case she is, then like the rest of us, she will still have a lot to learn from the old ways.)

This does not mean that we should accept everything a tradition offers. It does mean that we should stop dismissing other approaches as automatically inferior. Further, we should stop reifying religions or cultures as if they have a permanent essence or clearly defined conditions for membership which cannot be crossed.

There are some values in the dominant Western paradigm, which should be retained. All cultures have their values and can contribute to the rich tapestry of the council of all beings. All cultures need to be approached with a mixture of appreciation and suspicion. Especially, we need to be appreciative and suspicious of our own culture (whatever that is). No one is sufficient for this task, of course, but let us begin.

A common question is, "Which is the true religion?" or "Which religion shall I follow?" These are questions with a monotheistic background, assuming that there is one true God and one true religion. One does not imagine the possibility of being a follower of the Jewish religion and a Christian at the same time. Likewise, one is either a Christian or a Muslim. On the other hand, there is no difficulty in following Daoist, Buddhist, and Confucian ways at the same time, as the exclusivity of monotheism is not operative in the typical Chinese outlook. In many ways, these are also modern questions, in that they recognize a variety of outlooks, assume that one of them is correct or more correct, and that a person has some autonomy in recognizing truth or giving commitment. Presupposed here are the principles of identity and non-contradiction. Of any two outlooks, if one is true, the other must be false, and also, there is a distinction between them, so that a person cannot adopt both at the same time. Boundaries between positions can be crossed, but the boundaries themselves are not permeable. The outlook or religion has become reified. One is either a Christian or not, either a believer or not. These assumptions are not always clearly made nor held by all modern thinkers. Nevertheless, these presuppositions are typical of the modernist period.

I suggest changing the question. Instead of "Which is the true religion?," let us ask, "What can we learn from another religion?" This starts without the assumption that either my religion or another is better. It does assume that it is possible and desirable to learn from another. Note also that this question does not commit one to relativism. It does not assume that there is no truth or aspect that is better or more adequate. It does assume that truth, goodness, or adequacy is not one's possession. It also assumes that we can learn from each other. (Norton-Smith reminded me that even "truth" can mean something different in various traditions. In the Western tradition, truth is generally a property of propositions, while in Native traditions, truth is a property of respectful and successful performance.)

Many gods

One major obstacle to learning from the older ways is that indigenous peoples often have many gods. This can be horrifying both to monotheists and to children of the enlightenment. Indeed, Norton-Smith argues that to speak of the "gods" of indigenous peoples is not accurate. American Indian "deities" are just like other animate beings in kind—just different in power. Indeed, his point is well taken.

The polytheism of indigenous peoples should not be overstated. There is a tension between the plurality of the gods and their unity. To some extent, the One God and the many gods are fluid concepts. John Mbiti, for example, has argued that it is inappropriate to characterize traditional African religions as polytheistic, as above the many gods, there is a highest God (Mbiti, 1970). It is common in the Hindu world to refer to the various deities as manifestations of the One ultimate reality. The Lakota seer Black Elk also was quite clear that the various gods are, in some sense, one God. (The fact that Black Elk had been a Roman Catholic catechumen for many years when he told his story to John Neihardt may call for some caution.)

If the plurality of the gods should not be overemphasized, neither should the unity of the God of monotheism. Officially, the monotheists stress one god, yet popular piety in at least some branches of Christianity seems functionally equivalent to polytheism. The petition of the aid of saints and angels in Roman Catholicism seems quite similar to the invocation of gods and deified heroes in traditional Africa. And, in both Catholic and Protestant churches, the prayers to Jesus seem remarkably akin to the bhakti's personal devotion to Lord Krishna. At the farthest end of unmitigated monotheism, in Judaism, Islam, and sometimes, Christianity, the Shekinah (divine presence), the Quran and Jesus seem to function as subordinate divine agents or powers. If the monotheist wishes to make a clear distinction between god and lesser agents or powers, then why cannot the supposed polytheist make a similar distinction between the supreme deity and lesser divine powers? *The contrast between monotheism and polytheism is not as stark and definite as the monotheists (and the sons and daughters of the European enlightenment) have claimed.*

Many religious naturalists suggest that the key category to be used in thinking about religion, at least in European languages, is "the sacred" or perhaps "the divine." Likewise, when American Indian scholars wished in a 1977 study to use a generic/technical term, they often did not refer to god or gods, but rather to "the sacred" in their book of that title (Beck et al., 1992).

One way to think about the sacred is that it is the quality of events, processes, or experiences, which seem to transcend the ordinary (to use a spatial metaphor) to manifest or point beyond the surface of things to their depths. Any god or goddess is a focal point of the sacred. So also are certain natural events or processes. The sacred, like any quality, may take different hues in its diverse appearances, and yet, has some unity amidst its diversity. Thus, we can assume that there is diversity as well as unity in the sacred. This fits well with the writer's own approach to religious naturalism, which places a strong emphasis on the plurality of the divine [Stone, 1992, 14 (Number 1) and 16 (Number 1)].

Just perhaps, the many goddesses and gods of the indigenous religions are the same as or at least analogs of the angels of monotheism. They function in many of the same ways. They both have power, more or less specific functions, and sometimes, may be petitioned. A crucial difference between gods and angels is that angels are clearly servants of the high god. However, when the many gods are seen as manifestations of the one ultimate god (as in some Hindu discussions of Brahman), their role is similar to that of servants. On the other hand, for many religious naturalists, the gods are loci of the sacred in its diverse aspects, while god or the divine is the unified aspect of the sacred.

Monotheism, of course, gives philosophical coherence to the world. If there is a single Creator, governor, and redeemer, then there is a unity and integrity to the cosmos. The many gods of paganism seem to be constantly fighting. However, this is a narrow reading of the stories of the gods. Only in some religious narratives, as in Homer and Hesiod, is the realm of the gods characterized by strife. This is not the picture we receive from the stories of many of the native peoples of the earth. Indeed, this emphasis on the strife between the gods may be a factor of European scholars, with their classical training focusing on the struggle between the Trojans and the Hellenes or perhaps between the earlier goddess religion and the later conquering tribes with their patriarchal ways. Besides, if we want a picture of strife, we need look no further than the warlike Yahweh of Judaism before the Unified Kingdom under Saul, David, and Solomon. Again, the picture of the difference between the pagans and the One True God is overdrawn. However, the world seems to have varying degrees of unity and diversity. (Following William James and some recent ecologists, it does seem to be a patchwork.) If one takes the suggestion that the gods of the early peoples are analogous to the angels of the monotheists (and perhaps also to the saints of the Roman Catholic tradition), then the one god can be seen as governing the multiple servants of the most high. On the other hand, if one takes the more radical speculation of my own pluralistic brand of religious naturalism, the world is a mosaic, and we do not need a unifying principle beyond or behind the mosaic itself. In any case, we need not reject the religious paths of the indigenous peoples just because they seem to have many gods and goddesses.

The goddess

Another serious obstacle to learning from the older ways is the prominence of a goddess among some indigenous stories. [For one of many examples, see Paula Gunn Allen, *The Sacred Hoop*, (Allen, 1986, 13–29).]

Perhaps, it would help if I made my starting point clear. My feeling has always been that the divine transcends gender, that god is neither female nor male. However, I have been listening to feminist reflection on religion and have tried to be open to what seems to be creative movements in our contemporary world. It seems that the gender neutrality of the divine is not the last word on this matter.

If, indeed, there are strong elements of patriarchy in the images and institutions of Western religion and the Abrahamic religions in general, and it seems obvious that there are, then a stance of assumed neutrality leaves this bias unchallenged and reinforces it by leaving it unchallenged.

We must use symbols, images, and metaphors for the divine if we are to speak of it at all. Surely, images of mother, sister, and feminine lover and friend are just as appropriate for the divine as images of father, brother, and masculine lover and friend. Further, these symbols are as inadequate and need to be transcended as do any symbols. We are probably at the moment when these feminine symbols can be received and need to be used.

If the divine is a quality, as I have suggested, then it can be a quality of the physical and even of the sexual. Perhaps, one of the reasons for some of our personal and social neuroses is that we separate sex and religion, that we do not combine prayer and our love life.

As a religious naturalist, I have a strong sense of the inadequacy of all religious symbols. Nevertheless, they have a place, and a very important place, in our cultural and personal lives. *She who is speaks and bodies forth with power today.*

Bodies and spirits

Some of us find it difficult to believe in unembodied spirits. That would be superstition. Others of us find it hard to believe that bodies could be gods. That would be sheer idolatry.

However, suppose that our major religious category is not "god" or "spirit," but "the sacred" or "the divine." As a quality or adjective, there is much less of a problem in conceiving of a material organism or process as having a divine quality. Furthermore, if there are spirits, one or more of them might be divine also.

Furthermore, corresponding to the sacred is "veneration," rather than worship. In official Roman Catholic theology, a person is allowed to have worship (*latria*) only for God, but to have veneration (*dulia*) for the saints. A monotheist has trouble worshipping more than one god or worshipping anything with a body. However, "veneration" of a tree does not detract from worship of god. Veneration need not be exclusive nor anti-material.

Animal deities

Some of the old ways had deities in the form of animals. When encountered, this can be a further stumbling block to a serious encounter with the primary religions. In addition to the issue of idolatry, that is, of identifying god with a finite existent, and the apparent trapping of the spiritual within the physical, we have the additional factor that in the modern world, animals have generally been considered to be inferior to humans, often with a focus on inferior rationality or morality.

Two comments can be made. In the *first place*, serious thought should be given to the alleged inferiority of animals. Clearly, animals are different. Indeed, each species is different from all of the others. In many respects, difference, not inferiority, is the category that should be used. An ascription of inferiority can easily lead to a justification for domination and mistreatment. To be sure, animals are inferior to humans in many ways, but this is an aspect of difference. By the same token, we are inferior to animals in other ways.

When two species or individuals differ, one species or individual may be said to be superior in respect to the difference. I am larger than the male Northern cardinal in the horse chestnut tree, and he can call more clearly and beautifully. I am superior in size, and he is superior in song.

For these types of superiority, "difference" is a better term. Furthermore, for any superiority on the part of one species, there is often a corresponding superiority in the other. I can camouflage myself to hide from or make weapons to kill my enemies. However, the cardinal can warn his enemies off or can fly from them. It is a trade-off. Neither of us is clearly superior in relation to our enemies (except possibly for a moral superiority in the cardinal, in that he normally does not kill his enemy, if we can speak of morality here).

To be sure, we are more rational than other animals. Possibly. Rationality is a complex notion involving several intellectual skills. Dolphins, elephants, corvids (crows and related birds), and of course, chimpanzees and bonobos all exhibit high degrees of some intellectual skills, and I have heard amazing anecdotes about pigs. The thinking of humans is possibly more plastic or variable and possibly more abstract than other species, allowing for more novelty and abstraction than that of other animals. But, both of these strengths have corresponding weaknesses. Plasticity allows a great degree of error and abstraction can lose touch with concrete actuality. To focus on morality, humans are possibly capable of more freely chosen or habitual moral behavior than most other species, but at the same time, are capable of more immoral behavior.

In the *second place*, most indigenous people do not *identify* the one monotheistic god with an animal. Often, the plant or animal is a manifestation of a god or the divine in general. There is a difference between identity and manifestation. The general comments made above on the relation of "spirit" and body" hold here.

Finally, religious naturalism suggests that the old ways can best be appropriated not as the worship of many gods in nature, but as the veneration of and reception to the divine quality of some or all aspects of this world.

Pre-scientific modes of thought?

The religious ways of the primary people are often rejected as basically unscientific. This is a complex issue, and I can only sketch some tentative solutions. These issues should not be sidestepped, however.

In the first place, many apparently unscientific practices of the primary peoples achieve results, which are not explainable with current scientific theories, but scientific theories could, in principle, be developed to account for them. Many healing practices, herbalism, and acupuncture, for example, have a high rate of success, as far as we can tell from the evidence. (See my comments on traditional African healing practices in Stone, 1982.) Some of the cures or mitigations are not fully understood by current Western scientific knowledge, but we can envision the direction research could take and the fair possibility of achieving such understanding. The cures often seem legitimate. We have here cases of Western scientific thought not yet caught up with the facts. No major revolution in our understanding of science will probably be indicated by successful pursuit of empirical investigation in these areas.

More difficult are cases, such as the complex phenomenon of shamanism, which do seem to run counter to Western scientific notions. Here is a genuine tension pulling in opposite directions. On the one hand, it is well to give up a naive notion of the superiority of science as a closed system, especially with the corollary relegation of other cultures to the limbo of alleged inferior intellect. On the other hand, there are values to the pursuit of intelligence and careful inquiry, which we neglect at our peril. Some of Aldo Leopold's most significant environmental insights came as the result of his careful attention to the facts as he could best discern them. Feminist philosophers of science have been attempting to develop a theory of evidence within a holistic epistemology (Harding, 1986; 1987; Nelson, 1990, especially the Introduction and Chapter 6).

It is important to understand that scientific theories are extrapolations from observations and experiments. Unconsidered variables may very well make these theories inapplicable to regions not yet observed. My own scientific understanding does not encourage me to anticipate that I will be visited by birds or animals in the flesh if I waited on a mountain for a vision. However, it would be foolish of me to maintain that such a visit would not occur. Vertebrates have greater awareness of us and are ready to communicate on more levels than Western moderns often are prone to credit.

In addition, much occurs in dreams. It would be foolish to dismiss all dreams as subjective in the sense of arbitrary and unsubstantiated. I have come to enough insight and resolution of conflict in my dreams not to dismiss their significance automatically. Further, when a student of mine reported that a wolf appeared to her in a vision, while I do not think that either a physical wolf or the spirit of a wolf (defining spirit narrowly) visited her, it would be narrow-minded of me to say that the cultural and experiential materials, which wolves supply, had no objective bearing on her vision. Indeed, viewed generously, it was the spirit of the wolf that came to her.

Finally, the old ways should not be taken simply as either pro- or anti-scientific. The issues are far more complex. We can, at certain times, say that in our best judgment, a cognitive judgment can be reached on scientific grounds. For example, I find it reasonable to affirm that levitation does not occur. However, I would not immediately ostracize a Hindu philosopher who assumed it was a matter of course. And, if I found Jesus walking the streets, I would look for the mirrors, or at least into my psyche. Having made such a judgment, we need to remember that thoughtful and rational people, operating from different epistemic principles, could arrive at different judgments. While holding fast to our judgments, if need be, we need not automatically cast those people into the limbo of intellectual darkness.

Time

It is customary to distinguish between the Biblical and later Western outlooks from other worldviews by differentiating between a linear as opposed to a cyclical view of time. Indeed, this distinction goes back at least to Augustine. The linear view of time has, of course, been secularized in the modern view of progress and in the Marxist dialectic of history. These linear views are usually accompanied with the assumption of the superiority of the linear view as supporting a forward-looking dynamism.

Perhaps, we should take a new look at the cyclical view. There is much routine and repetition in our daily lives. The linear view treats much of this as drudgery, chores to be finished, perhaps derogated as women's work or for the janitors or clerical staff, so that the rest of us can get on with the real work. Changing images will not bring new life to maintenance or nurturance functions, but a linear view of time can easily exacerbate their drudgery. One problem with a linear view is that when a forward movement is frustrated, everything that leads up to it seems pointless. Also, the present seems to have value only from the future. For a thoughtful position on how a cyclical view of time has a stronger pragmatic adequacy than the religious and secular apocalyptic versions of the linear view, see Starhawk (1979).

Much of our life is a dynamic movement among myriad things. It is inevitable that much of our work will be cyclical or nearly so. Some of it is very repetitious, such as doing laundry or driving to work. Some of it is quasi-cyclical, as in exercise or rest or in correcting a personal or social pendulum swing. Much of this is the yin–yang restoration of a balance. None of this is *ipso facto* meaningless.

Many primary peoples give great importance to the practice of the dance and to the dance as a major image for life. In a dance, there is value in both the repetition and the innovation, in both dancing alone, as couples, or in a group. The dance can give significance to both the individual and the group. It makes reconciliation as important as competition. Normally, there are no winners in a dance. For a bioregionalist view, a dance celebrates place, not journey.

The dance is not the only appropriate metaphor. Conflict and decay are realities, as well as boredom and frustration, loneliness and despair. There is a need for hope as well as for repetition. We need a plurality of metaphors for life. But, surely, we need to restore the view that when a forward movement is frustrated, everything that leads up to it is not pointless. The present has a value of its own, which does not derive from the future. The dying infant has its value. (For comments on dance, see "The Ceremonial Motion of Indian Time: Long Ago, So Far," in Allen, 1986, 147–154; LaChapelle, 1988; Gary Snyder, "The Same Old Song and Dance," in Snyder, 1990, 48–53; Peters, 2002.)

Sacred places

To recapture the spirit of the older ways, we shall need a sense of sacred places: trees, rocks, prairies, rivers, and mountains. Part of the problem is that we do not wish to tie down the sacred to one place. If god is everywhere, we say, then god cannot be localized. On the other hand, we build sanctuaries where we often feel the presence of the divine. If we can go to special places, built by humans, which are designated as sacred, surely we can go to special places, shaped naturally, which are recognized as sacred. Indeed, the human and the natural can cooperate, as when tradition or an act of consecration acknowledge the sacred place. There is a strong monotheistic tradition of cutting down the sacred groves. What we need is to realize that to have a sense of sacred place is not tree worship, in the sense of confusing the one Creator with a plant, but is rather the acknowledgment of the awesome, of the overriding and overwhelming. To recover some sense of the meaningfulness of the primal traditions, we need to rethink the notion of sacred place. For a religious naturalist, it is not hard to recover the sense of sacred place. The religious naturalist is, to begin with, open to sacred qualities of some experiences. Sometimes, this sacred dimension will be especially evoked by the qualities of a special location. For a theist, there can be Bethels, places associated with epiphanies. There is no theoretical reason, if the sacred dimension of life is recognized, for the sacredness of certain places not to be recognized by theists or religious naturalists.

When the sacred is recognized, there is a very strong motive to preserve, even defend it. For this reason, the recognition and also the nurture of these experiences has a key place in the recovery of an appreciative stance toward the special places of this world.

Gary Snyder has a word of wisdom about sacred places. We have lost much. Some places we can once again find to be sacred ground if we turn off the electronics, slow down, walk, and listen. However, we may have to wait until the places speak to us. Our ears are weak. But, if we wait, some of these places may yet name themselves to us. (See Gary Snyder, "Good, Wild, Sacred," in Snyder, 1990, 78–96.)

There is a danger of idolatry, of course. The Nazis sacralized place, blood, and soil. However, monotheists can idolize the finite as easily as anyone else.

Ritual

Delores LaChapelle has given thoughtful attention to re-establishing ritual. Ed Eagle Man McGaa has devoted much care to making the essentials of Lakota ceremony available to non-Indian audiences, although there is controversy about his work (LaChapelle, 1976; LaChapelle, 1988, 54–109; McGaa, 1990; McGaa, 1992; Gill 1987).

Although some people are eager to try out exotic rituals or "play Indian," some of these rituals are obstacles to observers. Sometimes, a person of one tradition can find rituals from another heritage to be alien. Sometimes, a person from the enlightenment or puritan tradition will disdain ritual in principle. However, the rituals of nature should be no more of an obstacle than any set of rituals. As we come to recognize the importance of ritual in human life, the rituals of indigenous peoples will become more appreciated. However, these rituals should not be appropriated. Rather, they should be used as inspiration for the development of analogous ceremonies.

Non-natives and indigenous ideas and ways: appropriation or learning?

There is a very serious objection to this entire project of learning from old ways by non-natives. It has come from a variety of sources and is often presented in a thoughtful manner. The general drift is that it is disrespectful of native peoples to treat their ideas as "resources." Also, when an idea is taken from one culture, it loses its meaning when set in a new context. "Cultural cannibalism" is what Greta Gaard calls it. Particular mention may be made of Greta Gaard's objection to the use of American Indian ideas by ecofeminists. A similar objection is made by Ward Churchill of the American Indian Movement. Likewise, Gerald Larson inveighs against mining Asian traditions for environmental thinking (Gaard, 1993, 295–314; Churchill, 1993, 43–48; Larson, 1989, 267–278). More recently, Laurelyn Whitt has mounted a sophisticated attack on extractive biocolonialism, whereby indigenous agricultural and medical knowledge is legally converted into private intellectual property and sold in the marketplace (Whitt, 2009).

My response to these objections is first that seeking to learn from another is most respectful. It is a recognition that one has something to learn and that the other has important insights that need to be explored. To be sure, such learning can be done arrogantly or flippantly. However, the danger of abuse does not mean that you should not do it.

In the second place, the thing to do is to admit that we are transforming these ideas. We are not "going native." Rather, we are developing new ways, hopefully creative ways. There is much precedent for one culture to learn from another. Chinese, Korean, Japanese, Indonesian, modern African, Arabic, Jewish, European, Plains Indian, indeed most cultures have learned from other cultures, and in so doing, transformed what they learned, often in creative ways.

There are understandable historical reasons for cultural provincialism and the frequent temptation to ethnocentrism. My proposal is that we overcome this provincialism, not because the others are right and we are wrong, but because we all have much to learn from each other.

Norton-Smith advised me that it is wrong to appropriate for two reasons. One is that, following Nelson Goodman, because radically different linguistic traditions will have radically different ontologies, then appropriating a notion from an indigenous tradition will be plucking an item of that tradition from its original context and giving it a Western interpretation. Indeed, this will be a double misinterpretation. Second, in indigenous traditions, knowledge is a gift, not an appropriation.

Perhaps, the answer is that, rather than seeking to appropriate ideas and rituals, we modern Westerners can learn from indigenous peoples some general directions in which to travel, but that we will be venturing on our own roads. We can learn from them the importance of rethinking what we mean by gods and deities. We can learn from them the importance of rethinking our own relation to place and land, to ritual and dance, to time and tradition. This would indeed be a great gift.

Notes

1 Parts of this chapter are adapted from my "On Listening to Indigenous Peoples and Neo-Pagans: Obstacles to Appropriating the Older Ways," (Stone, 1997).
2 Professor Thomas Norton-Smith, former Chair of the Committee for Indigenous Philosophy of the American Philosophical Association and a member of the Shawnee tribe of American Indians, has challenged me to rethink my viewpoint in this chapter (Norton-Smith, 2010). There are profound experiential differences as well as deep philosophical differences at work here. Norton-Smith has lived experience in both the Western academic world and contemporary American Indian life. He has a PhD from the University of Illinois and teaches at Kent State University. He is also an enrolled member of the Piqua Sept Shawnee Tribe. He can speak, from first-hand knowledge, of the solemn responsibility of participating in the tribal Bread Dance. Besides his participation in both contexts, he has reflected on this dual heritage with the philosophical categories of Nelson Goodman. Drawing on Goodman's *Ways of Worldmaking*, Norton-Smith argues that "words make worlds," that symbol systems—language, ritual, etc.—create different ontologies, and radically different languages create radically different worlds (Goodman, 1978; Norton-Smith, 2010). Thus, the distinction between the Western and the indigenous worlds is a deep gulf.

In view of Norton-Smith's lived experiences, it is with some hesitation that I disagree with him. Although there are profound differences between the Western and the indigenous worlds, there is enough analogical similarity that the indigenous world can suggest that there are alternatives to the dominant contemporary Western outlook.

Chapters 4 through 7 of Norton-Smith's *The Dance of Person and Place* are a very helpful delineation of four themes, which he finds in American Indian philosophy: the importance of relatedness, the expansion of the concept of persons to include animals and other non-human beings, the semantic potency of performance, and circularity (rather than linearity) as a world-ordering principle. Three out of four of these themes have reinforced my own thinking, feeling, and acting to explore alternatives to contemporary Western outlook. This should be clear from this and the previous chapters. The one theme from which I have failed to draw inspiration is the semantic power of performance, as in naming and gifting.

Bibliography

Allen, Paula Gunn. 1986. *The Sacred Hoop: Recovering the Feminine in American Indian Traditions*. Boston, MA: Beacon Press.
Beck, Peggy V., Anna Lee Walters and Nia Francisco. 1992. *The Sacred: Ways of Knowledge, Sources of Life*. Tsaile, AZ: Navajo Community College Press.
Cotelli, Laura. 1990. *Winged Words: American Indian Writers Speak*. Lincoln, NB: University of Nebraska Press.
Christ, Carol P. and Judith Plaskow, Eds. 1979/1992. *Womanspirit Rising: A Feminist Reader in Religion*. New York: Harper Collins Publishers.
Churchill, Ward. 1993. "Another Dry White Season," *Z Magazine* 6, 10, 43–48.
Gaard, Greta. 1993. "Ecofeminism and Native American Cultures: Pushing the Limits of Cultural Impoverishment?" in *Ecofeminism: Women, Animals, Nature*. Edited by Greta Gaard. Philadelphia, PA: Temple University Press, 295–314.
Gill, Sam. 1987. *Native American Religious Action: A Performance Approach to Religion*. Columbia, SC: University of South Carolina Press.
Goodman, Nelson. 1978. *Ways of Worldmaking*. Indianapolis, IN: Hackett.
Harding, Sandra. 1986. *The Science Question in Feminism*. Ithaca, NY: Cornell University Press.
Harding, Sandra. 1987. "The Method Question," *Hypatia*, 2 (Fall).

Harding, Sandra. 1995. "Is Science Multicultural? Challenges, Resources, Opportunities, Uncertainties," in Edited by David Theo Goldberg, *Multiculturalism: A Reader*. London: Blackwell's.
Kidwell, Clara Sue, Homer Noley and Tinker, George E. 2001. *A Native American Theology*. Maryknoll, Orbis Books.
LaChapelle, Delores. 1976. *Earth Festivals*. Silverton, CO: Finn Hill Arts.
LaChapelle, Delores. 1988. *Sacred Land, Sacred Sex, Rapture of the Deep*. Durango, CO: Kivaki Press.
Larson, Gerald James. 1989. "'Conceptual Resources' in South Asia for 'Environmental Ethics,'" in Edited by J. Baird Callicott and Roger T. Ames, *Nature in Asian Traditions of Thought: Essays in Environmental Philosophy*. Albany: State University of New York Press; reprinted in Susan J. Armstrong and Richard G. Botzler, *Environmental Ethics: Divergence and Convergence* (New York: NY: McGraw-Hill).
Mbiti, John. 1970. *Concepts of God in Africa*. New York, NY: Praeger Publishing Company.
McGaa, Ed Eagle Man. 1990. *Mother Earth Spirituality: Native American Paths to Healing Ourselves and Our World*. San Francisco, CA: Harper Collins Publishers.
McGaa, Ed Eagle Man. 1992. *Rainbow Tribe: Ordinary People Journeying on the Red Road*. San Francisco, CA: Harper Collins Publishers.
Nelson, Lynn Hankinson. 1990. *Who Knows: From Quine to a Feminist Empiricism*. Philadelphia: Temple University Press.
Norris, Kathleen. 1993. *Dakota: A Spiritual Geography*. Boston, MA: Houghton Mifflin Company.
Peters, Karl E. 2002. *Dancing with the Sacred: Evolution, Ecology, and God*. Harrisburg, PA: Trinity Press International.
Snyder, Gary. 1990. "The Same Old Song and Dance," in *The Practice of the Wild*. San Francisco: CA: North Point Press, 48–53.
Starhawk. 1979. in Edited by Christ, Carol P. and Judith Plaskow, 1979, 1992. *Womanspirit Rising: A Feminist Reader in Religion*. New York: Harper Collins Publishers.
Stone, Jerome A. 1982. "A View of African Culture" in *AITIA: Philosophy-Humanities Magazine*.
Stone, Jerome A. 1992. *The Minimalist Vision of Transcendence: A Naturalist Philosophy of Religion*. Albany, NY: State University of New York Press.
Stone, Jerome A. 1997. "On Listening to Indigenous Peoples and Neo-pagans: Obstacles to Appropriating The Older Ways," in Edited by Charley D. Hardwick and Donald A. Crosby, *Pragmatism, Neo- Pragmatism and Religion: Conversations with Richard Rorty*. New York, NY: Peter Lang.
Whitt, Laurelyn. 2009. *Science, Colonialism, and Indigenous Peoples: The Cultural Politics of Law and Knowledge*. New York: Cambridge University Press.

8

RELIGIOUS NATURALISM IN THE PUBLIC SQUARE

Toward a public ecotheology

What is a public theologian? A public theologian, as I use the term, is a public intellectual who uses recognized images of transcendence, such as "sacred," "spirit," or "creation," in addressing major public issues.[1]

First of all, a public theologian is a kind of public intellectual, that is, she is a thinker who addresses significant issues faced by the public and who speaks to a major section of the public. This means that the public intellectual is addressing neither narrowly conceived ecclesiastical or academic problems nor speaking to denominational or academic audiences. The public intellectual, by the width of her issues and publics, will be transdisciplinary, willing to stick her neck out into areas where she is not expert. Among current theologians, John Cobb comes clearly into focus. Among environmental writers, I think of Aldo Leopold, Rachel Carson, the Ehrlichs, Gary Snyder, Charlene Spretnak, and Delores LaChapelle.[2] These are people who have the courage to explore away from the safety of a narrowly defined discipline. They are willing to make mistakes, to be wrong, in the desire to get a larger view of our complex home and what we are doing to it.

In the second place, as I conceive the idea, a public theologian is a special kind of public intellectual. Specifically, the public theologian is a public intellectual who uses religious symbols, that is, recognized symbols of transcendence, in addressing these issues.

The alternative to such a public theology, it seems to me, is to surrender these symbols to the dogmatists. Rather than surrender these symbols to the fundamentalists and the confessional theologians, I would rather fight to clarify and vivify these symbols, except for the key central symbol of god. I would rather we undertake the process of revising these symbols than throw in the towel. (I used to wish to preserve the god-symbol. However, in Chapter 5, I have indicated my reluctance to use this word, at least in most contexts. This is perhaps the major fault line separating me from my liberal Christian friends.)

What then is a naturalistic public theologian? A naturalistic public theologian is a public theologian who either avoids traditional religious symbols with their supernaturalistic baggage (such as the signers of the first *Humanist Manifesto*) or else revises them in a naturalistic manner (such as Henry Nelson Wieman, Gordon Kaufman, eventually, and Karl Peters). A naturalistic public theologian is likely to use such phrases as "the beloved community," "the inherent worth and dignity of all persons," and "sacred." John Dewey was a naturalistic philosopher who engaged in naturalistic public theology in his *A Common Faith* (1934). There, he used the word god in a revised, deliberately naturalistic sense, which shocked many of his humanistically inclined contemporaries.

Not everyone will take the route of public theology, of course. The major competing options to public theology are, it seems, confessional, kerygmatic, or authoritarian theologies on the one hand, and secular ideologies on the other. The problem with confessional theologies is that they do not speak outside of their own communities, and there are too many of us outside confessional boundaries. The problem I have with authoritarian theologies, which overlap with the confessional, is that they are dogmatic, they seem to have all of the answers. Thus public theology, as I conceive it, is not what many Evangelicals, Catholics, Jews, and Muslims are doing. On the other hand, a public theologian should be able to speak in a way that many traditionally oriented people could resonate with, even agree with, what the public theologian affirms. How what such a theologian has to say would translate to the non-theistic and the indigenous religious traditions is more problematic and will take time to sort out. However, in principle, good public theology should be intelligible to persons of any religious background, given a willingness to listen.

On the other hand, public theology is also an alternative to a secular framework. The symbols of transcendence have power. Such symbols address the problem of overall meaning and significance. Like any ruling metaphor, they can supply that sense of the whole, which at least some people seem to crave. Also, such symbols give direction. They lure in a direction that could be called the affirmation of life and existence, or wonder and appreciation.

How do you proceed in public theology? You use logical rigor and detailed empirical inquiry as much as you can, but there are limits, due to the complexity of the problems, the shortness of the time, and the multiplicity of listeners with diverse backgrounds. Finally, you have to appeal, to invoke, and to speak. While doing what you can to inform and demonstrate to your audience, finally, you have to appeal to the audience's own understanding, insight, and good sense.

You also proceed in public theology by invoking the symbols of transcendence. You often cannot stop to clarify thoroughly or justify sufficiently these symbols. You have to assume that these symbols are sufficiently understood and have enough cogency and power to function in the dialog.

We must say, each in our own way, "This is the way it seems to me, what does it look like to you?" or "I think we should do this now, what do you say?" Some of us might even say, invoking the key Abrahamic symbol of transcendence,

"This is where God seems to be calling us" or perhaps in a more animistic vein, "Ley us tread softly, for surely a spirit lives here. What do you sense?" Or, in language I usually prefer, "Here seems to be the creative edge. What do you discern?"

In using these symbols of transcendence, we do not have infallible oracles from the mouth of god, or a scriptural blueprint or pronouncements *ex cathedra*. What we do have is our own responsibility for these symbols of transcendence.

In all of this talk of public theology, this attempt to make connections with the religious beliefs of a wide variety of people, in no way do I wish to substitute religious judgment for appropriate scientific or common sense judgments. We are responsible for our choices, our actions, and even our images within the context of our genetic and cultural inheritance. When former U.S. Secretary of the Interior, James Watt, said that we need not do anything about the environmental crisis because the end of the world was coming soon, he was speaking irresponsibly. When the Pope in Mexico spoke about the need to have more Catholic children, he was acting irresponsibly. The time is long past for us to tolerate any religious idea.

While this entire book has been an attempt at public theology, this chapter develops the notion of public theology explicitly. The remainder of this chapter gives further precision to this idea of public theology by dialog with some outstanding recent public theologians.

Paul Tillich

Paul Tillich was a prominent philosopher of religion and Lutheran theologian who made a strong effort to bridge the gap between secular culture and Christian thought. His academic career stretched from Germany in the 1920s to Union Theological Seminary in New York, Harvard, and the University of Chicago roughly from the 1930s to the mid-1960s. He delved deeply into art, literature, and psychology. He was active in the socialist movement in Germany, and later in New York he was in frequent dialog with psychotherapists and leaders in personality theory.[3]

Tillich has a rich and very complex social ethic. His treatment of the loss of humanness in contemporary society and his analyses of capitalism, Marxism, and religious socialism are important. However, I wish to concentrate on his concepts of "the Protestant Principle" (Tillich, 1948, xiii–xxix, 161–181, 273–316). By the Protestant Principle, he means that no human social organization or program should be absolutized. Nothing is sacrosanct, in the sense of being above question or criticism. (This does not contradict the basic theme of this book that nature is sacred, and its many things might be considered sacred. I insist that sacredness does not imply methodological insulation.) This Protestant Principle is a symbol of transcendence, although within the context of his concept of god as the ground of being, it is not a naturalistic symbol. It is a powerful tool of prophetic critique against the idolatrous pretentions of totalitarianism, religious fanaticism, national chauvinism, and corporate capitalism. Of course, living by means of this principle is not easy.

Tillich's notion of the Protestant Principle is related to his notion of god. Tillich is known for his definition of god as the "object of our ultimate concern." But, right now, I wish to focus on other ways that Tillich spoke of god. He often spoke of god as being-itself, the power of being, or the unconditional. But, for our purposes, the phrase to concentrate on is his oft-repeated statement that "God is the ground of being" or "God is the ground and abyss of being" (Tillich, 1951, 235–238).

By the metaphor of "ground," Tillich suggests two lines for our imagination. First, as the ground of being, god is not a being among other beings, even the highest being. Thus, to speak of god as the supreme being is to reduce god to the level of beings, making god just another being, even if the supreme being. Thus, Tillich was sympathetic toward atheists who deny that there is a supreme being.

Now, Tillich will sometimes speak of god as the ground *and* abyss of being. Thus, "abyss" is another metaphor paired with "ground." It suggests that the ground of all things is "infinitely" removed from them, that because god is not a being, god cannot be found within the realm of beings, that god does not literally act in history or interfere with the natural order of events (here Tillich comes close to religious naturalism), that the existence of god (a blasphemous phrase!) cannot be the conclusion of any proof, certainly that evidence for god cannot be found empirically, and that when religion is understood properly, there can be no conflict between science and religion. All of this is suggested by the notion that god is the ground (and abyss) of being. All of these terms, such as ground of being, are metaphorical of, as Tillich would say, symbols. Indeed, even the term "God" is itself a symbol for which cannot be captured in language.

The Protestant Principle, when understood as a way of living in history in relation to the ground of being, thus attaches significance to particular moments of special importance, placing them in a paradoxical relation to the absolute, which charges them with absolute significance, and yet, by placing them under the judgment of the absolute prevents them from becoming absolutes themselves. The existential significance of this concept of the Protestant Principle is that it allows one to move beyond cynicism and indifference and to take seriously the task of making decisions and acting, without falling into utopianism or idolatry on the other. Thus, the great value of Tillich for public theology is that he points to a way between absolutizing any human movement or program, such as communism, capitalism, democracy, or religion and the cynical or despairing rejection of any significance to human endeavors. The Protestant Principle is one of his ways of stating this.

Tillich's method rests on his notion of god as the ground and abyss of being and meaning. God as ground gives being and meaning to human endeavors, but god as abyss withholds absolute being or meaning. Everything human stands under judgment, to use a traditional religious phrase. Naturalism does not employ the categories of ground and abyss. It only knows about beings and their processes and relations. But, like Tillich, it is faced with the problem of significance: how to avoid the Scylla of fanatic attachment and the Charybdis of indifference. The answer of religious naturalism, at least as this writer sees it, is to recognize relative worth and to refuse to grant absolute worth. There are things of importance, and some activities are worthwhile. We need not fall into indifference or despair. On the other hand, we must protest against any absolutizing or idolizing of our projects and plans. Nothing is beyond question or criticism, including our own glimpses of sacredness.

Jeffrey Stout

A significant contribution to the issue of using religious arguments in a public context in a democratic society comes from Princeton philosopher Jeffrey Stout in his *Democracy and Tradition* (Stout, 2004). While his entire argument is logically complex, set in a description of the nineteenth- and twentieth-century development of the democratic tradition, containing some passages of dense philosophical prose and in dialog with a number of contemporary philosophers and theologians, the outlines of his position can be stated fairly simply, as he does in his Introduction and Conclusion.

He is "trying to articulate a form of pluralism, one that citizens with strong religious commitments can accept and that welcomes their full participation in public life" (Stout, 2004, 296). He sees this pluralism, not as a philosophical theory, which needs to be imposed on our political life, but rather an already existing feature of our political life, but which needs articulation so that the current tendency of many Christians not to engage in public life can be overcome. Another of his aims is "to persuade seriously committed religious citizens . . . that identifying with the civic nation in a democratic republic like ours need not conflict with their theological convictions" (Stout, 2004, 297). Thus, a religious person can participate in our political discourse "wholeheartedly without implicitly discounting one's theological convictions" (Stout, 2004, 298).

A key part of Stout's approach is his development of the notion that there is a democratic tradition. Stout analyses a number of figures in this tradition, such as Ralph Waldo Emerson, Walt Whitman, John Dewey, and refers to many more, including William Cobbett, William Hazlitt, Mary Wollstonecraft, and Wendell Berry. Now, while it might seem obvious that there is such a tradition, there are a number of contemporary writers who elaborate a rational or contractual approach to democratic theory that downplays such a tradition. (Stout has in mind especially John Rawls. I cannot reproduce his detailed analysis of Rawls here. See Stout, 2004, 65–77.) Indeed, downplaying democracy as a tradition is not new. As Stout puts it: "Many early champions of modern democracy, influenced by Enlightenment philosophy, had portrayed themselves as the heralds of a complete break with the past; 'tradition was a name for what they opposed.'" In opposition to this, Stout claims that: "There is much to be gained by abandoning the image of democracy as essentially opposed to tradition, as a negative force that tends by its nature to undermine culture and the cultivation of virtue. Democracy is a culture, a tradition in its own right" (Stout, 2004, 13).

There are other writers who shy away from enthusiastic participation in the democratic process because they think that it really has no such tradition. (Stout has Stanley Hauerwas and Alasdair MacIntyre in mind. See Chapters 5 and 6 of

Stout, 2004). Indeed, such traditionalists "see democracy as an essentially negative, leveling force." Such traditionalists "are tempted to withdraw from democratic discourse with the heathen" (Stout, 2004, 12).

According to Stout, many democratic theorists as well as religious traditionalists, equate democracy with secularism. They hold that "the political culture of our democracy implicitly requires the policing or self-censorship of religious expression in the political arena" (Stout, 2004, 84). To challenge this view, Stout refers to a number of historical examples of persons in American history who do not shy away from using religious language in the political arena. His examples include the abolitionists, Abraham Lincoln, Dorothy Day, Martin Luther King, Jr., Rosemary Radford Ruether, and Wendell Berry.

Another idea that is important for Stout, although he does not give it thorough elaboration, is that democratic practices depend on and also help develop positive character traits or virtues. He defends "the notion that democratic questioning and reason-giving are a sort of practice, one that involves and inculcates virtues, including justice" (Stout, 2004, 152). Among the virtues that can guide "a citizen through the process of discursive exchange and political decision making" are "civility, or the ability to listen with an open mind, or the will to pursue justice where it leads, or the temperance to avoid taking and causing offense needlessly, or the practical wisdom to discern the subtleties of a discursive situation." They also include "the courage to speak candidly, . . . [and] the tact to avoid sanctimonious cant, . . . [and] the poise to respond to unexpected arguments, . . . [and] the humility to ask forgiveness from those who have been wronged" (Stout, 2004, 85). Among the champions of discourse about democratic virtues, Stout lists Walt Whitman, Mary Wollstonecraft, William Hazlitt, Ralph Waldo Emerson, Henry David Thoreau, and John Dewey (Stout, 2004, 28).

In looking at the contemporary American scene, Stout suggests that many secular liberals might wish to argue that "the only way to save our democracy from the religious Right is to inhibit the expression of religious reasons in the public square." However, he goes on, "Aside from whatever theoretical errors might lie behind this argument, it is foolhardy to suppose that anything" like this "will succeed in a country with our religious and political history." Indeed, "secular liberalism has unwittingly fostered the decline of the religious Left by persuading religious intellectuals that liberal society is intent on excluding the expression of their most strongly felt convictions. The new traditionalism portrays the religious Left as *a mutation of secular liberalism* that is infecting the churches like a deadly virus." However, Stout points out that:

> This picture gets all of the relevant historical patterns wrong. The first modern revolutionaries were not secular liberals; they were radical Calvinists. Among the most important democratic movements in American history were Abolitionism and the Civil Rights movement; both of these were based largely in the religious communities.
>
> (Stout, 2004, 299–330)

Thus, Stout is asking us to recognize that:

> Democracy involves substantive normative commitments, but does not presume to settle in advance the ranking of our highest values. . . . It takes for granted that reasonable people will differ in their conceptions of piety, in their grounds for hope, in their ultimate concerns, and in their speculations about salvation. Yet it holds that people who differ on such matters can still exchange reasons with one another intelligibly, cooperate in crafting political arrangements that promote justice and decency in their relations with one another, and do both of these things without compromising their integrity.
> (Stout, 2004, 298)

Stout is very helpful in his reminder that there is a tradition of using religious language in the political arena to foster progressive directions. This tradition includes the abolitionists, Lincoln, Dorothy Day, Martin Luther King, Rosemary Radford Ruether, and Wendell Berry. What needs to be added is that there is a growing tradition of religious naturalists who either use non-theistic religious language or else use naturalistic god-language in political discourse. Among these are Henry Nelson Wieman, Victor Anderson, Gordon Kaufman (in his later writings), and Carol Wayne White's use of religious naturalism to articulate the liberation struggle of African Americans (Wieman, 1958; Anderson, 2008; Kaufman, 2004, Chapter 2, 32–52; Kaufman, 2006, Chapter 3, 63–88; White, 2016). Stout's treatment of democratic virtues could also profitably be extended in a naturalistic direction.

William Dean

In his book, *The Religious Critic in American Culture*, William Dean argues that America needs religious critics. By this term, he does not refer to what goes on in churches, synagogues, or mosques. By religious critic, he means public intellectuals who critically analyze and perhaps reinterpret a people's sense of the whole and what is of ultimate importance in that whole.

In this book, he argues that "the sacred" is a convention composed of images in the spiritual culture of a people, images of what is ultimately important (Dean, 1994, 133–139).[4] This set of images is subject to constant reinterpretation. However, in its turn, it also influences the people themselves. In this way, it is partially independent of the people and their interpretations. To illustrate this, Dean refers to the Constitution of the United States, which, he suggests, is not reducible either to a written document or to the interpretations of the U.S. Supreme Court. Thus, the Constitution functions as a sacred convention. Likewise, god is a social convention, a social construction with a life of its own, which has unpredictable effects on the society within which it operates. (Dean also deftly analyzes jazz, football, and the movies as part of America's "spiritual culture," a technical term for him.)

The partial independence of a sacred convention is shown in that the effects of a sacred convention exceed what is predictable from the images that contribute to that convention. The sacred, like any socially constructed reality, can turn back on the society and act in ways that were not intended. The sacred, then, is a living tradition about what is ultimately significant, is constantly being reinterpreted, is completely historical, and is partially independent of its society. [For further development of Dean's notion of god as a social convention, including analogies with common law as well as constitutional law, and for his use of American pragmatism and the early twentieth-century Chicago theologians, especially Shailer Mathews, see his *The American Spiritual Culture* (Dean, 2002, 70–86). For his argument that the empirical American philosophers, William James, John Dewey, and Alfred North Whitehead and their "theological proteges" offer to Martin Heidegger, Jacques Derrida, and Michel Foucault and the theologies rooted in them a "cosmological foundation," see his *American Religious Empiricism* (Dean, 1986, 48–50). For a similar argument that American philosophy, especially that of Charles Sanders Peirce, offers such a foundation to theologians and philosophers taking inspiration from European continental sources, see Robert Neville's *The Highroad Around Modernism* (Neville, 1992).]

Such a convention is not a mere projection, first because it has effects on its society, and second, because it works in ways that cannot be strictly predicted. The sacredness of the sacred depends both on its partial independence and on the fact that it involves what is ultimately important, responding to a people's deepest questions and suggesting ultimately important answers. God is such a convention within the life of the American public.

Although it is subject to continual reinterpretation and its effects are unpredictable, a sacred convention is conservative in its own way, as it stands in a line of past conventions. A convention is tied to its previous interpretations with a rather short leash. As a public construction in a chain of interpretations, a sacred convention is neither subjective nor objective. Rather, it is formed by an objective public past interacting with current subjectivity creativity, but reducible to neither.

I have learned much from Dean. He is valuable, in that he analyzes the ongoing life of a convention and its continuing role in the history of people in a direction farther than I have taken it. Our fundamental difference is that he focuses on the god-symbol, whereas I am willing to use less theistic symbols such as "the Beloved Community," or "Justice." His recent concern with mystery and "the irony of atheism" may or may not be far removed from the religious naturalist's sense of the sacred. When secular culture is pursued all the way, Dean finds a religious ground at the end, a view with a strong sense of the *via negativa* (See Dean, 2002, 189–198). He has recently published a series of significant papers on the poets Wallace Stevens, W.H. Auden, and T.S. Eliot, which explore these issues and how these poets can form resources for liberal Christian theology (Dean, 2012; Dean, 2014; Dean, 2016).

Bruce Ledewitz

In his book, *Church, State, and the Crisis in American Secularism*, legal scholar Bruce Ledewitz argues that the government can and should use non-sectarian religious language and imagery to promote such ideas as the objectivity of values and the universality of human rights, ideas that both religious and secular people should be able to agree on. For example, the United States Declaration of Independence's commitment to the idea that humans (or at least free men) have certain unalienable rights is a claim that human rights are not gifts from government, especially not a gift from the king.

Ledewitz begins his argument with the claim that the government of the United States can establish what he calls higher law in the public square. It is a settled principle of U.S. constitutional law, called the "government speech" doctrine, that government can make substantive moral and philosophical pronouncements, provided that it does not coerce people into believing them. It may persuade, but not coerce. It is "free to praise democracy and the free market. The government may condemn the deprivation of human rights around the globe. Public officials can criticize premarital sex and the taking of illegal drugs.... All of this is government communication of ideas" (Ledewitz, 2011, 99). More to his point, the government itself may legitimately assert the claims that there is a higher law, that values are objectively real.

The next step in Ledewitz's argument is that government may use religious symbols in affirming the objectivity of values. Indeed, the Supreme Court can reinterpret religious symbols "along deeply meaningful secular lines that differ from, but do not conflict with, their original religious meaning" (Ledewitz, 2011, 124). This, asserts Ledewitz, would preserve the court's religious neutrality, and hence, would be constitutional.

He suggests that thorough and consistent government neutrality, such as the complete elimination of religious references by public officials, would be impossible. And, if it were attempted, millions of Americans would be convinced that our present court system was evil and would probably lead to a constitutional amendment that would enshrine monotheism and maybe Christianity as the national religion. If we do not find common ground amidst our religious diversity, "we will end up voting for and against God in all future elections. This promises continuing political strife" (Ledewitz, 2011, 136).

"The question now becomes, can government, consistently with the Establishment Clause," use a religious word such as "'God' to represent the higher law position? Can the words 'under God' in the Pledge of Allegiance, for example, plausibly mean anything other than an endorsement of the God of the Bible?" (Ledewitz, 2011, 128). In answering this, Ledewitz distinguishes between a secular and a religious sense of such a word. To claim that human rights are god-given is to embody the claim that such rights are absolute, that "the majority can be objectively wrong and that government, even though supported by the will of the majority, might violate our fundamental rights" (Ledewitz, 2011, 129). That is the secular meaning. For the religious believer, or at least the monotheist, this meaning overlaps with the religious meaning. The answer to the question as to why use religious language to express the secular meaning can now be answered. "The believer hears the truth of objective value as religiously supported, while the nonbeliever also hears the claim of objective value," even though without religious support (Ledewitz, 2011, 130). This promises genuine community among disparate believers as well as between believers and non-believers.

Ledewitz points out that despite the growth of secularism, this is not and may never be a secular society.

> Any effort to force religious imagery out of the public square promises political and legal strife for years to come. Any contrary effort to use government to promote religion promises the same. But recognizing that religious language is rich in its connotations and can be understood as promoting very broad claims about reality, including secular claims, might allow a new kind of consensus to emerge. We might come to agree as a nation that much religious expression can be accepted for its secular content, despite its continuing, genuine religious content.
>
> (Ledewitz, 2011, 135–136)

Ledewitz has a vision of America's future, in which the dual content of god-language, secular or higher law, and religion heals the polarization of American politics (Ledewitz, 2011, 140–142).

Most crucial for Ledewitz's project is to clarify the secular meaning of the term "God." He refers to the work of Mordecai Kaplan, John Dewey, Stuart Kauffman, and various religious naturalists. [See my *Religious Naturalism Today* for a treatment of these thinkers (Stone, 2008, 44–51, 111–119, 220–221).] Secularism should not be afraid of this word. It can help ward off nihilism and relativism. Religious believers have been using the word to express the hope that "the ways of freedom, justice and peace have power to change the world" [Ledewitz, 2011, 228, quoted from Ledewitz *Hallowed Secularism* (Ledewitz, 2009, 198)]. Secularism can also join in that hope. He also affirms that the phrase "one Nation under God" can be understood as a bulwark against arbitrary human power. If values are objective and real, this "means real apart from the will of human beings. The word 'God' in this context stands as a placeholder for, as John Dewey would say, the power of the ideal" (Ledewitz, 2011, 223). In the Pledge of Allegiance, you really cannot, he claims, use the phrase, "one Nation under the mystery of existence" or under "the ground of being," or refer to "the ontological status of rights." "God may just be the deepest and most inclusive word we have for the expression of the objectivity of meaning" (Ledewitz, 2011, 223).

Ledewitz has a thoughtful analysis of these issues and is an important legal scholar, or so it appears to me as a layperson. My chief disagreement with him is that for him morality is objective, which seems to mean that it is not arbitrary and has truth-value independent of human vagaries. "America stands for the proposition that there is a morality that is not a human invention. This is indeed the power of the higher law position. And it is a fully American creed" (Ledewitz, 2011, 153).

However, there is a third possibility besides morality being objectively true and subjectively arbitrary. I suggest that morality involves a *transaction* between objective and subjective poles. It involves an *interplay* between the objective facts about human and ecological flourishing and subjective desires and interests. Morality is neither invented nor discovered. It is *constructed* by human subjects from objective factors in the situations in which we find ourselves. Values are the result of transactions.

Paul Rasor

Reclaiming Prophetic Witness, by Paul Rasor, is an attempt to show how liberal religion can regain its prophetic role in America. A key theme is that religious liberals must be clear about the *religious* principles that support and guide their basic social justice work. This is not easy for religious liberals, because of their commitment to religious freedom.

For Rasor, liberal religion seeks to be in tune with modern knowledge and culture, and has a commitment to free religious inquiry. Religious liberalism's positive orientation toward modern culture is in tension with the needed critical distance required to maintain a critical orientation. Further, religious liberals often come from the educated middle and upper-middle classes, and thus, belong to the classes they need to critique. Their social location can interfere with a sustained commitment to social justice work and with an ability to see the downside of the status quo. The liberal commitment to free religious inquiry also makes it difficult for religious liberals to embrace the kind of clear theological commitments needed for a strong prophetic voice. Another problem arises from the broad range of theological perspectives found in religious liberalism. This makes it hard to make communal affirmations. Fearful of saying something that might offend someone, they often say nothing at all. In addition, in today's highly charged media climate, with its focus on high-volume sound bites, reflective religious liberals have difficulty finding room for their voices.

The discomfort of religious liberals with religious discourse means that their religious commitments are frequently disguised. This can weaken prophetic practice. Some people think that the liberal tradition requires not only the institutional separation of church and state, but also a separation of religious ideas and political deliberation.

One political philosophy holds that religious reasons do not belong in public discourse. Another holds that religiously grounded arguments should be welcome in public discourse, even when conflicting values and assumptions are brought to the table. The question is why the first position came to be called *liberal*. Religion has always been part of American public life and seeking to exclude religious arguments seems *illiberal*.

Many political theorists assume that religious convictions are always grounded in sources that lie beyond the reach of reason or in texts or institutions whose authority is limited to particular groups. However, prophetic practice grounded in liberal religion always strives to satisfy the principle of accessibility. Rasor cites a number of political theorists who argue for an inclusivist view, which allows for public religious arguments.

Rasor notes that there is an impulse toward American global military, economic, and cultural influence. This impulse is combined with a concentration of corporate and political power. These impulses are rooted in the ideologies of militarism and capitalism, ideologies that function as theologies shared by both conservatives and liberals. Our militarism is rooted in a soteriology of violence evident in the narratives of western novels, detective stories, and superheroes. "Bad violence" is overcome by "good violence." Free market fundamentalism is the theology that supports the unlimited accumulation of wealth and power by global corporations plus obscene inequality. The market is the god, which creates order and will bring us salvation. Like any god, it is self-justifying and has no need of moral accountability.

The union of global corporations and U.S. government is anti-democratic and undermines the spiritual dimension of democracy. It expects patriotism and resists an engaged citizenry that asks hard questions, encouraging shallow public discourse and low political engagement. The impulse toward democracy is still beating in the American breast, but work is needed to keep it alive. We need to nurture a prophetic counterweight to the impulse toward expansion and domination.

The deep core of both democracy and religious liberalism includes their mutual commitment to freedom and equality. Religious liberalism's understanding of democracy is grounded in its affirmation of the inherent worth and dignity of all persons, rooted in the biblical concept of the *imago Dei*. This understanding includes a commitment to human equality and the creation of just institutions.

This emphasis on freedom and equality is shared with democracy. However, there is a difference in how the two traditions understand freedom. In religious liberalism, freedom is seen as an attribute of the person. In liberal political theory, freedom specifies the relationship between the individual and the state. Contemporary political philosophers usually do not elaborate a philosophical anthropology. For religious liberals, the understanding of freedom and equality is rooted in a claim about the nature of persons, and therefore, is a theological affirmation. This rooting can infuse our political struggles with a spiritual vitality that can sustain our struggle over the long haul.

Beneath the theological diversity of religious liberalism, there is a shared set of religious values. These must be named—or renamed—for our time. Rasor articulates nine core religious principles, which he thinks religious liberals in fact affirm. They include such things as "*the inherent worth and dignity of all persons*" and the importance of "*cooperative power*" and adds the principle of human liberation. "As religious liberals, we know that . . . our diversity is something to celebrate rather than fear, and that we can build just and liberating human communities.

This is the message of healing and hope that our prophetic social justice practice brings to the world" (Rasor, 2012, 105).

Rasor provides valuable insight regarding the prophetic role of liberal religion in political discourse. What is not quite clear is what makes a religious principle *religious*. What I have suggested is that public discourse employs recognized symbols of transcendence, vertical or horizontal. To speak of "inherent worth and dignity" is, I believe, a recognized symbol of transcendence. It is open to a minimalist or naturalistic interpretation, but it also is open to a reading in a more theistic direction. If we said that "human rights are God-given rights," this would probably not be capable of a naturalistic interpretation, whereas "inherent worth and dignity" is. Another of Rasor's religious principles is the importance of "cooperative power." This does not seem to carry a sense of transcendence, naturalistic or otherwise. To speak of "building the beloved community" does, however, I suggest, carry with it a note of transcendence. Whether another one of Rasor's religious principles, that of human liberation, is a symbol of transcendence is not easy to discern. I think that it might be. In any event, I wish to claim that a religious principle for use in the public square, is not just a deeply held conviction, but one that is a symbol of transcendence, whether minimally naturalistic or maximally supernaturalistic.

Conclusion

A public intellectual is a thinker who addresses significant issues faced by the public and who speaks to a major section of the public. This means that the public intellectual is addressing neither narrowly conceived ecclesiastical or academic problems nor speaking to denominational or academic audiences. The public intellectual, by the width of her issues and publics, will be transdisciplinary, willing to stick her neck out into areas where she is not expert.

A public theologian, as I use the term, is a public intellectual who uses recognized images of transcendence, such as "sacred," "spirit," or "creation," in addressing major public issues.[5] A naturalistic public theologian will use only naturalistic images of transcendence.

Paul Tillich has shown the importance of a third way between absolutizing and idolizing any human social or political movement or institution and an indifference to or despair of engaging in such movements. This third is epitomized in his concept of the Protestant Principle. We have found that this idea rests on his notion of god as the ground of being, a notion not employable by a naturalist. However, by recognizing the relative worth of our endeavors, without absolutizing (even though we may dedicate our lives to one of them!), a naturalist can also thread the narrow way between fanaticism and despair.

Jeffrey Stout, by developing his depiction of the democratic tradition, is able to claim that religious language can be used in the political arena by progressives. What we have suggested is that Stout needs to recognize that there is a growing tradition of religious naturalists who either use non-theistic religious language (such as myself) or else naturalistic god-language in the public political arena.

William Dean has valuable insights on the role of the god-symbol as a semi-autonomous convention in the ongoing life of a people. I shift away from his focus on the god-symbol to the use of symbols, which can be employed non-theistically, such as "the Beloved Community," or "Justice."

Bruce Ledewitz claims that government may make reference to "higher law" in the public square and affirm that values are objectively real, and he claims further that religious symbols can be used by government in making these assertions. He claims further that complete government neutrality and the total elimination of religious references by government figures would be impossible, and in fact, counterproductive, if attempted. These assertions are thought-provoking and worth considering. My disagreement with him is that I do not think that values are objectively real. Rather, they are constructed through an ongoing interplay between the objective facts about human and ecological flourishing and the desires and interests of various living things. (In other words, food is a value to any living thing. Amoebae, as well as humans, have values.)

Paul Rasor has important things to say about reclaiming prophetic witness in the public sphere. My suggestion is that the religious principles, which can undergird this witness, are not just deeply held convictions, but rather are recognized symbols of transcendence. Religious naturalism is able to use some of these symbols with both caution and conviction.

All of these writers give serious thought on how to use religious language in the public sphere in a democracy. Yet, none of their attempts quite accomplish the task. My claim is that certain recognizable symbols of transcendence can be used in a naturalistic fashion to engage both with those who employ traditional religious language and those who do not. Some of these symbols may easily be fitted into a naturalistic framework, such as "Higher Law," "building the Beloved Community," and "the inherent worth and dignity of every person."

The symbol of "God" has been used by some writers, such as Spinoza, Wieman, Peters, and Kaufman, in a naturalistic framework. I must acknowledge their use as genuinely naturalistic. However, I am reluctant to take this direction, as I think that the symbol of "God" is dangerous and too easily misunderstood. I would rather not speak of god. That said, there are other symbols of transcendence that can and should be used in the public sphere in a naturalistic framework.

Further reflection on public theology from a religious naturalist position could profitably be gained from reflection on the Earth Charter and the worldwide cross-cultural process that went into its drafting [www.earthcharter.org; Peter Miller and Laura Westra, *Just Ecological Integrity* (Miller and Westra, 2002); see especially J. Ronald Engel, "The Earth Charter as a New Covenant for Democracy," Chapter 4, 37–52 in that book]. Also, Michael S. Hogue's forthcoming *American Immanence: Democracy in an Uncertain World* is an important statement of how religious naturalism (Hogue prefers to use the term "immanence" to naturalism) can develop an astute political theology relevant to today's world (Hogue, 2018).

Notes

1 Parts of this chapter are based on my "Caring for the Web of Life: Towards a Public Ecotheology," Religious Experience and Ecological Responsibility, edited by Donald A. Crosby and Charley D. Hardwick. (New York: Peter Lang, 1996) 277–285. However, I now depart from this earlier writing in my reluctance to use the symbol of god.
2 For representative writings of these writers, see Rachel Carson, *Silent Spring* (Boston: Houghton Mifflin, 1962); John B. Cobb. Jr., *Is It Too Late?: A Theology of Ecology* (Beverly Hills: Benziger Bruce and Glencoe, Inc., 1972): Herman E. Daly and John B. Cobb, Jr., *For the Common Good: Redirecting the Economy Toward Community, the Environment, and a Sustainable Future* (Boston: Beacon Press, 1989); Paul R. Ehrlich, *The Population Bomb* (New York: Ballantine Books, 1968).
3 For a slightly different analysis of Tillich from my naturalistic perspective, see my "A Tillichian Contribution to Contemporary Moral Philosophy: The Unconditional Element in the Content of the Moral Imperative," John J. Carey, Ed. *Being and Doing: Paul Tillich as Ethicist.* (Macon, GA: Mercer University Press, 1987, 69–85).
4 Parts of this section are taken from my *Religious Naturalism Today* (Stone, 2008, 197).
5 Parts of this section are based on my "Caring for the Web of Life: Towards a Public Ecotheology," *Religious Experience and Ecological Responsibility*, edited by Donald A. Crosby and Charley D. Hardwick. (New York: Peter Lang, 1996) 277–285. However, I depart from this earlier writing in my current reluctance to use the "God-symbol."

Bibliography

Anderson, Victor. 2008. *Creative Exchange: a Constructive Theology of African American Experience*. Minneapolis, MN: Fortress Press.
Dean, William. 1986. *American Religious Empiricism*. Albany, NY: State University of New York Press.
Dean, William. 1994. *The Religious Critic in American Culture*. Albany: State University of New York Press.
Dean, William. 2012. "Even Stevens: A Poet for Liberal Theology," *The Journal of Religion*, (April), 177–198.
Dean, William. 2014. "Liberal Piety: W.H. Auden among the Theologians," *The Journal of Religion* (October), 436–456.
Dean, William. 2016. "Liberal Realism: T.S. Eliot and the Ambiguity of God," *The Journal of Religion* (April), 212–233.
Dewey, John. 1934. *A Common Faith*. New Haven, CT: Yale University Press. Earth Charter. 2002. www.earthcharter.org.
Hogue, Michael S. 2018. *American Immanence: Democracy for an Uncertain World*. New York: Columbia University Press.
Kaufman, Gordon. 2004. *In the beginning . . . Creativity*. Minneapolis, MN: Fortress Press.
Kaufman, Gordon. 2006. *Jesus and Creativity*. Minneapolis, MN: Fortress Press.
Ledewitz, Bruce. 2009. *Hallowed Secularism: Theory, Belief, Practice*. New York: Palgrave Macmillan.
Ledewitz, Bruce. 2011. *Church, State, and the Crisis in American Secularism*. Bloomington, IN: Indiana University Press.
Miller, Peter and Laura Westra, Eds. 2002. *Just Ecological Integrity: The Ethics of Maintaining Planetary Life*. Lanham, MD: Rowman & Littlefield Publishers.
Neville, Robert Cummings. 1992. *The Highroad Around Modernism*. Albany, NY: State University of New York Press.

Rasor, Paul. 2012. *Reclaiming Prophetic Witness: Liberal Religion in the Public Square*. Boston: Skinner House Books.
Stone, Jerome A. 2008. *Religious Naturalism Today: The Rebirth of a Forgotten Alternative*. Albany: State University of New York Press.
Stout, Jeffrey. 2004. *Democracy and Tradition*. Princeton: Princeton University Press.
Tillich, Paul. 1948. *The Protestant Era*. Chicago: The University of Chicago Press.
Tillich, Paul. 1951. *Systematic Theology*, Volume One. Chicago: The University of Chicago Press.
White, Carol Wayne. 2016. *Black Lives and Sacred Humanity: Toward an African American Religious Naturalism*. New York: Fordham University Press.
Wieman, Henry Nelson. 1958. *Man's Ultimate Commitment*. Carbondale: Southern Illinois University Press.

CONCLUSION

Emily Brontë recalled "seeing a caterpillar destroying a flower: 'at that moment the universe appeared to me a vast machine constructed solely to produce evil.' Nature, she concludes, 'exists on a principle of destruction: every being must be the tireless instrument of death in others, or itself ceases to live'." . . . However, "[I]n the same realm of nature that Emily Brontë in some moods saw as a machine for producing cruelty and destruction, in different moods she also found the soothing consolations found by other romantic pantheists, from Wordsworth among the English lakes to Victor Frankenstein in the Swiss Alps" [quoted in Edward Mendelson, *The Things That Matter* (Mendelson, 2006, 63–64, 66)].

Is nature enough? No. Nature will not satisfy our deepest longings. Nature will not give us immortality, as far as we know, except metaphorically as our elements return. Nature will not satisfy our deepest longings. It will not satisfy our deepest hunger for metaphysical ultimates. Nature includes all the parasites, bacteria harmful to us, and viruses which can and will kill us. Nature generates tsunamis, volcanoes, earthquakes, and forest fires. And, as nature includes serial killers, horrendous dictators, conquering heroes, and other killing things, nature will finally kill us. Nature is not enough. But, it is all we have and it will have to do. And, so far it has done well enough.

Religious naturalism, holding nature sacred, will not solve some of the thorny issues that confront us concerning the environment. Religious naturalism will not solve issues in environmental policy such as the best method of contingent valuation or what the discount rate of the future should be. Religious naturalism will not solve some of the dilemmas in conservation biology concerning preservation versus sustainable development or the reintroduction of predators into ecosystems. Religious naturalism will not solve the nitty-gritty issues of the tension between humans and other life forms.

However, if we hold nature to be sacred, it will introduce an added dimension into our thinking. If we hold the natural world, including ourselves, as of very great importance, we will be cautious in our actions. If we train our perception and our feelings to recover the sacredness of the interconnected web of all beings, there will be a pragmatic effect on our behavior.

Any religious or philosophical viewpoint must be judged partly in terms of its potential for liberation and empowerment. On the whole, religious naturalism has not grown out of a context in which the struggle for caste, gender, or class justice has been paramount. However, it does have emancipatory power in at least two respects. First, it helps in the dismantling of the oppressive aspects of traditional theism. In addition, it articulates an alternative position that is at least as fulfilling and empowering as much traditional theism. Second, by being more in tune with the approaches and results of the natural sciences, it challenges the authoritative stance of some of the more religiously oriented conservative political and social movements. As nature bats last, if we do not stop fouling our nest there will be no hope for any of us. But, I think we may have cautious hope in working with the creative powers of the universe.

As a final teaser, I recall from Chapter 2 that the physicist Stanley Klein of Berkeley thinks that religious naturalists miss the boat by ignoring quantum mechanics. I wonder what it would be like if the weirdness or craziness of QM (Klein's words) were to be basic in religious naturalism. I am certainly open to suggestion. I think that it is weird that there is something, rather than nothing. Perhaps, this is where god comes in. However, in my considered judgment, using god is not really an explanation, but rather another name for the weirdness of existence. Anyway, the word "God" is too dangerous. I do have to be cautious, however. We are at the edges of human rationality. It would be arrogant of me to insist on my view.

At the church where I am a member, every other year, the curriculum for the seventh and eighth graders involves the study of other faith traditions with visits to neighboring synagogues, churches, mosques, and meditation halls. But, when it comes to agnosticism and atheism, I am invited to visit the class as a representative of these viewpoints. Now the attention span of even the best seventh and eighth graders being what it is, I give a very short talk. It goes like this.

"An *agnostic* is someone who is not sure whether God exists or not. And I am an agnostic. But when it comes down to it, for all practical purposes, I guess I'm really an atheist. An *atheist* is someone who doesn't think there is a God. But atheism is a pretty negative position, so I like to think of myself as a humanist. A *humanist* is someone who places a high value on humans. But in this day of environmental catastrophe we must value more than just humans. We need to place a high value on our home planet Earth and all of its habitats. So most of all I like to think of myself as a *religious naturalist*."

Nature will not satisfy our deepest yearnings for rational coherence and cosmic value. But, nature is all we have and it will have to do. And, it does. Even though it is indifferent to us and full of dangers, it is our home. The physical world is full of enchantment, if not magic. We must trade the grunge view of matter for the glitz view.

Bibliography

Mendelson, Edward. 2006. *The Things That Matter: What Seven Classic Novels Have to Say About the Stages of Life*. New York: Pantheon Books.

INDEX

Abram, David 59
abstraction 32
aesthetic indicator species 47, 57
affection 40
affordance 51, 62–63
After Empire (Welch) 75
after life, lack of belief in 1
agnosticism 138
Alexander, Samuel 4, 21, 84, 91
Allen, Paula Gunn 107
amateur naturalists 43–44
American Immanence (Hogue) xviii, 134
American Religious Empiricism (Dean) 128
American Spiritual Culture, The (Mathews) 128
Ames, Edward Scribner 84, 86, 90
Anderson, Victor 9–10, 84, 127
angels 110–111
animal deities 112–113
anthropomorphization 105
appreciative perception: communities and 104; introduction to 31–34; LaChapelle and 49–52; Leopold and 39–49; Snyder and 52–55; summary of discussion of xvii, 55–58; theory of 58–65; Thoreau and 34–39
Aquinas, Thomas 2–3
aspiration 75–76, 80
atheist 138
Auden, W. H. 128
Augustine 98, 115
authoritarian theologies 122
awareness 75

Barker, Elliott 44
Barlow, Connie 23–24, 28, 91
beauty 60
Becoming More Fully Human (Murry) 75
Being and Value (Ferré) 60
Beirstadt, Albert 42
benevolence 103–104
Bernhardt, William 84, 91
Berry, Thomas 25, 28
Berry, Wendell 125, 126, 127
big picture, scientific 14–15, 21–25
bioregionalism 52
Black Lives and Sacred Humanity (White) 10, 18
bodies and spirits 112
boundary issues 10–11
Broley, Charles 44
Brontë, Emily 137
Bruno, Giordano 4
Buddhism 70, 75, 78
Bumbaugh, David 93–94
Burhoe, Ralph Wendell 84, 88, 91

Callicott, J. Baird 41–42, 43, 47–48, 57, 99, 104
Cannon, Susan Faye 36
care, broadening 99–104
Carruth, William Herbert 83
Carson, Rachel 121
charity 69
Chicago Naturalists 85–88
Christ, Carol 105
Christian, David 28

Index

Christian Century, The 92
Church, Frederic 42
Church, State, and the Crisis in American Secularism (Ledewitz) 129
Churchill, Ward 117
Cloke, Paul 65
Cobb, John 121
Cobbett, William 125
Cohen, Jack 91
Color Purple, The (Walker) 91
Common Faith. A (Dewey) 19, 122
Comte-Sponville, André 75, 77
confessional theologies 122
connection 75–76, 77, 80
consequentialism 70
Constitution of the United States 127
cosmological arguments for existence of God 2–3
cosmology 22–23
Creative Exchange (Anderson) 10
creativity, serendipitous 89–91
Criddle, Norman and Stuart 44
critical eye 49
Crosby, Donald 8–10, 13–14, 15, 18, 99
cultural cannibalism 117
curiosity 40
cyclical view of time 115

Daly, Mary 105
dance 115
Darwin, Charles 36–37
Dawkins, Richard 28
Day, Dorothy 126, 127
Deacon, Terrence 74
Dean, William 33, 91, 127–128, 134
De Caro, Marco 67–68
Declaration of Independence 129
defamiliarization 38, 56
democracy 102–103, 125–127, 132
Democracy and Tradition (Stout) 125
"depth" dimension 19
Derrida, Jacques 128
Dewey, John: concept of "religious" and 79; Dean and 128; on empiricism 35; imagination and 21; influence of 19; Ledewitz and 130; as naturalistic theist 84; as religious naturalist 4; Stout and 125, 126; use of "god" and 122; Wieman and 92, 100
Dewsbury, J. D. 65
Dietrich, John 5
divine: feminine side of xviii, 104–105, 111–112; plurality of 20–21; Welch on 7–8, 74–75

Dowd, Michael 28, 84, 91
Dworkin, Ronald 7, 9

earth, resacralization of xvii, 97
Earth Charter 134
ecological perception 55
ecotheology, public xviii, 121–134
educated perception 57–58
Edwards, Jonathan 102, 103–104
Ehrlichs 121
Einstein, Albert 7, 84, 91
Eliot, Frederick May 84, 92
Eliot, T. S. 128
Elton, Charles S. 45
emergence 74
Emerson, Ralph Waldo 4, 35, 125, 126
empirical holism 36
empiricism 35
End of Faith, The (Harris) 69
Engel, J. Ronald 18
enthusiasm 40
envy 72
epic of evolution 24, 27–28
eroticism 63, 71, 72
Establishment Clause 129–130
ethics xv–xvi
evil, problem of 9
evocative power 17
evolution 23, 24, 27–28
experiential anchors 33, 34

familiarization 38, 56
fanaticism 69
feminine divine 104–105, 111–112
Ferré, Frederick 60
Feynman, Richard 8
field studies 43–44
Finality of the Christian Religion, The (Foster) 85
First Nations 75
Flader, Susan L. 43
Flanagan, Owen 70–71, 77
Foster, George Burman 84, 85, 90
Foucault, Michel 128
freedom 132
functional ultimacy 93
Function of Religion in Man's Struggle for Existence, The (Foster) 85

Gaard, Greta 117
Game Management (Leopold) 55
gender 104–105, 111–112
generous empiricism 33
Gibson, James 50, 51, 63

Gilpin, William 37, 42
"glitz" theory of matter 98
God: arguments for 2–3; lack of belief in 1; Ledewitz and 130; naturalistic conception of xvii, 83; naturalistic theism and 84–91; question of 92–95; Spinoza on 68; Tillich on 124
goddess 111–112
gods, many 109–111
good and evil 9
Goodenough, Ursula 14, 18, 19, 22–23, 28, 73–74, 76, 80, 93
Goodman, Nelson 117
"government speech" doctrine 129
Green Space, Green Time (Barlow) 23–24
"ground of being" theologies 11
Growth of Religion, The (Wieman and Horton) 87
"grunge" theory of matter 98

Hardwick, Charley 91
Hargrove, Eugene 31
Harris, Sam 69–70, 77
Hartshorne, Charles 2, 11
Haydon, Harold 34
Hazlitt, William 125, 126
Hefner, Philip 3
Heidegger, Martin 128
Hick, John 2
Highroad Around Modernism, The (Neville) 128
Hinduism 78
Hitler, Adolf 26
Hocking, William 77
Hogue, Michael S. xviii, 10, 134
Homer, Winslow 35
Horicon Marsh 14–15, 19
horizontal transcendence 18, 73, 76
Hughes, Chief Justice 103
Humanist Manifesto 5, 79
humanists 5–7, 10, 93, 138
humans: place of 15; in universe–process 25
Humboldt, Alexander von 36–37
husbandry 44–45
Hussey, Christopher 42
Huxley, Julian 5, 84

Idea of the Holy, The (Otto) 99
idolatry 77, 112, 116, 124
inclusivity 132
indigenous people: animal deities and 112–113; appropriation versus learning from xviii, 117–118; bodies and spirits of 112; goddess and 111–112; introduction to 107–109; polytheism and 109–111; rituals of 116; sacred places and 115–116; scientific thought and 113–114; time and 115
In Face of Mystery (Kaufman) 88
Ingold, Tim 64–65
intentionality 38, 56
interconnectedness 25
In the Beginning . . . Creativity (Kaufman) 88
Irenaeus 100

James, William 128
Jeffers, Robinson 73
Jesusism 70
Johnson, Elizabeth 105
Jones, William 93
journal assignment 32–33
Journals (Thoreau) 34, 35–36, 37, 76

Kant, Immanuel 33, 86
Kaplan, Mordecai 91, 130
Katahdin (Ktaadn), Mount 15, 31–32
Kauffman, Stuart xvi, 28, 90, 130
Kaufman, Gordon 84, 88–91, 127, 134
Kidwell, Clara Sue 108
Kidwell, Jeremy 64–65
Kilmer, Joyce 20
King, Martin Luther, Jr. 18, 126, 127
Klein, Stanley 23, 138

LaChapelle, Delores 49–52, 62, 63, 116, 121
landscape painting 42
language 32, 34, 52–54, 56–59
languages of nature 59
Larson, Gerald 117
Lawrence, D. H. 52
Ledewitz, Bruce 129–131, 134
Leopold, Aldo 39–49, 55, 56–57, 62, 64, 99, 104, 114, 121
Leopold, Luna 39
liberal naturalism 67–68
Lincoln, Abraham 126, 127
linear view of time 115
Little Book of Atheist Spirituality, The (Comte-Sponville) 75
Living with Ambiguity (Crosby) 9
Locke, John 35
Loomer, Bernard 84, 87–88, 92, 98
Lorraine, Claude 42
Lowie, Robert 6
loyalty 102–103, 104

Macarthur, David 67–68
Macintosh case 103
Man's Hidden Search (Patton) 6
Man's Ultimate Commitment (Wieman) 87
Marett, R. R. 6
materialism 10
material spirits 98–99
Mathews, Shailer 84, 86–87, 100, 128
Mbiti, Joseph 110
McFague, Sally 105
McGaa, Ed Eagle Man 116
Mead, George Herbert 102
meaning, science and 24, 26
Means, Russell 108
meditation 69–71
Meland, Bernard 23, 33, 64, 88, 92, 99, 100
Mind, Self, and Society (Mead) 102
mindful reverence 73–74
minimal experiences of transcendence 17, 94
Minimalist Vision of Transcendence, The (Stone) 20, 27, 102
modal logic 2
Momaday, N. Scott xvi
Monet, Claude 35
monotheism 102, 110–111, 112
Monroe, Harriet 91
morality 1–2, 22–23, 33, 113, 130–131
Moran, Thomas 42
More than Discourse (Crosby) 9
motivation 39–41, 60–61
Muir, John 35, 42
Murry, William R. 10, 75–76

Native American Theology, A (Kidwell, Noley, and Tinker) 108
Naturalism and Normativity (De Caro and Macarthur) 67
Naturalism in Question (De Caro and Macarthur) 67
naturalistic mysticism 6
naturalistic public theologian 122
naturalistic theism 84–92
naturalized spirituality xvii, 67–68, 76–80
Nature (Emerson) 35
Nature as Sacred Ground (Crosby) 9, 18
Nature is Enough (Rue) 98
Nature of True Virtue, The (Edwards) 103
Neville, Robert 11, 128
New Atheists 69
New Genesis 27–28
Nice, Margaret Morse 44
Niebuhr, H. Richard 102–103

Nixon, Rob 60
Noley, Homer 108
Normative Psychology of Religion (Wieman) 87
Norris, Kathleen 64, 107–108
Norton-Smith, Thomas 108, 109, 110, 117
no-self, concept of 78
noumenon 47–48, 57

observation: LaChapelle and 49–50; Leopold and 43; Thoreau and 35–39; *see also* perception
Ogden, Schubert 2
Oliver, Mary 79
ontological arguments for existence of God 2
openness 19
Otto, Rudolf 6, 99

pantheism 4, 10
paradigm shifts 97–105
Patton, Kenneth 6–7
Paul, Colonel 31
Paul of Tarsus 98
Peirce, Charles Sanders 128
pelican, brown 13–14, 15
perception: development of 55–56; educated 57–58; focus of 56–57; Leopold and 39, 44–46, 48; motivation and 60–61; values and 59–60; *see also* observation
perspective 50, 62
Peters, Karl 17, 84, 90–91, 134
Phenix, Philip 91
physicalism 10
piety 69
Place in Space, A (Snyder) 54
planetary ethic 22–23
Plaskow, Judith 105
Platonic dualism 98
Pledge of Allegiance 130
pluralism 125
plurality 20–21
poetic metaphor 25
poiesis 22
polar bear photos 32
polytheism 109–111
Popper, Karl 26
positivists 26
practical absolute 86, 90
pre-scientific modes of thought 113–114
Price, Uvedale 42
pride of knowing 40

process theology 11
Promise of Religious Naturalism, The (Hogue) xviii, 10
Protestant Principle 123–124, 133
public theologian: conclusions regarding 133–134; examples of 123–133; overview of 121–123

quantum mechanics 23, 138

Radest, Howard 77
radical monotheism 102
Randall, John Herman 4
Rasor, Paul 131–133, 134
rationality 72, 113
Rawls, John 125
Raymo, Chet 8
reading landscape 45–46
Really Hard Problem, The (Flanagan) 70
Reason and Reverence (Murray) 10
Reason in Religion (Santayana) 69
Reclaiming Prophetic Witness (Rasor) 131
Reese, Curtis 5
reflection 75–76, 80
Reinventing the Sacred (Kauffman) 90–91
religion, working definition of 1
Religion of Nature, A (Crosby) 8
Religion without God (Dworkin) 7, 10
Religion without Revelation (Huxley) 5
Religious Critic in American Culture, The (Dean) 127
religious liberalism 131–133
religious naturalism: boundary issues and 10–11; case for 2–4; downsides to 3–4; emancipatory power of 138; introduction to 1–2; overview of xv–xviii; practitioners of 4–10; in public square 121–134; sacred and 13–21; scientific big picture and 21–25
Religious Naturalism Today (Stone) 9, 10, 93
Remarks on Forest Scenery (Gilpin) 37
reverence 72, 73–74, 75, 93–94
ritual 116–117
Robinson, Edward Arlington 91
Rosa, Salvatore 42
Round River (Leopold) 39, 64
Royce, Josiah 102
Rue, Loyal 28, 91, 98
Ruether, Rosemary Radford 105, 126, 127
Russell, Bertrand 28

sacred: experiences of 17–21; illustrations of 13, 15–16; implications of theory of 19–21; meaning of xv–xvi; overview of 13–17; plurality of 20–21; restraint and 77–78, 97; technical theory of 18; two aspects of 99–101; use of term 16–17
sacred conventions 127–128
Sacred Depths of Nature, The (Goodenough) 14, 22, 73
sacred places 115–116
sacred reality 84
Sacred Sands (Engel) 18
Sand County Almanac, A (Leopold) 44–45, 46
Santayana, George 4, 69
science: meanings and 26–27; needs of 27; Sideris on 27–28
Science in Culture (Cannon) 36
scientific explanations 113–114
scientific naturalism 67, 68
secular liberalism 126
Seeing New Worlds (Walls) 34
selection 91
self-expression 40–41
Sellars, Ray Wood 4, 79
sensitive discernment 33
separateness 69
serendipitous creativity 89–91
shamanism/shamanistic discourse 55, 114
side of eye approach 38
Sideris, Lisa 27–28
skepticism 77
Skepticism and True Believers (Raymo) 8
Slow Violence and the Environmentalism of the Poor (Nixon) 60
Smith, Gerald Birney 88
Smith, John Maynard 24
Smuts, Jan Christiaan 4
Snyder, Gary 35, 52–55, 57, 58, 116, 121
social conventions 127–128
Social Darwinism 26
social justice 21
Solomon, Robert C. 71–73
soul, lack of belief in 1
Source of Human Good. The (Wieman) 87
Spinoza, Baruch 4, 7, 21, 68, 77, 83, 84, 92, 134
spirit and matter, reconceptualization of xvii, 98–99
spirituality: naturalistic theory of 76–80; theories of 68–76
Spirituality for the Skeptic (Solomon) 70
spiritual landscapes 65
Spretnak, Charlene 121
Starhawk 115
Stevens, Wallace 128

Stone, Jerome A. 9, 10, 20, 27, 93, 102
Stout, Jeffrey 125–127, 133–134
suffering 73
Sutherland, Justice 103
Swimme, Brian 25, 28

terminology 79
Thank God for Evolution (Dowd) 91
Thoreau, Henry David 4, 15, 32, 34–39, 42, 55, 57, 76, 77, 126
Thou of Nature, The (Crosby) 9, 99
Tillich, Paul 11, 19, 123–125, 133
time 115
Tinker, George E. "Tink" 108
Tobin, John 78
Toland, John 4
training appreciation 32
transcendence: horizontal 18, 73, 76; ideal aspect of 100–101; minimal experiences of 17, 94; real aspect of 100; symbols of 122–123, 134; vertical 73
trust 72
Tyson, Neil DeGrasse 28

U.S. v. Macintosh 103
utilitarianism 70

values 59–60, 63
veneration 112
vertical transcendence 73
virtues 126

Walker, Alice 91
Walls, Laura Dassow 34, 36–37, 38, 57, 59
Watt, James 123
Welch, Sharon 7–8, 74–75
When God is Gone, Everything is Holy (Raymo) 8
White, Carol Wayne 9, 18, 127
Whitehead, Alfred North 11, 128
Whitman, Walt 125, 126
Whitt, Laurelyn 117
Wieman, Henry Nelson 84, 92, 100, 127, 134
wild language 58
Wildman, Wesley 11
wildness 53, 58
Wilson, E. O. 28
Wollstonecraft, Mary 125, 126
Woodruff, Paul 73–74, 75
Wordsworth, William 8, 137
worth, discernment of 60

yogin 54